Hemingway's Laboratory

Hemingway's Laboratory

The Paris *in our time*

Milton A. Cohen

THE UNIVERSITY OF ALABAMA PRESS
Tuscaloosa

Acknowledgments: I wish to thank Matthew Stewart and Susan Beegel for reading the text and making helpful suggestions, Esteban Egea for checking sentence identification, and, as always, Florence Chasey-Cohen for her keen-eyed editorial assistance and encouragement.

Tuscaloosa, Alabama 35487-0380

Manufactured in the United States of America

Hardcover edition published 2005.
Paperback and eBook editions published 2012.

Typeface: Bembo

Cover photograph: Ernest Hemingway's passport photograph from 1923. Courtesy of the John F. Kennedy Library, National Archives and Records Administration.
Cover design: Erin Bradley Dangar / Dangar Design

∞

The paper on which this book is printed meets the minimum requirements of American National Standard for Information Science–Permanence of Paper for Printed Library Materials, ANSI Z39.48—1984.

Paperback ISBN: 978-0-8173-5728-3
eBook ISBN: 978-0-8173-8636-8

A previous edition of this book has been catalogued by the Library of Congress as follows:
Library of Congress Cataloging-in-Publication Data
Cohen, Milton A.
Hemingway's laboratory : the Paris In our time / Milton A. Cohen.
p. cm.
Includes bibliographical references and index.
ISBN-13: 978-0-8173-1482-8 (alk. paper)
ISBN-10: 0-8173-1482-2 (alk. paper)
1. Hemingway, Ernest, 1899–1961. In our time—Criticism, Textual. 2. Hemingway, Ernest, 1899–1961—Technique. I. Title.
PS3515.E37I533 2005
813'.52—dc22

2005008767

for Florence

Contents

Introduction ix

PROLOGUE

1. Before *in our time:* Multiple Directions 3
2. A Coalescence of Pieces: Composing *in our time* 32

EXPERIMENTS

3. Narrative Modes 59
4. Voices 80
5. Sentence Rhythms 97

TEXTS

6. The Chapters 129

Epilogue 203

Appendix: Sentence Structure in *in our time* 217

Notes 221

Works Cited 249

Index 259

Introduction

Ernest Hemingway's books of fiction are commonly thought to begin with *In Our Time,* the remarkable collection of stories interspersed with short "chapters" that he published in 1925. Certainly, that book's acclaim launched his career among knowledgeable critics, journalists, and writers, just as *The Sun Also Rises* (1926) established Hemingway's popular success.

Less well known are two small books Hemingway produced before *In Our Time: Three Stories & Ten Poems* (1923) and *in our time* (1924).[1] Published by little presses in Paris, each book's publication run was tiny: 300 and 170 copies respectively. Except for small holograph editions that appeared in 1977, neither book has been reprinted to date, and extant copies of the originals can be found only in rare book collections.[2] Understandably, these books have attracted relatively few readers, and even Hemingway scholars tend to neglect them, typically discussing their contents in the context of later collections containing them—*In Our Time, The First Forty-nine Stories, The Complete Short Stories of Ernest Hemingway, Ernest Hemingway: 88 Poems*—rather than in their original provenance. To date, no scholarly book before this one has focused exclusively on either *Three Stories & Ten Poems* or *in our time.*[3]

But do these slender books merit critical studies? Here, the case for each book must be considered separately, and I shall argue only for *in our time.* Three related questions bear on this issue: Are the contents of *in our time*—eighteen brief chapters—important to Hemingway's work? Do the chapters acquire a different meaning when considered as an integral unit rather than interspersed with short stories, as in *In Our Time?* And have these chapters, taken together, received their just due from critics and scholars?

The first question—the importance of the chapters to Hemingway's oeuvre—is easiest. From their first appearance in 1924, the *in our time* chapters have been recognized by their author, readers, and critics as profoundly compelling prose in an altogether new form. "[I]t is where I think I have gotten hold of it," Hemingway wrote to Edmund Wilson a few months after finishing them (25 Nov. 1923, in *Selected Letters* 105). Wilson, the most influential critic of his time for Hemingway's generation, agreed: "[H]is prose is of the first distinction," Wilson declared in one of the book's first reviews and added, "he is . . . strikingly original, and in the dry compressed little vignettes of *In Our Time* [sic], has almost invented a form of his own" ("Dry Points" 120). As I will show in Chapter Two, numerous other reviewers, who had never heard of Ernest Hemingway, shared Wilson's enthusiasm, and even those repelled by Hemingway's violent subject matter acknowledged the power of his prose. Fellow writers, too, recognized that, as Scott Fitzgerald put it in recommending the book to his publisher, "He's the real thing."[4]

In the ensuing eight decades, scholars and critics have confirmed these judgments overwhelmingly—but usually in studies that examine the chapters in the context of the *In Our Time* stories. To be sure, this format was Hemingway's final choice for the chapters, and he even went so far as to declare that he had *composed* them as "chapter headings" to be interspersed with the *In Our Time* stories[5]—a dubious claim considering that he wrote them in 1923 for a commissioned book to consist only of these chapters, well before he envisioned a story-chapter book or had written the stories to fill it.

Leaving aside important textual differences between the two versions, are the chapters of *in our time* really the same in their impact and in the cumulative effect of their subject and style as the chapters interspersed with stories in *In Our Time?* Hemingway himself provides the answer in describing to Edward O'Brien how the two forms intertwined. The chapters, he felt, had more explosive power:

> in between each [story] comes bang! the In Our Time [chapter]. . . . I've tried to do it so you get the close up [of the stories] very quietly but absolutely solid and the real thing but very close, and then through it all between every story comes the rhythm of the in our time chapters. (12 Sept. 1924, *Selected Letters* 123).

The perspective of the chapters—pointillistic glimpses of four realms "in our time": war, crime, politics, and the bullfight—sharply contrasts with the "quiet," close-up narratives of individuals in the stories. The chapters "give the picture of the whole between examining it in detail [in the stories]," Hemingway explained to Edmund Wilson. "Like looking with your eyes at something, say a passing coast line, and then looking at it with 15X binoculars" (18 Oct. 1924, *Selected Letters* 128).

The common denominator of the chapters is violence and responses to it, while the stories (though certainly not bereft of violence) more typically explore relationships, often between family members or couples. Where the chapters focus on recent and often cataclysmic events (World War I, postwar revolutions, and the aftermath of the Greco-Turkish War), several stories reach back into the childhood of their protagonist, Nick Adams, to form a chronological bildungsroman. If the chapters thus served to jolt the quieter stories with the impact of their bloody subjects and their boldly compressed form, the opposite could also be claimed: the stories (in their civilian settings, comparatively slower, more gradual development, and understated emotion) muffle the explosive chapters. Without those dampers, then, the impact of the chapters would be like the climax of a fireworks display—a series of continuous explosions, each succeeding the last without giving readers time to catch their breath—surely a very different effect from their cumulative impact when interspersed with stories.

Studying the chapters together, moreover, brings into sharp relief the development and contrast of their themes and techniques—progressions that the intervening stories can obscure. The six bullfight chapters, for example, contrast impressionable and knowledgeable narrators, and juxtapose bullfighters who are incompetent and skillful, escapist and fatalistic, while the obstreperous, intrusive crowd runs through the chapters like a leitmotif. The botched execution of the cabinet ministers in chapter 6 anticipates the travesty of Sam Cardinella's execution in chapter 17. Imagistic motifs linking rain with misery and death, tranquil settings and violent action, join chapters across the span of the book. These interconnections apply also to Hemingway's technical experiments—his sentence rhythms, for instance, or his narrative voices, his multiple perspectives, or his ways of handling of emotion. Parallels, contrasts, and variations of these techniques appear throughout. The conjunctive run-ons of one bullfight narrative (chapter 2) appear again in another (chapter 13); yet the very next bullfight chapter (14) employs a quite different combination of complex-compound sentences and fragments. The soldier-narrator who coolly describes the praying soldier in chapter 8 anticipates the narrator of chapter 11, who skeptically relates the naive absolutism of his younger comrade. Both tones are far removed from that of the bemused kitchen corporal in chapter 1 describing the drunken antics of his battery and the officer in chapter 4 numbly recalling unexpected combat. Significantly, the sentence rhythms in each of these chapters evoke the speaker's particular mood and thus vary sharply among themselves. Studying the chapters in sequence brings out the range and scope of these explorations—Hemingway's experimental brio. In turn, the question of the book's essential nature grows more acute: is it a series of experiments and self-instructive exercises or a unified whole?[6]

This issue of the book's identity brings us to the third question of how critics have dealt with the chapters. Critical studies have related the chapters to each other, to the *In Our Time* stories, and to Hemingway's work as a whole. Scholars have traced the chapters' historical bases and examined their internal themes and (less commonly) their styles.[7] But one assumption runs through most of the criticism: that in these chapters Hemingway finally, as he put it, "got hold of it" and found his métier—consolidated his style, found his typical subject matter, determined his narrative approaches, and solidified particular techniques such as understatement and omission—the hallmarks, in short, of *the* Hemingway style.[8]

There is much to support this critical assumption since the chapters contain virtually all the components of the mature writing: the violent subjects; the study of how men respond, physically and psychologically, to danger; the stripped-down, uncluttered prose; the careful attention to the rhythms of action; and the muted handling of emotion and themes. Indeed, if this book does mark the consolidation of Hemingway's mature style and subject, its importance for that reason alone would merit a scholarly monograph.

But alongside these characteristically "Hemingway" elements are others more modernist and experimental that he either dropped or modified in his subsequent writing: sentence fragments, syntactical elisions (for example, "and each swing the crowd roaring"), long run-ons linked by *and,* intentionally ambiguous narrators and contexts, quick shifts of narrative voice, and even a self-consciously modernist look, such as using dashes instead of quotation marks to separate dialogue speeches.[9] Equally important, the chapter texts and drafts reveal how tirelessly Hemingway revised, explored alternatives to or variants of each technical element, and tried out differing combinations of several elements. Experienced Hemingway readers will recognize the deadpan objectivity in the voice narrating chapter 6: "They shot the six cabinet ministers at half-past six in the morning against the wall of a hospital."

But these readers may also wonder why an author subsequently famed for clarity and precision fails to identify who "They" are. Variants of this vagueness in several other chapters show that Hemingway was tinkering with opening sentences that were at once mimetic and semiabstract, journalistically precise and ominously vague in omitting explanatory context. Readers will also hear a plethora of voices in these eighteen brief chapters. Twenty-six different speakers, eight of whom are first-person narrators, reveal an author not only diversifying his characters and finding a credible voice for each, but also trying out multiple perspectives in mini-narratives rather than the single, consistent perspective typical of the short story.

This same exploring of alternatives can be seen in the narrative modes of these chapters, where parodies of fairy tales mingle with quasi-journalistic reporting, where first-person experiential narratives bump up against detached descriptions of action. In sentence rhythms, likewise, Hemingway explores diverse combinations of simple, compound, and complex structures to achieve particular rhythmic and thematic effects. The pervasiveness of this experimentation thus changes the identity of these chapters from a finished work employing a unified style to something far more open-ended and exploratory that tries out multiple styles and narrative techniques.

For this reason, I have titled this study *Hemingway's Laboratory.* Its chief aim is to explore the range, individual effect, and outcome of his experiments in narrative mode (Chapter Three), voice (Chapter Four), and sentence rhythm (Chapter Five). Chapters One and Two, as prologue, provide historical and biographical context, tracing Hemingway's styles and competing professional identities (journalist, author of slick fiction, poet, satirist, realist, modernist) before *in our time,* the key influences on his modernist experiments, the composition of the book itself, and critical responses to it. The final chapter—almost half the book—examines the individual chapters of *in our time:* their historical origins, themes, and styles, including a listing of their sentence structures (which are tabulated in an appendix). In addition, I compare the published text to unpublished drafts, not only to trace the chapter's development but also to reveal Hemingway's evolution as a stylist. Finally, the epilogue considers how the *in our time* experiments fared in his subsequent work: which ones were dropped or modified; how others were polished and developed to form the prose we've come to recognize as inimitably Hemingway's.

Ultimately, in this study I hope to change the way *in our time* is viewed within the Hemingway canon: not as the consolidation of his mature style, but as the experiments that made that consolidation possible. The same provisional status I impute to the book I also depict in Hemingway's career during the crucial year of 1923; his authorial identity now appears far less calculated and self-determined than is usually thought—than Hemingway wanted us to think—and far more susceptible to the external influence of immediate commissions and potential publications, and to the conflicting tensions of artistic and popular success. Although he gradually sorted out the competing professional identities mentioned above, he continued to waver between avant-garde modernist and popular writer until he discovered, in resolving the multiplicity of these experiments into a single style, that he could be both. Finally, if this study succeeds in establishing a new importance for the chapters of *in our time,* I hope that it will lead to a new trade edition of this seminal work. Hemingway deserves no less.

Hemingway's Laboratory

PART I

PROLOGUE

1
Before *in our time*
Multiple Directions

When Hemingway and his wife embarked for Paris in December 1921, his literary career was very much up in the air. His publications thus far were virtually nil, and he was uncertain about his intentions. But if he did not know what sort of writer he would become, he knew that he was putting behind him the literary identity he had striven for over the past three and a half years: he packed few of his stories and poems.

Those years had witnessed false starts, multiple directions, wasted effort. Their lodestar was his determination to be a successful writer. Besides his high school juvenilia, he wrote stories and poems continuously after he was wounded in July 1918: in Milan while recuperating; at home in Oak Park, Illinois, and at the family cottage on Walloon Lake, Michigan, in 1919 and summer 1920; and when he lived on his own in Petoskey, Michigan (fall 1919), in Toronto (winter–spring 1920), and finally in Chicago (fall 1920 to fall 1921).[1] Concurrently, since leaving high school in 1917, he had worked on and off as a journalist, writing straight news stories as a cub reporter for the *Kansas City Star,* short articles for the *Co-operative Commonwealth* magazine in Chicago, and human interest features as a freelancer for the *Toronto Star.*

This divided identity—journalist, poet, fiction writer—partly explains Hemingway's uncertain direction in 1921, but the *kind* of fiction and poetry he should pursue—popular? modernist? satirical?—was also in flux. Failure as a popular writer and exposure to modernist literature in Chicago had already begun to change his thinking. It would change further in Paris, under the tutelage of Gertrude Stein and Ezra Pound and the influence of several other modernists. But the ambivalence in his literary identity did not resolve itself immediately. During his first year in Paris, he wrote more poems but finished only two stories, "Up in Michigan" (begun in Chicago) and "My Old Man." His primary occupation was still journalism. This chapter will briefly trace these various stages in Hemingway's development and look closely at the formative influences of Anderson, Stein, Pound, Eliot, and journalism on his early experimental writing in Europe. His first serious story, "Up in Michigan," is a touchstone for gauging these influences.

Stories for the *Saturday Evening Post:* Oak Park and Petoskey, 1919–20

The modernist who composed *in our time* in 1923 is scarcely recognizable in the Hemingway of four years earlier, who expected to storm the popular market for short stories. So different are the two, in fact, that his creative writing in Europe amounts to almost a clean break. For this reason, his writing for the popular market needs only brief summary, except for one potential link to the chapters of *in our time.*

The Hemingway who returned to America with his war wounds and Italian cape in 1919 had no intention of becoming an innovative "artist"—his eye was fixed on the popular market of the *Saturday Evening Post* and *Red Book.* He brought home stories he had written while recovering from his wounds in Milan, and he wrote new ones at home in Oak Park. When his family returned home from their cottage on Walloon Lake, Michigan, Hemingway stayed on, then rented a room in nearby Petoskey in fall 1919 to continue writing. When he moved to Chicago a year later, he was still writing stories. In them, as Michael Reynolds observes, Hemingway "was imitating what he took to be marketplace fiction . . . his eye from the beginning was fixed on the bottom line: would the piece sell?" Reynolds continues:

> [T]hese juvenilia read like O. Henry and Ring Lardner, if those two had combined to write for *St. Nicholas* magazine. The heroes are all young, audacious, and successful. Punk Alford, a crime-solving newspaper reporter; Rinaldi Rinaldo, an Italian-American war vet; Jack Marvin, a much decorated pilot; Nick Grainger, a wounded soldier in Milan. The settings are either Italy or Chicago. . . . the plots are serious, romantic, sometimes humorous, and frequently revolve around either winning a girl's heart or a father's approval. Jack Marvin, son of an ex-champion boxer, must prove to his father that he is not yellow. Stuy, a rich boy, must become middle-weight champion to win his girl's hand. ("Looking Backward" 2–3)

The style that has become so thoroughly associated with Hemingway—rhythms of sparsely modified simple and compound sentences—is nowhere to be found in these stories. Instead, ornate complex sentences, often narrated in a facetious tone, proliferate. For example: "I came out of the wind scoured nakedness of Wabash Avenue in January into the cosy bar of the Cambrinus and, armed with a smile from Cambrinus himself, passed through the dining room where the waiters were clearing away the debris of the table d'hotes and sweeping out into the little back room" ("The Mercenaries" 105). Like many novice writers, Hemingway expected the *Saturday Evening Post* to gobble up these stories. When it did not, he kept on cranking them out while finding various ways to support himself.

Over the fall and winter of 1919, however, he did try out one form that Reynolds calls "the seed bed for the interchapters of *in our time* and the subject matter for many of the Nick Adams stories in *In Our Time*" ("Looking Backward" 4). These were brief sketches, most just a few paragraphs long, each about a single character living in a small town. Each sketch is titled with that character's name and presents his or her personality or situation in narrative that mostly summarizes, dramatizing only a key speech or moment. As Reynolds notes, Hemingway's immediate source for these eight "Cross Roads" sketches was E. W. Howe's "The Anthology of Another Town," which the *Saturday Evening Post* began to serialize in fall 1919. A more prominent source for both Howe and Hemingway was Edgar Lee Masters's *Spoon River Anthology* (1916), whose small-town characters recall from the grave their disappointments and dreary lives.

Although the brevity of the "Cross Roads" sketches anticipates the compressed chapters of *in our time,* the latter are not simply "polished extensions of 'Cross Roads'" ("Looking Backward" 6). The narrative style of the two works is almost antithetical: the "Cross Roads" sketches are *told* stories, heavily narrated. "Pauline Snow," for example, concludes after the protagonist's walk into the countryside with Art Simons:

> After a while some of the neighbors made a complaint, and they sent Pauline away to the correction school down at Coldwater. Art was away for awhile [sic], and then came back and married one of the Jenkins girls. (*Along With Youth* 124)

By contrast, nearly all of the *in our time* chapters *present* scenes that start in the middle, often lack an ending, and depend on description and dramatization rather than narrative summary. Nonetheless, Hemingway was to recycle several of the "Cross Roads" characters and situations into his mature stories. "Pauline Snow," for example, is the model for the brutal seduction story "Up in Michigan," which begins with the same summarized character history:

> Jim Gilmore came to Hortons Bay from Canada. He bought the blacksmith shop from old man Horton. Jim was short and dark with big mustaches and big hands. He was a good horseshoer and did not look much like a blacksmith, even with his leather apron on. He lived upstairs above the blacksmith shop and took his meals at D. J. Smith's. ("Up in Michigan" 59)

> Pauline Snow was the only beautiful girl we ever had out at the Bay. She was like an Easter Lily coming up straight and lithe and beautiful out of a dung heap. When her father and mother died she came to live with the Blodgetts. Then Art Simons started coming around to the Blodgetts' in the evening.[2] (*Along with Youth* 124)

Although Hemingway's friend Bill Horne encouraged him to keep at these sketches, he quit them after a few months, having finished eight. Reynolds feels that "the young writer did not fully realize the possibilities of what he had written" ("Looking Backward" 6). But arguably, Hemingway did recognize that these sketches were just as derivative as the stories he was trying to publish and that their setting and theme—the constricted life in rural and small-town America—was not one he found congenial. Moreover, he was about to encounter a writer in Chicago who was hard to top in this genre: Sherwood Anderson.

Hemingway, Anderson, and the Chicago Renaissance: Chicago, 1920–21

The avant-garde of Paris was not the first that Hemingway encountered, for Chicago, too, had experienced a creative surge and a lively intermingling of artists, writers, publishers, and journalists. In 1920, when Hemingway moved there, the Chicago Renaissance was well past its prewar prime, however, and several of its leading figures, such as Margaret Anderson and her *Little Review,* had moved on to the more active hubs of the avant-garde in New York and Paris. Nonetheless, the Chicago literary community could still boast Harriet Monroe's pioneering *Poetry* magazine and perhaps the most controversial of new novelists, Sherwood Anderson, who had just published *Winesburg, Ohio* the year before. More important, at Y. K. Smith's large apartment, Hemingway lived and associated with young writers keenly interested in literature as an art and modernism in all the arts, eager to discuss the most recent psychosexual theories of Freud, Kraft-Ebbing, and Havelock Ellis, and well-connected to Anderson and other Chicago luminaries. Still intent on achieving practical success as a writer, Hemingway was skeptical of much of the "art-for-art's-sake" talk, but he was nonetheless eager to read the writers whose names were so frequently discussed—Anderson, Conrad, Joyce, Lawrence, Floyd Dell, Knut Hamsun, and the Russian novelists, particularly Turgeniev. They all had something to teach him about craft, particularly the successful yet innovative Anderson, who visited the apartment often and took a liking to Hemingway (Fenton 88–90; Reynolds, "Biography of a Book" 36–37).

In Anderson, as in Mark Twain, Hemingway saw how colloquial American English could become a powerful narrative device, particularly in the first-person voices of young narrators, whose colorful expressions, broken sentences, and stammering repetitions betray a naive, unprotected sensibility. Anderson's *Winesburg,* moreover, like Joyce's *Dubliners* and Turgeniev's *A Sportsman's Sketches,* gave the short story new respectability, and Anderson's collection showed how the experiences of a central character—a young man—could link the stories thematically. In many of the Winesburg stories and others, such as "I'm a Fool" and "I Want to Know Why," the protagonists do not fully understand the meaning of their experience, creating dramatic irony, and often this meaning is sexual. Repeatedly, sex appears as a disruptive and disturbing force that protagonists can neither repress nor fully understand.

Hemingway was to adapt and transform several of these qualities in his first artistically serious short story, "Up in Michigan," which he began in Chicago in 1921 and revised in Paris. Defying the conventional wisdom that an author should not make the point-of-view character a member of the opposite sex, Hemingway makes his protagonist a naive servant girl who does not understand how her infatuation with the town's blacksmith, Jim Gilmore, is increasingly tinged with sexual desire. In a paragraph that lists the various physical qualities she liked about Jim, the last is sexually suggestive:

> One day she found that she liked it the way the hair was black on his arms and how white they were above the tanned line when he

> washed up in the wash basin outside the house. Liking that made her feel funny. (*Complete Short Stories* 59)

Her viewing this surrogate of private parts recalls the voyeurism in Anderson's "The Strength of God" and the insistent, homoerotic energy of Wing Biddlebaum's hands. Like Anderson's protagonists, Liz does not understand why she "found herself liking" this glimpse. And the narrative expresses her puzzlement ("made her feel funny") in her own unsophisticated, ambiguous colloquialism—a technique Hemingway would use again near the end of chapter 1 of *in our time:* "It was funny going along that road." If "Up in Michigan" surpasses Anderson (and virtually every other living writer) in its sexual explicitness, and in its blatantly sexual images of "hard" and "tight" anticipating the actual encounter, it borrows outright an image of sexual desire—"shining eyes"—that Anderson made central to "I Want to Know Why." And like so many of Anderson's protagonists, Liz Coates feels thoroughly disillusioned and abandoned following an encounter that Jim has brutalized into near rape. In attempting to out-Anderson Anderson, however, Hemingway falters with point of view, shifting it to Jim at times ("Jim began to feel great"), and drops into the rhetoric of a boy's locker-room to describe Liz's growing desire: "She was frightened but she wanted it. She had to have it."

The naive protagonist also appears in "My Old Man," a 1922 story which, more than any other, helped launch Hemingway's career but also haunted him for years to come with its obvious debts to Anderson. The racetrack setting, the young narrator who does not fully understand the corruption around him but nonetheless grows disillusioned by the end, his narrative voice—full of *gee*'s and "I was nuts about the horses" and "[It] was the swellest course"—all of these elements are Andersonian trademarks. Less obvious was what made the story Hemingway's: the mastery of a particular subculture—here, the world of European thoroughbred racing—down to its fine details—for example, the differences between the Italian and French tracks, and a story that is far more carefully and fully plotted than one typically finds in Anderson.

Three years later, Hemingway acknowledged to Scott Fitzgerald that this fictional mastery of a subculture—applying, as well, to his stories about boxing and bullfighting—was "not the kind of thing I'm shooting for" (*Selected Letters* 180). He might have added that the story's heavily narrated plot (young Joe mostly tells it) also proved uncongenial to an aesthetic that increasingly stressed imagistic presentation. But "telling" was very much Anderson's style, and Anderson's fingerprints were what the early critics fixed on, to Hemingway's increasing irritation. Edmund Wilson, for example, immediately noted the similarity in a letter acknowledging receipt of *Three Stories & Ten Poems.* Hemingway's reply exudes the "anxiety of influence":

> No, I don't think "My Old Man" derives from Anderson. It is about a boy and his father and race horses. Sherwood has written about boys and horses. But very differently. It derives from boys and horses. Anderson derives from boys and horses. I don't think they're anything alike. I know I wasn't inspired by him. (25 Nov. 1923, *Selected Letters* 105)[3]

What unquestionably did inspire Hemingway in 1920–21 was Anderson's kindness, professional encouragement, and generosity, which, like Y. K. Smith's literary circle in Chicago, had much to do with changing the younger writer's literary aims. Anderson recognized and encouraged Hemingway's talent—"He's going to go someplace" he predicted after their first meeting (qtd. in Fenton 89). He urged the writer and his bride to join the migration of artists and writers to Paris,[4] where he could develop his craft in a milieu friendly to artists and American dollars. Most important, he opened crucially important doors to Hemingway in Paris with letters of introduction to Gertrude Stein, Ezra Pound, Lewis Galantière, and Sylvia Beach. The Hemingway who left for Paris in December 1921 may well have had "no clear conception of what he wanted to do," as Y. K. Smith described him in Chicago (Fenton 86). But he at least knew that he would not be an author of slick fiction. Just what identity he would pursue instead—professional journalist, modernist poet, satirist, avant-garde writer—remained to be determined.

Hemingway and Stein: Paris, 1922–23

Hemingway's relationship with Gertrude Stein has been recounted many times but never with enough attention to Stein's theories and styles to show how profoundly they influenced Hemingway's prose experiments and emerging style in 1923. Of course, her influence went beyond aesthetics, style, and technique to help shape the young writer's professional identity. It was Stein who told him, after looking over the stories and unfinished novel he had brought with him from Chicago, "begin again and concentrate." He did. It was Stein who told him he would have to cut the journalistic umbilical cord if he hoped to be reborn as a serious writer. He did. Her influence in these formative years can scarcely be overestimated and was matched only by Pound's.

Very likely, Hemingway had started reading Stein's *Three Lives* before he even left the States since Sherwood Anderson, a close friend of Stein's and an enthusiastic promoter of her work, would certainly have recommended the book to Hemingway. If so, her stylistic influence made itself felt at once in the story Hemingway had begun before leaving Chicago, "Up in Michigan."[5] Arriving in Paris with Hadley in late December 1921, he continued reading Stein (as well as Joyce, Pound, and the Russians), checking out *Tender Buttons* from Sylvia Beach's bookstore, Shakespeare and Company (Reynolds, *The Paris Years* 14). One wonders what, if anything, he made of Stein's experiments in abstract description. In any case, he was well prepared in Steinian prose, intermediate and advanced, when he and his wife paid their first social call to 27 rue de Fleurus in March 1922. There, teacher and tyro mutually impressed each other: the formidable and self-assured Stein, the serious and self-effacing Hemingway virtually sitting at her feet to absorb what she could teach him about writing.[6] Stein's collection of modernist art—the best in Paris—also impressed Hemingway deeply. On her atelier's crowded walls, he could observe works by Matisse, Picasso, Braque, Gris, Derain, Dufy, and, most impressive for Hemingway, Cézanne—each painter stripping the medium to color, line, texture, and mass, and in his own way reconfiguring those elements into increasingly abstract arrangements of material reality. This sumptuous visual display powerfully reinforced Stein's own persona as an innovator and imbued her own experiments in prose—as well as her weighty pronouncements on modernist literature—with an authority that seemed to parallel her knowledgeable discussions of the painters and their work. Hemingway was not excluding himself when he wrote in *A Moveable Feast:* "critics who met her and saw her pictures took on trust writing of hers that they could not understand because of their enthusiasm for her as a person, and because of their confidence in her judgment" (17).

Since biographers have often told the personal side of their friendship and falling-out, this chapter will concentrate on Stein's stylistic and thematic influence. Stein's close and prescient contact with avant-garde painting (and, secondarily, her reading of Flaubert and her Radcliffe studies in psychology under William James) made her increasingly aware that the narrative conventions of nineteenth-century literature were inadequate for capturing a contemporary experience of time and space as increasingly fragmented and disjointed.[7] She expressed this new sense of fictional time in several prose works throughout her career. In one of her American lectures in 1935, she states:

> When one used to think of narrative one meant a telling of what is happening in the successive moments of its happening . . . that one thing happened after something else . . . [and] it really did not make any difference where you were at what moment you were in your happening since the important part of the telling was that anything that everything was progressively happening. But now we have changed all that. . . . We . . . do not really know that anything is progressively happening. (*Narration: Four Lectures By Gertrude Stein* 17)

Progressive narration, moving from beginning to middle to end, must now yield to a time sense in which each moment becomes self-contained and, freed of a linear hierarchy, as important as any other moment. For Stein, the change was epistemological as well as experiential and literary. Knowing something, she asserts, always occurs completely in the present, in the now, and does not rely on succession. Therefore to know something one must reject the succession of things to concentrate on the individual moment (*Narration* 20–21).

Stein's analysis of Cubism in her 1938 book on Picasso describes the same alinear shift in virtually the same words:

> [The composition of Cubism] had neither a beginning nor an end, a composition of which one corner was as important as another corner. . . . [B]ecause the way of living had changed, the composition of living had extended and each thing was as important as any other thing. (*Picasso* 37–38)

In her creative writing, as early as *Three Lives* (1905), Stein began devising techniques to express this alinear and acentric narrative and "to concentrate on the individual moment." One technique—which she called "beginning again" and her critics have subsequently labeled as "the continuous present"—was to construct overlapping sentences that each seemed to fold both a character's recent past and implied future into the present moment through juxtaposed verb tenses:

> Melanctha Herbert's mother was now always getting sicker. (*Selected Writings* 362)

In this sentence—a paradigmatic structure in "Melanctha"—"was getting," the past progressive, describes an action without clear temporal boundaries: it overlaps past ("was") and present ("getting"). The relative "sicker," likewise, contributes to this progressive process. But "always" projects the process into the future, while "now," conversely, focuses it on the present moment. When this same sentence appears ten pages later, Stein's technique becomes clearer. Because it folds past and future into present, each moment seems temporally self-contained, but its status is always provisional and progressive, conveying an ongoing process that lacks clear temporal boundaries. Thus, in encountering the same—or, more often, slightly changed—statement further on in the narrative, the reader *experiences,* rather than is told, both the momentary self-sufficiency of the condition and its incremental, almost imperceptible change. Stein explains:

> In ["Melanctha"] there was a consistent recurring and beginning there was a marked direction in the direction of being in the present although naturally I had been accustomed to past present and future, and why, because the composition forming around me was a prolonged present. . . . [which is] a natural composition in the world as it has been these thirty years. ("Composition as Explanation" 517)

Central to this "prolonged present" is the participial verb, either as past or present progressive, which continues an action even as it obscures its temporal boundaries. To get this "present immediacy," Stein writes elsewhere, "I had to use present participles, new constructions of grammar. The grammar constructions are correct, but they are changed in order to get this immediacy" (*How Writing is Written* 155).

"Melanctha"'s subject is well-suited to this incremental style. Although it mostly describes the love affair between a reckless free spirit, Melanctha Herbert, and a cautious, socially responsible doctor, Jeff Campbell, the story is also a psychological study of how one gains worldly experience. The experience is sexual, scarcely concealed by euphemisms like "wisdom" and "knowledge," and (as in Stein's earlier *Q.E.D.*) both protagonists are guided through this experience by a tutor: the aptly named Jane Harden for Melanctha, and Melanctha herself for Jeff. Thus, the glacially slow movement in Stein's "beginning again" style psychologically mirrors the character's gradual awakening, even as its components, particularly absolute adverbs ("always," "never"), suggest static time in a "continuous present":

> Jeff was coming always each time closer to be really understanding, but Melanctha was so bad in her suffering with him, that he knew she could not any longer have him with her while he was always showing that he never really yet was sure what it was, the right way, for them to be really loving. (400)

Hemingway's "Up in Michigan" is heavily indebted to Stein's "Melanctha." Critics have long noted the derivative repetitions in the third paragraph:

> Liz liked it the way he walked over from the shop. . . . She liked it about his mustache. She liked it about how white his teeth were when he smiled. She liked it very much that he didn't look like a blacksmith. She liked it how D. J. Smith and Mrs. Smith liked Jim. One day she found that she liked it the way the hair was black on his arms and how white they were above the tanned line. . . . Liking that made her feel funny.

Hemingway repeated this mannerism, even the verb "like," in two other early stories, "Soldier's Home" and "Cat in the Rain" (and fortunately dropped it there). But Stein's influence extended further. Like "Melanctha," "Up in Michigan" traces an unworldly young woman's sexual awakening, as Liz's infatuation with Jim slowly turns to unrecognized desire. As in "Melanctha," "Up in Michigan" imbues neutral verbs, "think" and "come," with increasingly sexual connotations. Paragraph 6 begins with an exact copy of the typical "Melanctha" sentence: "All the time now Liz was thinking about Jim Gilmore." Paragraph 7 reiterates "thinking" and gradually evolves it into "coming":

> All the time Jim was gone on the deer hunting trip Liz thought about him. It was awful while he was gone. She couldn't sleep well from thinking about him but she discovered it was fun to think about him too. If she let herself go it was better. The night before they were to come back she didn't think she slept because it was all mixed up in a dream about not sleeping and really not sleeping.

> When she saw the wagon coming down the road she felt weak and sick sort of inside. She couldn't wait till she saw Jim and it seemed as though everything would be all right when he came.

Liz's lovesick expectations inevitably collapse during the homecoming—a foreshadowing of the ending—but as the men finish dinner and Liz her chores, she returns to "thinking" about him from the next room:

> Liz was sitting in the kitchen next to the stove pretending to read a book and thinking about Jim. She didn't want to go to bed yet because she knew Jim would be coming out and she wanted to see him as he went out so she could take the way he looked up to bed with her.
>
> She was thinking about him hard and then Jim came out.

In double entendre, their sexual encounter has already occurred before Jim even approaches her. Thus, although critics have viewed Jim's crude actions as a kind of "date rape" that victimizes her,[8] Liz's obsessive "thinking" about Jim "coming" and her wanting to take his image to bed with her shows that, unknowingly, she has been moving in the same direction. Even as she is "terribly frightened" by Jim's fondling her, "she thought, 'He's come to me finally. He's really come.'" And Jim concludes the kitchen encounter by whispering, "Come on for a walk."

Steinian participles dominate this passage as well as the ending: "where Jim was lying. . . . She was crying. . . . A cold mist was coming up." Far more than the crudely repetitious sentence pattern in paragraph 3 ("She liked. . . . "), these techniques of using coded language to convey a psychological condition and participles to create an ongoing action in ambiguous time were ones that Hemingway brought into his mature writing. The first chapter of *in our time* shows how thoroughly participles of "the continuous present" inform his experiments and how skillfully he adapts Stein's overlapping repetition to capture the ongoingness of a night march:

> Everybody was drunk. The whole battery was drunk going along the road in the dark. We were going to the Champagne. The lieutenant kept riding his horse out into the fields and saying to him. . . . We went along the road all night in the dark and the adjutant kept riding up alongside my kitchen and saying, . . . It was funny going along that road.

In chapter 14, Hemingway pushes the participial technique even further, sacrificing grammatical correctness for temporal precision:

> The bull looking at him straight in front, hating. . . .
> Villalta standing straight and the red hilt of the sword sticking out dully between the bull's shoulders. . . .
> the bull roaring blood, looking straight at Villalta and his legs caving.

In *A Moveable Feast,* Hemingway writes that Stein had "discovered many truths about rhythms and the uses of words in repetition that were valid and valuable and she talked well about them" (17). In a letter to W. G. Rogers in 1948, he acknowledges that she had taught him "wonderful rhythms in prose" (*Selected Letters* 649). One might well assume these sentence rhythms encouraged long, unfolding compounds, interlaced with repetitions of key words and kept fluid by participials, such as this one beginning chapter 11:

> In 1919 he was travelling on the railroads in Italy carrying a square of oilcloth from the headquarters of the party written in indelible pencil and saying here was a comrade who had suffered very much under the whites in Budapest and requesting comrades to aid him in any way.

But, arguably, Stein also modeled for him in *Tender Buttons* writing so bereft of explanatory context and referential meaning as to seem abstract, in which the sounds and textures of words, and the rhythms they form, function in place of semantic meanings. In describing his indebtedness to Stein, Hemingway several times mentions learning from her "the abstract relationship of words" (see, for example, Plimpton, "Interview" 27). Like the critics he described, Hemingway may not have understood *Tender Buttons,* but he could still learn from its statements that perfectly described Stein's technique and her modernist sense of asymmetry:

> Act so there is no use in a centre ("Rooms," *Selected Writings* 498)
> A whole is in a part. ("Salad Dressing And An Artichoke" 496)

While other writers, notably Pound, encouraged this attention to parts, Stein's most radically fragmented writing may have inspired Hemingway to cut explanatory contexts from his own brief sketches in *in our time* and to begin many of his narratives in the middle.

Hemingway and Pound: Paris, 1922–23

Hemingway took nearly three months to work up the courage to meet Gertrude Stein. With Ezra Pound, it was easier, for the relationship of mentor and disciple came naturally to Pound, whose record as a talent scout and promoter of genius over the previous decade was remarkable. In fact, during his first visit to Pound's apartment in February 1922, Hemingway could have seen on Pound's desk a draft of Eliot's long poem, soon to be titled *The Waste Land,* which Eliot (en route from Lausanne to London) had left for Pound to mark up. Almost certainly, Pound discussed the poem with Hemingway, and its influence would soon appear in *in our time.* As he would with Stein, Hemingway "listened at E. P.'s feet, as to an oracle," Hadley Hemingway recalled, while the bearded eccentric discoursed on poetry and fiction.[9] In exchange, Hemingway gave Pound boxing and tennis lessons.

In many respects, Pound's technical advice and exemplars seem antithetical to Stein's. "Melanctha"'s prose rhythms lumber in lengthy, overlapping compound sentences:

> He loved his people and he never hurt them, and he always did everything they wanted and that he could to please them, but he really loved best science and experimenting and to learn things, and he early wanted to be a doctor, and he was always very interested in the life of the colored people. (360)

Pound's Imagist principles, by contrast, demand maximal compression ("Use no superfluous word") by *presenting* through the image ("that which presents an intellectual or emotional complex in an instant of time") rather than describing with numerous adjectives. "The point of Imagisme," Pound wrote in 1916, "is that it does not use images as ornaments. The image is itself the speech." Cut from Imagist poetry are explanation, abstractions ("language is made out of concrete things"), philosophizing ("Don't be 'viewy'"), singsong metronomic meters ("rhythm must have meaning"), and likewise the filler necessary to make regular meters scan.[10] In its most radical form, Imagism even omitted connectives and verbs, relying on juxtaposition (or, as Pound later called it, superposition) of images to present the poem's meaning:

The apparition of these faces in the crowd;
Petals on a wet, black bough.

Although these principles were already a decade old in 1922, and Pound was now writing long Cantos rather than two-line poems, he had never abandoned the principles of maximal compression and presentation through the image. They were, in fact, the essence of the "ideogrammic method" that now structured his Cantos.

Since Hemingway considered himself in 1922 as much a poet as a prose writer, Pound's advice and models were immediately valuable. In fact, Hemingway had probably encountered both in the issues of *Poetry* he read in Chicago; moreover, he had written Imagist poems before coming to Paris. Now, however, the master himself could critique his work, such as "Oily Weather," a rather unsubtle Imagist piece that Pound recommended to the *Dial* and Hemingway included in *Three Stories & Ten Poems:*

The sea desires deep hulls—
It swells and rolls.
The screw churns a throb—
Driving, throbbing, progressing.
The sea rolls with love.
Surging, caressing.
Undulating its great loving belly,
The sea is big and old—
Throbbing ships scorn it. (*88 Poems* 44)

Although he also selected "Roosevelt" for the *Dial,* Pound was probably less enthused about Hemingway's satirical poems—and Gertrude Stein would have despised them had she read his nasty parody of her style in "The Soul of Spain":

In the rain in the rain in the rain in the rain in Spain.
Does it rain in Spain?
Oh yes my dear on the contrary and there are no bull fights.
The dancers dance in long white pants
It isn't right to yence your aunts
Come Uncle, let's go home.
Home is where the heart is, home is where the fart is.
Come let us fart in the home.

There is no art in a fart.
Still a fart may not be artless.
Let us fart and artless fart in the home.

(*88 Poems* 70)

Despite his heavy-handedness with the genre (and in this case adolescent crudeness), satire and parody appealed to Hemingway early on. He wrote several such pieces in Chicago and Paris as poems, brief sketches, journalistic dispatches, and in 1925, a novel, *The Torrents of Spring,* parodying Sherwood Anderson's writing.

Hemingway recalled in *A Moveable Feast* how much he valued Pound's advice: Ezra "was the man I liked and trusted the most as a critic then, the man who believed in the *mot juste*—the one and only correct word to use—the man who had taught me to distrust adjectives" (132). Clearly, this discipline applied to prose as well as to poetry. As Michael Reynolds summarizes:

> It was Pound who told Hemingway that symbols first must be natural objects, their symbolic function not obtruding into the work . . . [L]et the action speak for itself. Without telling readers how to respond, what to feel, how to judge, let images convey meaning. If action is presented truly, precisely, using only its essential elements, then readers, without being told, will respond emotionally as the writer intended. . . . Hemingway arrived in Paris using some of the technique unconsciously. Pound and, a little later, Stein made him see clearly what he was doing. (*The Paris Years* 31)

"Up in Michigan," that litmus test of stylistic influence, shows Pound's Imagism intermingling with Anderson's themes and Stein's rhythms and repetitions. Like the repeated words "think" and "come" (discussed above), symbolic images foreshadow Liz's sexual encounter. "Big," "hard," and "stiff" recur often, first to describe the dead buck Jim has bagged (as he will "bag" Liz), then to describe what Liz feels as he holds her against the chair. Complementing these phallic images, "warmer and softer" images, such as "the water lapping in the piles," suggest Liz's physical arousal that fights against her fear and rigidity. Finally, Hemingway imagistically anticipates the intercourse itself from Liz's perspective: Jim holds her "tight hard against the chair" and "it was such a sharp, aching hurting feeling that she thought she couldn't stand it and then something clicked inside of her and the feeling was warmer and softer."

One aspect of the story—its graphic depictions—Hemingway did not learn from anybody. In their actual encounter on the "hard" hemlock planks, symbolic imagery becomes literal, as Liz cries, "Oh, it's so big and it hurts so." This was the passage that probably prompted Stein to predict to Hemingway that the story was not publishable. And she was correct—for a time: though it appears in *Three Stories & Ten Poems,* Boni & Liveright had the story replaced for their 1925 publication of *In Our Time,* and Scribner's did not publish it until *The First Forty-nine Stories* appeared in 1938. To mention the unmentionable in print was not merely the naughtiness of an enfant terrible, nor was it simply trendy subversion, though Joyce, Cummings, Lawrence, and others were simultaneously challenging these limits. Rather, Hemingway's frankness was central to his emerging aesthetics: to depict elemental realities that earlier authors had softened through euphemism and indirect handling. As subsequent chapters will discuss, *in our time* forces its readers to look at sordid, brutal, and gory images: the returning soldier contracting gonorrhea, the horse with its intestines hanging out, the terrified prisoner messing his pants. These images were shocking in 1923 and still retain the power to shock readers with their unblinking directness.

Pound's response to "Up in Michigan" is unrecorded, but he did not promote the story. He did like some of Hemingway's poems enough to recommend them to Scofield Thayer at the *Dial.* When Thayer rejected them, Pound sent them to Harriet Monroe, who accepted six for *Poetry.* Here was another realm—arguably, the most important—in which Pound could and did help the aspiring writer, just as he had so many before him. As foreign correspondent for the *Dial,* poetry editor for the *Little Review,* and an influential associate of Harriet Monroe, Pound was unquestionably the best connected and most influential advocate for the avant-garde in Paris. Since the early teens, he had used that influence tirelessly to promote those he felt would help raise the quality of new art to his own exacting standards. Hemingway recounts in *A Moveable Feast:* "Ezra was the most generous writer I have ever known and the most disinterested. He helped poets, painters, sculptors and prose writers that he believed in and he would help anyone whether he believed in them or not if they were in trouble" (110). The assistance he offered Hemingway was crucial to the young writer's nascent career. Besides placing his poems, Pound recommended Hemingway in 1924 as associate editor for the *transatlantic review* (under the editorship of Pound's friend, Ford Madox Ford). The review quickly became the most prominent among the American expatriates and did much to establish Hemingway's name in that community, printing several of his stories and editorial pieces. More important (as will be described in the next chapter), Pound commissioned Hemingway directly (through the Three Mountains Press) and indirectly (via the *Little Review*) to create his most experimental writing, which became *in our time.*

Just as Eliot had done with drafts of *The Waste Land,* Hemingway consulted Pound regularly while writing *in our time.* His letter to Pound c. 5 August 1923 is a progress report of the chapters and shows that Pound had critiqued them carefully with suggestions that Hemingway followed: "I will do the hanging [of Sam Cardinella—chapter 17]. Have *redone the death* of Maera [chapter 16] altogether different and *fixed the others.* The new death is good" (*Selected Letters* 91, emphasis mine). In his oft-quoted description of the chapters' unity (see Chapter Two), Hemingway was apparently responding to Pound's questions about their order and coherence. Although we can only infer from Hemingway's revisions the passages that Pound wanted fixed (and Pound certainly did not inspire all of these changes), the draft of Maera's death that he disliked *is* inferior to Hemingway's final version. Based on this fact and Pound's excellent editing of *The Waste Land,* it is safe to assume that his critical suggestions were beneficial.

In sum, the separate influences Pound and Stein exerted on Hemingway's evolving prose style seem antithetical but were actually complementary. Stein's overlapping compounds and participles interchanged with Pound's taut image fragments to create a whiplash effect of a rhythm unrolling, then snapping back sharply:

> There was a woman having a kid with a young girl holding a blanket over her and crying. Scared sick looking at it. (chapter 3)

> He had so much equipment on and looked awfully surprised and fell down into the garden. Then three more came over further down the wall. (chapter 4)

> They shot the six cabinet ministers at half past six in the morning against the wall of a hospital. There were pools of water in the courtyard. There were wet dead leaves on the paving of the courtyard. (chapter 6)

Where Stein and Pound concurred is in seeing that modern writing—prose and poetry both—required the same restructuring of its basic elements that modern painting and music had undergone to convey the freshness and intensity of physical experience within the tension and tautness of constructed form. To renew itself, writing had to slough off the accumulated habits of earlier prose: explaining, sentimentalizing, softening ugliness, editorializing. New prose *presented* experience without introducing or explaining or softening it. The interpretive work earlier authors had done was now the reader's responsibility.

Hemingway and Eliot: Paris, 1922–23

Pound and Stein were mentors Hemingway freely acknowledged; T. S. Eliot was one he did not. In fact, Hemingway repeatedly ridiculed Eliot in print. In his memorial to Joseph Conrad, he wrote:

> If I knew that by grinding Mr. Eliot into a fine dry powder and sprinkling that powder over Mr. Conrad's grave Mr. Conrad would shortly appear, looking very annoyed at the forced return and commence writing I would leave for London tomorrow morning with a sausage grinder. One should not be funny over the death of a great man, but you cannot couple T. S. Eliot and Joseph Conrad in a sentence seriously . . . and not laugh. (*transatlantic review* 341–42)

In his "Homage to Ezra" in *This Quarter* (Spring 1925), he took another swipe, calling Eliot "a minor poet" who took few chances, compared to Pound's daring innovations (221–25). As Michael Reynolds explains, Hemingway was no doubt jealous of Eliot's status then among the American avant-garde (*The Paris Years* 272–73). Hemingway may also have felt a kind of sibling rivalry with Eliot, vying for Papa Pound's attention (Pound launched his Bel Esprit plan to subsidize Eliot while still consulting with Hemingway about *in our time*).

Given these attitudes, Hemingway would not have readily acknowledged Eliot's influence on his experimental writing, but it is there nonetheless. The most obvious example occurs in a stream-of-consciousness piece Hemingway sketched in Rapallo at the same time he was composing his first *in our time* chapters:

> Cats love in the garden. On the green tea table to be exact. The big cat gets on the small cat. Sweeney gets on Mrs. Porter. Ezra gets nowhere except artistically of course. ("Rapallo," KL[11] 670.4)

Sweeney and Mrs. Porter appear in *The Waste Land,* but the Sweeney of an earlier poem, "Sweeney Among the Nightingales," may well have informed a curious revision Hemingway made to chapter 17 of *in our time.* Eliot's poem is masked in veiled references to characters engaged in ambiguous actions:

> The person in the Spanish cape. . . .
> The silent man in mocha brown. . . .
> The silent vertebrate in brown. . . .
> the man with heavy eyes

In chapter 17, the two guards who carry, then drop, Sam Cardinella are identified thus: "They were both disgusted. 'How about a chair, Will?' asked one of the guards. 'Better get one,' said a man in a derby hat." In an earlier draft, "a man in a derby hat" was clearly identified as the "deputy sherriff" [sic]. Hemingway thus intentionally obscured his identity à la Eliot in the final version.

Without question, Eliot's strongest influence on *in our time* appears in its multiple voices (discussed in Chapter Four). In eighteen small chapters, some twenty-six different voices speak. Many voices, including several first-person narrators, are anonymous or identified only by their occupations: a kitchen corporal, two British officers, a fellow soldier, a comrade of a young revolutionist, and so on. Frequently, the voices narrate in medias res and refer to themselves and others with ambiguous pronouns: "Everybody was drunk"; "We were in a garden"; "They shot . . . "; "They hanged . . . "; "We went to work on the trench." Michael Reynolds has identified Eliot as a likely source of this technique:

> That was the thing, lots of different voices. Eliot used so many voices in *The Waste Land* that it was hard to say when he was speaking. When Hemingway finished *in our time,* he achieved something of the same effect. (*The Paris Years* 125)[12]

"Paris 1922"

Eliot's depictions of lonely workingmen are strikingly similar to one of the six experimental sentences Hemingway composed in the late spring or summer of 1922, which he entitled "Paris 1922."[13] Compare:

> I have stood on the crowded back platform of a seven o'clock Batignolles bus as it lurched along the wet lamp lit street while men who were going home to supper never looked up from their

newspapers as we passed Notre Dame gray and dripping in the rain. (Hemingway)

and:

Shall I say, I have gone at dusk through narrow streets
And watched the smoke that rises from the pipes
Of lonely men in shirt-sleeves, leaning out of windows?
("The Love Song of J. Alfred Prufrock")

And short square fingers stuffing pipes,
And evening newspapers, and eyes
assured of certain certainties
("Preludes" IV)

A crowd flowed over London Bridge, so many
I had not thought death had undone so many,
Sighs, short and infrequent, were exhaled,
And each man fixed his eyes before his feet.
(*The Waste Land* I)

The other "Paris 1922" sentences each begin with "I have seen" and describe in compressed, vivid detail six scenes or actions the narrator has witnessed: (1) a steeplechase accident at Auteuil, which the crowd ignores in its haste to see the finish; (2) a quarrel at a late-night dance club between Peggy Joyce and a "shellac haired" young Chilean, who shoots himself later that night; (3) a battle between police and a crowd on May Day, in which a sixteen-year-old boy has shot two policeman; (4) the workingmen on the Batignolles bus (quoted above); (5) a one-legged prostitute sheltered from the rainy night by an Episcopal clergyman holding an umbrella over her; and (6) two Senegalese soldiers teasing a king cobra in the snake house of the Jardin des Plantes.

Hemingway himself "fancied" these sentences.[14] When they were lost with his other writings in the suitcase theft of December 1922, he immediately set about recreating them from memory, and their several drafts (KL 647, 647a) show the pains he took to get them exactly right. Before he started composing his chapters, he thought of using "Paris 1922" for his contribution to the *Little Review* "Exiles" issue.[15]

Scholars have made much of these "Paris 1922" sentences partly because they appear to anticipate the experimental chapters he started writing half a year later and because Hemingway had written so little else in 1922 that was not journalism. Both Carlos Baker and Michael Reynolds identify them with the "true sentence" Hemingway famously described in recalling his early Paris writing in *A Moveable Feast*.[16] Baker, for example, writes:

> He had set about in January to write one true sentence. By the end of May he had managed to write six—declarative, straightforward, and forceful. . . . After all the false starts in Petoskey and Chicago, he was on his way at last. (*A Life Story* 91)

Hemingway's "one true sentence" passage, however, does not refer specifically to these sentences and clearly links the "true" sentences to short stories: "So finally I would write one true sentence, and go on from there. . . . Up in that room I decided that I would write one story about each thing I knew about" (12).

Nonetheless, "Paris 1922" is an important step between Hemingway's earlier work and the *in our time* chapters. Formally, they are more elementary—sentences as compared to *in our time*'s paragraphs—in Hemingway's construction of a new style. Yet, the sentences are not simply stylistic exercises but an embryonic version of "unwritten stories" that he would approach quite differently in *in our time.* At their core are vivid images that convey the essence of each scene: the "the white, beaten up face of the sixteen year old kid who looked like a prep school quarter back"; the shellac hair of Peggy Joyce's Chilean companion; the cobra's "tense, erect rage" versus the snakelike crouching and weaving soldier in the red fez.

Each image implies a fuller story, much the way Pound's images do in "The Jewel Stairs' Grievance"; uncharacteristically, Pound made the implication explicit:

> Note.—Jewel stairs, therefore a palace. Grievance, therefore there is something to complain of. Gauze stockings, therefore a court lady, not a servant who complains. Clear autumn, therefore . . . [17]

Consider the "Peggy Joyce" sentence. The draft reads:

> ~~quarrelling~~
> I have seen Peggy Joyce at 2 a.m. in a Dancing in the Rue
> quarreling

> Caumartin with the shellac~~ed~~ haired young Chilean who
> (had ~~a little[?]~~ manicured fingernails
> ~~danced like Rudolph Valentino and hot~~ / blew a puff of cigarette
> smoke into her face, wrote something in a note book) and shot
> himself at 3.30 the same morning
>
> (KL 647 ms.)

Hemingway's revision cuts several revealing details:

> I have seen Peggy Joyce at 2 A.M. in a dancing in the Rue Caumartin quarreling with the shallaced haired young Chilean who had long pointed finger nails, danced like Rudolph Valentino and shot himself at 3.30 that same morning. (KL 647a ts.)

Taken together, the images condense a dissolving and distorted relationship:

Image	*Implications*
2 A.M. / dancing	keeps late hours, socialite
quarreling	public display, unhappy relationship, breakup
shallac haired	dandified, Valentino-like
long pointed finger nails	effeminate, homosexual or bisexual?
young	gigolo? kept man? Joyce desperate for male attention?
danced like Valentino	see above
blew puff of smoke in her face	cruel act, final farewell: coup de grâce. Did she send him away?
shot himself	Yes. Latin temperament: extremes

The unnarrated story here anticipates Hemingway's technique of omission. But the repetitive first-person opener—"I have seen"—severely limits the potential of these sentences to expand into narrative by distracting us from the scene to the superfluous narrator. By contrast, the typical *in our time* chapter presents an action that may span a few moments or several hours (for instance, the civilian evacuation from Adrianople). Although the action often begins and sometimes ends in medias res, its presentation makes it appear self-contained, a single experience. And in the chapters, Hemingway learned to diminish the dominance of first-person narrators—either by making them peripheral to the action (chapter 8), masking them in anonymity (chapter 13), or by changing them to third person (chapter 10). In sum, the "Paris 1922" sentences are a stage in Hemingway's reteaching himself narrative beginning with the sentence. But they are rudimentary compared to the narrative paragraphs he developed in *in our time.*

Journalistic Style: 1918–23

Hemingway's extensive experience writing for newspapers has been thoroughly examined by critics and biographers and needs only summary here.[18] In Charles Fenton's view, Hemingway's experience with the *Kansas City Star* and the *Toronto Star* did more to shape his style and tone than any other influence (*Apprenticeship* vii).[19] As a cub reporter for the *Kansas City Star* fresh out of high school, Hemingway quickly learned what reporters traditionally have learned: see things firsthand (hence, get to the scene of the action); present the story accurately and objectively, leaving out your personal response to the event; and find the telling details that recreate the scene. Given the police and general hospital beat, he brushed the demimonde of criminals and cops, pimps and hookers, and crimes of violence. The more action he could find, the better he liked it. This real-world experience gave him a considerable edge over college-educated contemporaries such as Dos Passos and Cummings, who first had to shuck off the upper-class gentility of their college education before they could begin to see the seamier sides of life.

The *Kansas City Star* also imposed on its reporters a rigorous style sheet of rules for clear, vigorous writing. Among those that left indelible marks on Hemingway's style were:

- Use short sentences [declarative sentences, Hemingway amended later[20]]. Use short first paragraphs. Use vigorous English. Be positive, not negative.
- Never use old slang. . . . Slang to be enjoyable must be fresh.
- Avoid the use of adjectives, especially such extravagant ones as *splendid, gorgeous, grand, magnificent,* etc. (qtd. in Fenton 35–37)

Lest a reporter forget these rules, the blue pencil of a copy editor was always there to remind him. Hemingway later called them "the best rules I ever learned for the business of writing. I've never forgotten them."[21] It is worth noting, however, that he did not immediately apply them to the slick fiction he wrote in 1918–21, the sentences of which were often quite convoluted and heavily modified. Only later would he revisit these rules when he was forming his own style.

Hemingway's dispatches for the *Toronto Star* (1920–24) were quite different from the straight reporting he had done earlier. Now, he could put himself into the human interest feature pieces he was expected to produce. The writing could be more subjective and adjective-laden, provided it was entertaining and vivid. Hemingway could also gratify his bent toward satire and sharpen his skills at writing dialogue since both were welcome. As a freelancer and later a foreign correspondent, he had considerable freedom in selecting his material, although he also received assignments abroad to cover big stories.

Several of the chapters in *in our time* come from events that Hemingway either covered himself (for example, the evacuation from Eastern Thrace, chapter 3), or got secondhand from another reporter (the visit to the king and queen, chapter 18), or read in the newspaper: the executions of Sam Cardinella (17) and the Greek cabinet ministers (6), and the cigar store robbery foiled by the police (9). More important, these and other chapters are narrated in an intentionally dispassionate or "flat" prose, which, combined with their factual emphasis, gives the narratives a distinctly journalistic feel:

> They hanged Sam Cardinella at six o'clock in the morning in the corridor of the county jail. The corridor was high and narrow with tiers of cells on either side. All the cells were occupied. The men had been brought in for the hanging. Five men sentenced to be hanged were in the five top cells. Three of the men to be hanged were negroes. They were very frightened. One of the white men sat on his cot with his head in his hands. The other lay flat on his cot with a blanket wrapped around his head. (chapter 17)

The frisson between the violence in these chapters and the dispassionate, factual voice presenting it has always affected readers powerfully. As one early reviewer of *In Our Time* wrote: "his stories are almost too artfully disanchored from his own emotions. Vital and astringent they are to a surpassing degree. . . . In lean, spare sentences he always makes you *see* the thing he writes about."[22] The voice in chapter 17 (as in chapters 3, 6, 9, 12) is anonymous and "journalistic." But even when that detached voice gradually reveals itself as first person—as in chapters 8, 11, 13, and 18—the effect is nearly the same, with the focus on the subject rather than the narrator. Finally, in the passage quoted above, all of the sentences have simple structures, some with brief phrases ("to be hanged"). The other "journalistic" chapters also rely heavily on simple sentences (see appendix). This combination of factual statements focused on an outward event, ostensibly shorn of narrative sentiment, and conveyed in simple structures is what makes these narratives appear journalistic.

But "journalistic" is not journalism. While appearing dispassionate, the narratives cited above attempt to manipulate our responses, usually through stylized elements, such as symbolic images and sentence structure. The pervasive rain and wetness images in chapter 3, for example, heighten the misery of the marchers, just as the chapter's participles and fragments emphasize the ongoing endlessness of their trek. Similarly, the provocatively ambiguous pronouns that begin these same chapters oppose journalistic clarity and omit explanatory context (why the refugees march, why the horse prances around with his intestines hanging out). These omissions create a scene abstracted from the causal world of journalism and focused on the nowness of the events themselves. As with the influences of Stein, Pound, Eliot, and Anderson, Hemingway selected and blended journalistic elements into stylistic experiments of his own.

"Cablese"

Hemingway once advised his fellow journalist Lincoln Steffens to concentrate on the "cablese" style (rather than on the political themes) of Hemingway's dispatch covering the civilian evacuation from Eastern Thrace ("A Silently, Ghastly Procession"): "Look at the cablese. Only the cablese. Isn't it a great language?" Steffens also recalls Hemingway telling him that he had quit journalism because "he was becoming too deeply fascinated with the lingo of the transatlantic cable."[23] These casual remarks have led to some confusion about the influence of "cablese" in Hemingway's creative writing.

Technically, cablese was a specialized style intended to save newspapers money on expensive transatlantic cables that were billed by the word. Hemingway sent such cables to the *Toronto Star* to be rewritten for immediate release. An example appears in his papers:

> TURKS POSTCHILD CONFERENCE ARRIVED COMPROMISE PLAN STOP PRESENT TOMORROW ADAMANT REFUSAL XXXX NATIONAL ARMENIAN HOME REFUSE ALLOW GREEK PATRIARCHATE STAY CONSTANTINOPLE BUT WILLING COMPROMISE IN-

> TERNATIONAL COMMISSION PROSUPERVISION XX MINORITIES AS YUGOSLAVIA BULGARIA CZECHOSLOVAKIA STOP WILL ASK TIME XX DECIDE WHETHER TO ACCEPT LEAGUE NATIONS PLANNING REFER ANGORAWARDS STOP LEARN EXBRITISH SOURCES CURZON ANGRIEST CONSTANT INGIVINGS FORCED HIM TURKWARDS BROKEN WITH SIR WILLIAM TYRELL PERMANENT HEAD FOREIGN OFFICE INTENDS MAKE STAND PRONATIONAL ARMENIAN HOME GREEK PATRIARCHATE AND LET CONFERENCE UPBREAK IF XXXXX NECESSARY THOSE POINTS STOP BRITISH TONIGHT TRYING UPPATCH[24]

Sentence fragments include only key words—thus, the Turkish position that adamantly refuses to allow the Greek Patriarchate to remain at Constantinople becomes "refuse allow Greek patriarchate stay Constantinople." The style economically compresses idiomatic phrases like "patch up" and "break up" into inverted fusions: "uppatch," "upbreak." Similarly, "from British" becomes "exBritish"; "giving in" becomes "ingivings"; "towards [the] Turk[ish position]" shrinks to the admirably concise "Turkwards."[25]

Because he did not cable his feature stories for the *Toronto Star,* Hemingway had no need to compress their prose this radically. "A Silent, Ghastly Procession," for example, contains numerous examples of colorful adjectives that Hemingway later cut when he rewrote it for *in our time.* His creative writing, likewise, contains no such cablese inversions as "ingivings." In fact, the simple sentences of *in our time* are less economical than cables, since each complete sentence requires its own subject and verb. Nonetheless, cablese did influence his creative prose, most obviously in requiring that superfluous modifiers be cut. Hemingway also experimented with the cable's fragmentary style. One draft of chapter 3 reads:

> Carts ~~were~~ jammed for thirty miles on the Karagatch road. Rain coming down. Mud splashed water buffalo and cattle hauling carts. No end and no beginning. Just carts piled with everything they owned. Old men and women soaked through walking along keeping the cattle moving. The Maritza rising and running yellow. Carts jammed solid on the bridge with camels bobbing along

> through. Greek cavalry riding herd on the procession. ~~Wayxoffxxx~~ Women , kids , in the carts crouched with mattresses,mirrors, sewing machines ,bundles. All in the rain. A woman having a kid with her little girl holding a xxxxxxx blanket over her and crying. Scared to death. That was the beginning of the retreat.
>
> 110 wds[26]

Although the final version was more conventional, several fragments remained: "No end and no beginning. Just carts loaded with everything they owned. . . . Scared sick looking at it."

Thus, when Hemingway spoke of "cablese" in his writing, he was really referring to his adapting some of its compressions, just as he was adapting and transforming, at the same time, the simultaneous influences of Pound, Stein, Eliot, Anderson, and journalism. Pure "cablese" would have looked very strange as prose fiction.

Conclusion

A year after Hemingway had arrived in Paris, December 1922, his creative style—indeed, his creative identity—was still in flux. He had definitely put behind him his early ambition to write slick fiction for the commercial magazines. But he was not yet certain of what new style should replace it. He knew he could write for newspapers and spent most of his first year in Paris doing just that. But he also knew he wanted more: to be a successful creative writer—successful artistically as well as financially. In Chicago, the artsy crowd he lived with started him thinking about modernism. Sherwood Anderson, the hero of this group, showed him how to use colloquial English, naive narrators, and sexual themes. Anderson's success also demonstrated that a writer could be applauded by the avant-garde and read by the masses. And in accepting Anderson's advice that Paris is the best place for a serious writer, Hemingway tacitly accepted that identity: He would be not merely a professional writer, but an artist.

But what kind of an artist? Much of the creative work he brought with him, and most of his 1922 writing, was poetry. His poems were split, however, between irreverent satires and short imagistic pieces, along with more than a trace of Victorian sentimentality in such Chicago poems as "Killed. Piave—July 8—1918." His fiction and prose sketches were also diffuse. The few stories and fragment of a novel he had brought with him from Chicago impressed neither Stein nor Pound.

In 1922, he had revised his first artistic story, "Up in Michigan," and its psychological realism, symbolic images, and sexual frankness showed promise and daring. But the story was also flawed in its abruptly shifting points of view and too obviously indebted to Anderson, Stein, and Pound. His other story that year, "My Old Man," showed how Hemingway could get inside of a particular world—here the subculture of European horse racing—and recreate with authority its everyday life, denizens, and language. He would soon do the same for bullfighting, boxing, fishing, and skiing. But he also recognized that the narrative perspective of "My Old Man," that of a naive, inarticulate, young narrator who becomes disillusioned, was not his bailiwick and was too reminiscent of Anderson's.

Meanwhile, Stein's advice to "begin again and concentrate" lingered. If he were to transform himself into a modernist, he certainly had two excellent mentors helping him. Stylistically, however, Stein's and Pound's examples seemed to pull in opposite directions. In "Melanctha," Stein's participles and long, compound sentences intentionally redound and overlap to gradually unfold a narrative in psychological time. Pound's Imagism demanded maximal compression of narrative into the "luminous detail." Both styles, however, defied the conventions of their genres to achieve a tension between formal abstraction and mimetic realism. With *Tender Buttons,* Stein shifted the fulcrum most of the way toward abstraction. And, like so many modernist painters and composers, both writers seemed to have formed their styles by starting from scratch—rethinking and recombining the basic elements of their crafts.

Hemingway's "Paris 1922" sentences were a first step in starting from scratch. But these "five-finger exercises," as Reynolds has called them (95), were too slight, their imagistic cores, while vivid, too undeveloped to become the "unwritten stories" that Hemingway would soon contemplate. The crucial questions of artistic identity thus remained: journalist, poet, satirist, or fiction writer? A detached analyst of psychosexual tensions or an insider-narrator, capturing the "fact and motion" of an action milieu? A stylist of unfolding sentences and overlapping repetition or of compressed, symbolic images that imply a larger narrative? Each of these personas—and, more likely, particular configurations of them—were viable for Hemingway by the end of 1922.

2
A Coalescence of Pieces
Composing *in our time*

It took Hemingway about seven months to write *in our time.* He began it in late January or early February 1923 at Chamby-sur-Montreux, where, after covering the Lausanne Conference for the *Toronto Star,* he enjoyed skiing and bobsledding with Hadley and friends. In late August, he finished revising the eighteen chapters just before he and Hadley boarded the boat for Canada. The book's immediate impetus derived from two profoundly contrasting developments in the last five months of 1922—events that combined to become a watershed in Hemingway's literary career.

The first development was exhilarating—and intimidating. In the late summer of 1922 (probably August), Ezra Pound invited Hemingway to contribute a short book to a series, "*The Inquest* into the state of contemporary English prose," that Pound had agreed to edit for Bill Bird's new Three Mountains Press. As Pound described the project to another potential contributor, William Carlos Williams, each book was to be short—about fifty pages—and consist of "strictly modern" prose. The "private limited [edition]" (Pound envisioned 350 copies) would free authors from having to write down to a public audience:

> One can be more intimate. . . . one is talking [not] to the public, but simply to one's friends. . . .
>
> The series is OPEN: Though I don't at the moment see much more than half a dozen names: Hueffer, you, Eliot, Lewis, Windeler, Hemingway, et moi même. (That's seven.) . . .
>
> This is a prose series. General success or point of the thng wd. lie in its being really interesting.[1]

Hemingway was especially well situated for this commission since Bird, a friend and fellow newsman, originally got the idea of contacting

Pound from Hemingway himself (Reynolds, *The Paris Years* 80). Nonetheless, Pound's invitation was a great vote of confidence—and a gamble. He could not have seen much of Hemingway's Parisian work since Hemingway had not written much in the seven months since he had arrived: the revised "Up in Michigan," "My Old Man," several poems, and the "Paris 1922" sentences. It was not Pound's first solicitation—he had promoted Hemingway's poems to the *Dial* and *Poetry* and a prose piece to the *Little Review,* where he served as coeditor. But this commission was for a book, and it was virtually a blank check. Even two months later in October, Pound still had no idea what Hemingway would write and was forced to list "Blank" by his name in a prospectus that Pound and Bird produced for the book.

Hemingway realized that he had not really earned this opportunity, and the prospect of measuring up to the standards of this great editor must have been daunting even for this naturally ebullient young man. After the prospectus was published, Hemingway acknowledged in a letter to Pound (c. November 1922)[2] that his inclusion in the *Inquest* group was due only to Pound's friendship; he grimly pledged not to disappoint the master and even offered Pound the chance to renege on his commission. Even though he had nothing *yet* worth submitting, Hemingway continued, he now knew what he wanted to achieve in prose and would be able to tell if he got it regardless of who praised it (he listed twenty-one different authors and critics). He should have some examples of the new prose ready in six months.[3]

A curious mixture, this letter, of assertive confidence, defensiveness, and procrastination—why a six-month delay? Hemingway may have known what he was after, but he seemed in no hurry to achieve it. To be sure, his other career was leaving him little time to write, as he covered the Christian retreat from Thrace in October and the Lausanne Conference in late November. All the while, he mulled over what his contribution to the *Inquest* would be.

At first, he thought of making his book a collection of his poems; to that end, he wrote Harriet Monroe in November for permission to republish the poems she had accepted for *Poetry* (*Selected Letters* 72). As Michael Reynolds observes, this notion shows how little he thought of his fiction to date (*The Paris Years* 81). It also shows that as late as November 1922 he was still thinking of himself—or at least his avant-garde self—as a poet as much as a prose writer. (His first book, *Three Stories & Ten Poems,* carries this mixed identity into 1923.) But Pound was directing his *Inquest* into prose, and the commission gave Hemingway a powerful incentive to create something new and to show the avant-garde in Paris and Chicago what kind of "contemporary English prose" this newcomer could construct.

Strengthening this incentive, the *Little Review* invited Hemingway to contribute to its spring "Exiles" issue. Although Hemingway biographers have credited Jane Heap, the *Little Review's* coeditor, with commissioning Hemingway (Baker, *A Life Story* 108; Reynolds, *The Paris Years* 113–14; Lynn 193), evidence clearly points to Pound.[4] As co-"Administrator" of the magazine, he suggested the idea for an "Exiles" number and included his newest discovery in the list of potential authors he would solicit:

> Do you want me to arrange a number? . . .
> The people I could bulldoze into contributing are
> possibly Cocteau
> B. M. G. Adams
> Hemingway
> Christian [Georges Herbiet], if I can find him
> [Robert] MacAlmon [sic] and I suppose Mina [Loy]. . . .
> (*Pound/The Little Review* 296–97)[5]

Pound's two commissions—the *Inquest* book and the *Little Review* contribution—could not have arrived more opportunely, not just to steer Hemingway back to prose, but to redefine the kind of prose he should write and the kind of writer he saw himself becoming. Both commissions sought innovative, experimental writing. The *Inquest* books would be "strictly modern"—"six works of invention."[6] And in that "Exiles" issue, Hemingway would rub shoulders with avant-gardists (his mentor, Stein, Cocteau, Léger) and enfants terrible, such as Antheil and Cummings.

Again, Hemingway was uncertain of what he would submit to this celebrated magazine that had serialized *Ulysses* and damned the common reader. According to Reynolds, he contemplated sending his most experimental writing to date, the "Paris 1922" sentences (*The Paris Years* 114). But they were too slight. Conventional stories obviously would not do for "contemporary" prose. And, unlike the book commission, the spring issue of the *Little Review* had a short deadline: April 1923. If he was to send them prose that represented "Ernest Hemingway, Paris 'exile,'" he would have to start right away.

The second major development for Hemingway was a catastrophe with a silver lining. In early December 1922, a valise containing nearly all the early work that he valued was stolen from Hadley on the train to Lausanne.[7] Without question, Hemingway was devastated by the loss; a month later, he wrote to Ezra Pound from Chamby:

> I suppose you heard about the loss of my Juvenilia? I went up to Paris last week to see what was left and found that Hadley had made the job complete by including all carbons, duplicates, etc. . . .
>
> You, naturally, would say, "Good" etc. But don't say it to me. I ain't yet reached that mood. 3 years on the damn stuff. Some like that Paris 1922 I fancied. (23 January 1923, *Selected Letters* 77)[8]

But beneath his devastation, his professional judgment may have been the voice he imputed to Pound, telling him that, ultimately, the loss might be a boon. After all, Gertrude Stein had urged him earlier that year to "begin again and concentrate" when she looked over his unfinished novel. The "Paris 1922" sentences he had composed that summer made a step in that direction. Now, with most of his older fiction and poems irretrievably lost, and two new commissions on his desk, both encouraging innovative prose, he was virtually forced to "begin again"—and he did so at once. In the very next sentence of this letter to Pound, he adds: "Am now working on new stuff"—which may well have been the opening chapters of *in our time.*

The combination of these two events—the commissions for innovative work and the suitcase debacle—thus acted as a carrot and stick for Hemingway's wavering determination to "begin again," cutting him off once and for all from his "juvenilia," his pre-Paris writing, encouraging new work in a "strictly modern" style and compressed format for an avant-garde audience, and promising two significant publications for that new work. The results were not long in coming.

The First Six Chapters: January–March 1923

Hemingway's frequent trips and correspondence over the next eight months, as well as his *Little Review* submission in late March, provide a rough chronology of the composition of these chapters, which he seems to have written approximately in the order they appear in *in our time.* From Chamby, he and Hadley visited Pound at Rapallo in February. There, Hemingway received further encouragement from a new acquaintance, Edward O'Brien, the anthologist of *Best Short Stories* for each year, who admired "My Old Man" and promised to try to place it.[9] In the stimulating company of Pound, Robert McAlmon, and the artist Henry ("Mike") Strater, who did two portraits of Hemingway at Rapallo, Hemingway's urge to innovate intensified. He writes Gertrude Stein on 18 February:

> I've been working hard and have two things done. I've thought a lot about the things you said about working and am starting that way at the beginning. If you think of anything else I wish you'd write it to me. Am working hard about creating and keep my mind going about it all the time. (*Selected Letters* 79)

Several details in this passage are provocatively ambiguous. What were these "two things"? "Things" suggests that they belonged to no conventional genre like the short story. Likewise, "creating" rather than "writing" implies he was thinking of himself as an artist constructing a work, not as a conventional storyteller. But what did Hemingway mean by "starting that way" at the beginning—the way, presumably, Gertrude Stein had advised. Reynolds explains it as Steinian stream-of-consciousness writing; as evidence, he points to an experimental piece Hemingway wrote in that style then, entitled "Rapallo" (KL 670.4; *The Paris Years* 103–04). But if at least one of the "things" Hemingway finished was a prose paragraph that would become part of *in our time,* then the Steinian technique he more likely appropriated "at the beginning" was not to have a beginning: to start in medias res. As he later described it in *A Moveable Feast:* "If I started to write elaborately, or like someone introducing or presenting something, I found that I could cut that scroll-work or ornament out and throw it away and start with the first true simple declarative sentence I had written" (12). Chapter 1 of *in our time* begins with just such a declarative sentence: "Everybody was drunk."

The new paragraphs came slowly, but by mid-March, he felt he had completed enough at least to represent his new writing for the *Little Review* "Exiles" issue. The paragraphs appeared there as six unnumbered pieces, internally separated by three spaced periods. All were untitled, except for the second of two narrated by a British solider, anomalously entitled "MONS (Two)." Eschewing numbers, Hemingway probably did not think of them as "chapters" of a larger work when he composed them. But the six pieces correspond to the sequence, and are almost identical to the texts, of the first six chapters of *in our time;* moreover, the *Little Review* collection bore the title "In Our Time" when the spring 1923 "Exiles" issue finally appeared in October 1923.

The editors did Hemingway a huge favor by omitting his subtitle, "I Am Not Interested in Artists," and Hemingway did himself another in rejecting the other titles he had contemplated for these pieces:

> Unwritten Stories Are Better
> Perhaps You Were There At The Time
> That Was Before I Knew You
> Romance is Dead
> The Good Guys See A Thing or Two
>
> (*The Paris Years* 116)

Although inferior, these titles reveal how Hemingway saw his project. "I Am Not Interested In Artists" is a self-conscious bit of posing that is false to the chapters' "artsy" style. But it also warns the reader that *this* "exile" was not writing about the hothouse Parisian world of artists. His world—war, crime, civilian suffering, political execution, the bullfight—is international, violent, often sordid, and devoid of romance. Even the hero of the bullfight chapter pukes. It is the world of political realities and tabloid headlines in *our* time—and the "our" includes anyone (not just the artist) who was there, who fought, who saw and experienced these events firsthand. "Perhaps You Were There At The Time," "That Was Before I Knew You," and "The Good Guys See a Thing or Two" all stress firsthand experience of real-world events of the recent past, now looked at retrospectively ("That Was Before . . . "). Ironically, Hemingway got nearly all of them secondhand.

Only one of the prospective titles, "Unwritten Stories Are Better," refers to the innovative style of these pieces. "Unwritten" suggests "unwriterly," stories that are not stories, shorn of the narrative conventions of traditional, "written" fiction: beginnings and endings, development of plot and characters, rising action and climax. In place of the "written" story is a fragment—the modernist form that best captures the ontology of modern experience. Accordingly, the six pieces lack conventional openings and begin in the middle. Their closings are deflated and ironical. What these six fragments most resemble are snatches of monologue, spoken by several distinct voices, each recalling an experience or describing an event. Like the missing contexts of these events (the "beginnings"), the voices lack character development; they are anonymous or sparsely identified: an unnamed kitchen corporal in a French battery, an excited observer of a bullfight, two British officers at Mons, and two anonymous narrators who impart scenes of civilian suffering and political execution with impassive detachment.

The diversity of these voices accurately reflects Hemingway's varied sources for this material. The sharply contrasting British voices came from his friend, Eric Dorman-Smith, who had served at Mons and skied with the Hemingways at Chamby. Mike Strater contributed the bullfight narrative, while the *Chicago Tribune Paris Edition* was the likely source of the political execution. The only event Hemingway had observed firsthand was the civilian evacuation from Adrianople.[10] Like their voices, their subjects and settings also varied: war on the Western Front, bullfighting in Spain, civilian evacuation in Thrace, political execution in Greece. Readers of the *Little Review* may have found this array disunified, but the thread running through the pieces is contemporary violence. Together, they are a set of variations on this theme: unexpected and unpredictable moments within the organized violence of war, responses to anticipated violence and recollections of past violence, and rituals of violence well performed or botched.

Rejected Pieces

The six *Little Review* pieces had already undergone some winnowing as Hemingway set aside some sketches. The two Mons chapters, for example, originally had a "MONS (Three)" companion, which picks up where "MONS (Two)" leaves off. The unit has to "fall back" from its perfect barricade to join the larger retreat; again, an officer narrates:

> We formed them in fours along the road. They were Gordons and very few of them were wounded. When we had lined up the last four the rest of them were gone along the road. "It's no good Charles," Buckley said. His face was red and he sounded sick. It wasn't at all like Sandhurst. We started along after them. The last of them were just going over the hill. They were keeping all together and they all had their rifles.[11]

As in the other two Mons chapters, the voice is unique: it is neither emotionally drained (like the soldier's in the garden) nor hyperbolically enthused (like the soldier's at the barricade). Rather, it is coolly sardonic in relating how "Young Buckley" (from the first Mons piece) is flummoxed by a retreat that does not conform to Sandhurst standards of orderliness. Just as in the sixth piece, an officer recognizes that "it was no good" trying to force messy realities into conventional molds. The retreat, at least, had not become a rout, and the concluding image is one of order and discipline: "They were keeping all together and they all had their rifles." Why Hemingway dropped this piece from the other two on Mons is unclear, but perhaps he felt that its action was slight, not sufficiently powerful. He also may have considered that it overemphasized the war vignettes in the *Little Review* submission, already half of the six.[12]

Another rejected war vignette introduces—and immediately kills off—the "Adams" whose name would later be resurrected into Nick Adams:

> Did You Ever Kill Anyone?
>
> We were moving along on the far right. The advance was going like clockwork. We'd shelled the shit out of everything. Adams and I and two men were on the extreme right of C Company. Cra-pung.
>
> Adams went down like a batter that has been beaned. There was an old boche in a round cap and spectacles standing up out of the shell hole with the rifle in his hands and a foolish look on his face. The men sort of hesitated for me to do the honors. (Qtd. in *The Paris Years* 127)

Once again, the speaker is an officer, now about to dispatch the German who has just picked off Adams. Although the shootings occur during an attack, killing this "old boche in . . . spectacles," who was foolish enough to pop up from his shell hole, seems particularly gratuitous (just as his shooting of Adams might be); thus, the other men leave the unpleasant chore to their officer. In this narration, as in the one that follows, the narrator's speech sounds exactly right for a soldier's—"shelled the shit out of everything"—but would have been unpublishable in 1924. As Reynolds points out, although Hemingway rejected the vignette, he later recycled it, sans obscenity, in the short story, "A Way You'll Never Be" (*The Paris Years* 127).

One final war vignette deserves mention for its more extreme frankness of speech and for the way it contrasts a leitmotif of the war chapters, fear under fire, to the manufactured "over the top" heroics of journalism:

> Heroes
>
> Some shit heel correspondent with a green brassard wrote that our top-kick hollered, "Come on you sons-of-bitches do you want to live forever?" Top-kick my ass, the top-kick was so god-damned scared that he was pissing in his pants if he wasn't praying. (*The Paris Years* 127)[13]

Even in an avant-garde magazine, Hemingway would have had trouble publishing this piece—it had only been a few years since the U. S. Post Office pinched *Little Review* issues carrying the serialized *Ulysses.* Although thoroughly convincing in its speech, this vignette was, in Stein's term, *inaccrochable.* Taken together, the rejected war pieces echo themes in the published war chapters: that in war nothing goes according to textbook; that within the larger logic of an attack, individual killings are often pointless; and that "Heroes" easily become manufactured propaganda for the home front. The true common denominator of combat is fear.

Chapters 7–11: March–June 1923

By the time Hemingway sent the six pieces to the *Little Review* in late March, he knew that their form would govern the remainder of the book that Pound had commissioned.[14] But he was still unsure what to call his "unwritten stories" or whether to leave them untitled and unnumbered as he had the first six. The issue went beyond naming, since a title shaped not only a reader's thematic expectations but also potential authorial strategies for subverting them through irony or satire. In the pieces he next composed during the spring and early summer of 1923, Hemingway initially tried out titles for each:

in our time	*chapter opening words or identification*	*original title*
7	"Nick sat against the wall"	Humour
8	"While the bombardment was knocking"	Religion
9	Drevitts and Boyle	Crime and Punishment Crime
10	"One hot evening in Milan"	Love
11	In 1919 he was travelling	Youth
12–16	bullfight chapters	Toros y Toreros

Except for the neutral "Toros y Toreros," all of these titles are bluntly, almost mechanically, ironic. "Love" heads a narrative of broken promises between lovers, a Dear John letter, and quickie sex (and gonorrhea) in a taxicab. "Religion" describes a soldier's broken promises to Jesus. Even the more neutral title "Youth" goes beyond merely describing the young revolutionist to suggest the immaturity of his political idealism. But as Hemingway soon recognized, the irony of these categorical titles is overbearing; indeed, each title makes the text following it little more than an easily summarized commentary on "Love" in our time, "Religion" in our time, etc. The all-important individuality and distinctiveness of each piece would be lost in this reductive irony. By early August, Hemingway had decided to drop the titles, instructing Pound: "They should each one be headed Chapter 1, Chapter 2 etc." (*Selected Letters* 91).

He remained uncertain, however, about what to call the two long pieces that could each pass as a short story: chapters 10 (the recovering soldier and Ag) and 11 (the revolutionist). After receiving proofs from Bill Bird in December, he crossed out "chapter 10" and wrote in "A Short Story." For "chapter 11" he substituted "The Revolutionist." Third—and wiser—thoughts prevailed, however, and he soon crossed out the titles, reinstated the chapter numbers, preserving the book's structural unity (Smith, *Reader's Guide* 26, 30). Still, when the book of chapters became a book of stories and chapters in the 1925 *In Our Time,* this problematic duo again shed their chapter status and became short stories, the former now titled "A Very Short Story."

More than titles were cut in chapters 7–11, for the war pieces in this group (chapters 7, 8, and 10) are more autobiographical than those of the first six chapters—Hemingway even wrote "Personal" atop a draft of chapter 10. In these chapters, the protagonist's experiences come very close to the author's: being shelled at night and fearfully praying for his life (8); being seriously wounded (7); recovering in a hospital, falling in love with his nurse, and making plans for marriage, only to receive a Dear John letter (10). These autobiographical roots show clearly in the early drafts of chapters 8 and 10, which are narrated in first-person. As will be discussed in Chapter Six, Hemingway took pains to conceal their potentially embarrassing content by shifting point of view and narrative voice in the revisions. In so doing, he maintained the multiple voices and perspectives he had developed in the first six chapters. He also continued to present images of war that run counter to popular clichés of courage, heroism, and nobility: the wounded Nick is happy to be out of the war; the terrified soldier, once safe, quickly forgets his promise to Jesus and prefers to follow prostitutes instead; unfaithful "Ag" betrays marriage plans with the recovering soldier, and he responds by pursuing sex with someone else.

Two of these middle chapters, 9 and 11, were free of autobiographical problems. Chapter 11 contrasts the gritty reality of the earlier political chapters (3 and 6) by studying the mentality of a revolutionary true believer and, by extension, the viability of political panaceas. The leitmotif of violence still lurks, however, in the revolutionary's tortured past and dismal future as a political prisoner. Chapter 9 introduces a new subject, crime, to depict not the criminals' violence but "legal" violence meted out to them. As in the other crime chapter (17), law-enforcers—here, the homicidal officer Boyle and his nervous partner—do not come off well. Like chapter 6, this one originated in a newspaper story, not a recent one like the ministers' execution, but one reaching back almost six years to the time Hemingway worked on the *Kansas City Star.* But as Chapter Six will show, the chapter changes the historical facts significantly to make the police seem no better than the criminals they shoot. This chapter also introduces dialogue—a change from the monologic narrative voices and from characters speaking, but getting no responses, in the earlier chapters.

Besides adding several new voices to the many already present, this group of chapters introduces a narrative technique Hemingway would develop extensively in his novels: a first-person narrator whose skepticism or detachment undercuts the attitudes of characters he describes. It is a short leap from the older revolutionary (11) and the soldier-narrator (8), whose narrative detachment undercuts their comrades, to Jake Barnes's contemptuously pitying descriptions of Robert Cohn.

The Bullfight Chapters (12–16): June–July 1923

In June 1923, Hemingway made his first trip to Spain, accompanied by his two publishers-to-be, Robert McAlmon (*Three Stories & 10 Poems*) and Bill Bird (*in our time*). The dozen or so bullfights they saw in Madrid, Seville, Ronda, and Granada deeply impressed Hemingway for life, and he returned to Spain with Hadley the following month to attend the fiesta at Pamplona and see several more bullfights (*The Paris Years* 131). His interest already piqued by Gertrude Stein and Mike Strater, he now threw himself thoroughly into the experience—even jumping into the ring in his white duck slacks during the "amateurs" to wave his sweater before a bull.

In his 1932 book on bullfighting, *Death in the Afternoon,* Hemingway explained at length (and critics, of course, have added their views) why the bullfight affected him so profoundly. Although certainly violent, the bullfight proved a kind of antidote to the random violence of modern war. A soldier's courage might be admirable, but it has little or no bearing on the chancy, often chaotic outcomes of combat. He might be spared—"The shelling moved further up the line" (8)—or hit, as Nick is (7), but his personal behavior has little to do with his fate. The *torero* also works close to death but can briefly—magically—seem to master it through his skill and courage. Moreover, the bullfight's structure and ritual, conducted properly, sharply contrasted with empty traditions and botched rituals of modern life, such as the political or criminal executions in chapters 6 and 17. The bullfight's fixed code of values, enforced by tradition and a demanding audience, thus opposed the moral flux of the postwar world. Ultimately, the bullfighter's ideal conduct—what Hemingway famously described as "grace under pressure"—modeled a code of behavior in Hemingway's later writings and even embodied the aesthetics of that writing.

In 1923, however, the bullfight provided Hemingway an entirely new realm in which to study—and describe—complex and simultaneous actions, behavior, and states of mind in life-and-death situations. As he explained:

> The only place where you could see life and death, i.e., violent death now that the wars were over, was in the bull ring and I wanted very much to go to Spain where I could study it. I was trying to learn to write, commencing with the simplest things, and one of the simplest things of all and the most fundamental is violent death. . . .
>
> So I went to Spain to see bullfights and to try to write about them for myself. I thought they would be simple and barbarous and cruel and that I would not like them, but that I would see certain definite action which would give me the feeling of life and death that I was working for. I found the definite action; but the bullfight was so far from simple and I liked it so much that it was much too complicated for my then equipment for writing to deal with and, aside from four [sic] very short sketches, I was not able to write anything about it for five [sic] years. (*Death in the Afternoon* 2–3)[15]

Even within these early "sketches," mostly written in late June and July, the bullfight evolves from a spectacle, conveyed by an uncritical enthusiast in chapter 2, to an art and a testing ground in chapters 12–16. While all the chapters ignore the surface glamour of the event—the pageantry, the costumes, and flourishes—the latter five focus on the complex dynamics of the bullfight's stages and performers: the bull and the horse, the bullfighter and the crowd, and, of course, the bullfighter and the bull. Paired contrasts sharpen this focus: the incompetent and cowardly *torero* (13) versus the masterful and courageous one (14); the badly gored horse—at once horrifying and grotesquely comic (12); the intrusive crowd, yelling, throwing things, even entering the ring, whether in approval (2, 14) or disgust (13); and the irresponsible bullfighter grasping for life (15) versus the responsible bullfighter accepting death (16). Hemingway did not intend merely to chronicle success or failure in the ring but to analyze what made bullfighters succeed or fail: their techniques, their states of mind.

With its descriptive challenges, this new realm stimulated Hemingway to continue the experiments of the preceding chapters, trying out different points of view and narrative voices, linking differing sentence structures to particular actions and types of perception. Unlike war, the bullfight is performed before spectators—"It's just like having a ringside seat at the war with nothing going to happen to you," Hemingway described it at the time (*Selected Letters* 88). Thus, the viewer's location and comprehension matter: We may be distant, uninformed spectators in chapter 2, but to appreciate Villalta's technique, we must be "right down close in front" (14) as engaged and knowing observers. We scale the *barrera* to experience the gored bullfighter's final sensations and fading consciousness in chapter 16, and are even privy to the bull's emotions: indecisive in chapter 12, "hating" in 14. Voices proliferate: Unnamed narrators speak in first and third person (13, 14); bullfighters also narrate and speak to each other; one narrative voice is detached and objective (12); another renders the bullfighter's interior consciousness (16). And all these voices depict multilayered action in a plethora of shifting sentence styles.

In one respect, the bullfight chapters are an anomaly in *in our time,* but one that became central to Hemingway's worldview. One prospective subtitle for the book—"Romance is Dead"—perfectly describes the thematic treatment of the book's other topics: war, politics, and crime. But romance survives in the bullfight—one might even say that its pageantry, ritualized actions, and formal expectations of conduct epitomize romance. In the disorderly world of 1923, these qualities must have seemed anachronistic, but for that very reason they fascinated Hemingway.

Chapters 17–18: Early August 1923

Hemingway's progress report to Pound, c. 5 August 1923, enables us to date precisely when he composed the concluding two chapters of *in our time.* "I will do the hanging," he begins cryptically, referring to the hanging of Chicago criminal Sam Cardinella. Further on, he states: "The whole [book] closes with the talk with the King of Greece and his Queen in their garden (just written)." (*Selected Letters* 92). As with chapter 9, he drew on his memory of tabloid city crime for chapter 17, and once again, he focused on the punishment phase: not rough police justice this time, but the chilling ceremonies of the state execution of Sam Cardinella, gang member and murderer. This interest in executions (recall chapter 6) might seem ghoulish except that it is not the moment of execution itself that concerns Hemingway, but the scene, the preparations, and most important, the behavior of the various participants. Just as he pairs cowardly and brave bullfighters, so he contrasts the quiet courage of the Greek cabinet ministers to Sam's abject terror that incapacitates first his legs, then his sphincter. The ceremonies of both executions are travesties: neither the sick minister nor Sam can be made to stand; Sam fouls himself and his disgusted executioners drop him; and, finally, the priests are more concerned with saving their mortal bodies than his immortal soul. Hemingway's fusion of the sordid, grotesque, and comical was never sharper.

The closing chapter, entitled "L'Envoi" in the 1925 *In Our Time,*[16] also comes from an external source, the newsreel cameraman Shorty Wornall, whom Hemingway had met while covering the Greek evacuation of Thrace. The strange *Alice in Wonderland* quality of this "very jolly" garden chat with a royal couple under house arrest, with the junta's guns lurking unmentioned beyond the garden walls, fittingly closes a series of mostly violent episodes that began with a kitchen corporal's recollection of a slightly surreal night march en route to a battlefield. And the deceptively tranquil garden setting recalls other pacific settings where violence erupts: the garden wall where overloaded German soldiers are shot, the hospital wall against which the Greek cabinet ministers are executed, the church wall where a badly wounded Nick is dragged. The violence may abate, but it never really goes away: "the great thing in this sort of an affair is not to be shot oneself," the king confides to the narrator, who, as in all the first-person chapters, is unnamed and begins his narrative in the middle. Hemingway was right to claim (in the letter to Pound quoted above) that "The king closes [the book] in swell shape" (*Selected Letters* 92).

The Question of Formal Unity

Hemingway had completed eighteen separate scenes, but what did they add up to? Were they a whole or merely a collection of pieces? Pound must have posed this question, for in the letter quoted above, Hemingway is at pains to explain the book's formal logic:

> When they are read altogether they all hook up. It seems funny but they do. The bulls start, then reappear and then finish off. The war starts clear and noble just like it did, Mons etc., gets close and blurred and finished with the feller who goes home and gets clap. The refugees leave Thrace, due to the Greek ministers, who are shot. The whole thing closes with the talk with the King of Greece and his Queen in the garden, (just written), which shows the king all right. . . .
>
> The radicals start noble in the young Magyar story and get bitched. America appears in the cops shooting the guys who robbed the cigar store. It has form all right. (*Selected Letters* 91–92)

Except for clarifying the linkages of the Greco-Turkish chapters, Hemingway's explanation raises more questions than it answers. The bullfighting chapters, for example, are imbalanced: one appears near the beginning (exactly as it did in the *Little Review*), six consecutive ones near the end. Hemingway tacitly acknowledged this imbalance in the 1925 *In Our Time,* when he grouped chapter 2 with the other bullfight chapters. The opening war chapters (1, 4, 5) seem neither "clear" (the drunken night march, the unexpected combat at the garden wall) nor "noble" (the easy "potting" of the Germans). They *do* progress, however, from relatively safe situations to ones of mortal danger, terror, and wounding, as protagonists are shelled (8) and wounded by enemy fire (7). If the war doesn't start "noble," it does "get close" and ends in the bitterness of the soldier disillusioned about "Love" and fidelity (10). Hemingway may have thought that the war chapters progress from idealism ("clear and noble") to disillusionment, but only the latter emerges clearly. The "young Magyar" chapter (11) encompasses both attitudes—though whether the revolutionist himself grows disillusioned is debatable.[17] Both crime chapters are sardonic (and, in Sam Cardinella's hanging, satiric), but their starting point is hardly idealism (unless it be the assumptions that the police should uphold the law impartially and state executions be conducted with dignity). This trend toward disillusionment and ultimately being "bitched" might well seem the unifying thread of the book. But pulling against it are the bullfight chapters that valorize the heroic. Here, Luis's irresponsibility and the bad bullfighter's resigned incompetence are violations of an enduring standard that Villalta and Maera epitomize.

In sum, Hemingway's rationale is unconvincing, and the formal cohesion of the chapters remains problematic. Some critics, following Hemingway's lead, have asserted a thematic logic to their arrangement, but not without some gerrymandering. Thus, Clinton Burhans Jr. writes:

> in their resulting order [in *In Our Time*], the vignettes reflect a clear pattern. The "Smyrna" sketch and the first seven are concerned with war, the next one with crime, the next six with bullfighting, the following one with crime, and the last one with war. From war to crime to bullfighting to crime to war—the pattern is definite and balanced; moreover, it suggests a unifying theme. By surrounding bullfighting with war and crime, Hemingway places violence and death on which man imposes order and meaning at the center of a world of chaotic disorder and violence, thus implying subtly that from the first—bullfighting—he can learn something about the second—the world—and about how to live in it.[18]

Apart from the question-begging assumption that the bullfight assumes a pedagogical role in an existential course on "how to live" in moral chaos—an assumption that was virtually a touchstone in Hemingway criticism of the 1950s and 1960s—Burhans's schema teeters on a rather arbitrary ordering that counts "On the Quai at Smyrna" as a chapter and categorizes the "Greek" chapters (3, 6, 18 in *in our time;* 2, 5, and "L'Envoi" in *In Our Time*) as "war" chapters even though all three depict civilians and occur *after* the Greco-Turkish War. Moreover, the generalization that all the war chapters represent a monolithic world of "chaotic disorder and violence" ignores real differences among these chapters, such as the "absolutely perfect barricade" of chapter 5 or the safety of the battery in chapter 1.

David Leigh's effort to impute "a new and expanded significance" to the chapters in their *In Our Time* interweaving with the stories makes similarly sweeping generalizations about "the stark violence of war" in the chapters (132). Like Burhans's, his division of the chapters seems rather arbitrary: all of the chapters preceding the bullfight chapters are lumped together as the first part; the bullfight chapters are the second part; and the two deaths following the bullfights (chapters 16 and 17) become the "final part," thus excluding the closing "L'Envoi" chapter.[19]

Although both of these articles address the chapters as they were reordered in *In Our Time,* the problem of trying to impose a formal logic on them is even greater in *in our time,* where they appear essentially in the order that Hemingway originally composed them.[20] Michael Reynolds argues persuasively that "the form [of the book] had not dictated content; rather, the sketches created the form. If there was a [unifying] principle involved, it came from the title, *in our time,* which itself had not appeared until the first six vignettes were finished." He concludes that "they were not written as a sequence but as an experiment." Reynolds does, however, find recurring themes that bind the "collage" of chapters and stories of *In Our Time:* "war, violence, water, darkness, isolation, babies, and most centrally, failed relationships."[21] To this list—and specifically regarding the chapters only—one could add more unifying themes and emotions: fear, disorientation, and the unpredictability of combat in the war chapters; civilian suffering and the irrelevance of both archaic tradition and revolutionary ideology in the political chapters; performers and crowds, courage and cowardice, skill and incompetence, responsibility and escapism, killing and being killed in the bullfight chapters; botched executions; and a corrosively ironic handling of patriotism, religion, love, and political idealism throughout. These themes, and the recurring stylistic experiments in narrative voice, perspective, mode, and sentence rhythms, are what unify the chapters of *in our time.*

From Manuscript to Book: August 1923–March 1924

Hemingway had already "fixed" the chapters Pound found faulty, so when he finished chapter 17, he was ready to send off the manuscript: now "she rides," he told Pound (*Selected Letters* 92). His timing seemed right: he and Hadley were leaving for Toronto to have their first child, and he wanted the manuscript in Bill Bird's hands before they left. But if he had expected a quick publication, he was to be disappointed. As new owner and editor of a handpress, Bird understandably wanted to make *in our time* something special. "I am going to pull something really fancy with your book, as a preparation for the great folio edition of the modern divina commedia," he wrote Hemingway on 4 September (KL 50). It was Bird's idea to make the book appear as modern as its title, subject, and style: to make the title page all lowercase and to keep Hemingway's dashes instead of quotation marks for dialogue.[22] He had a woodcut made from one of Mike Strater's Rapallo portraits of Hemingway to be used as a frontispiece. Bird's most imaginative idea was to surround each chapter with wide margins filled with newsprint: headlines and story text covering some of the same events described in the chapters and drawn from American and Greek newspapers, bullfight journals, and so forth. This collage of "actual" journalism would thus underscore the chapters' quasi-journalistic narrative style and its depiction of real-life events—a strong visual metaphor of "in our time." Ultimately, this plan proved too ambitious, and Bird limited the collage to the cover.

Hemingway's and Pound's responses to these ideas were cautiously supportive. Pound, having midwifed the book thus far, now left these issues to the author and publisher. He wrote Hemingway on 21 September: "Bill has noble plan for doing yr. book with MODERN typography. I wrote him he shd submit his ideas to you. I can not undertake the so delicate responsibility of this so delicate matter" (KL 69). Hemingway consented hesitantly. As he wrote back to Pound:

> I cabled Bill to commence firing on the newsprint borders. It all depends how it is done. It is a good hunch. If not well done it will sour quick as hell. That's up to Bill. Christnose he rates a little excitement out of the Press. I tell him to shoot. He is the man to do it. (13 October 1923, *Selected Letters* 96)

Considering how experimental Hemingway's prose was—the startling elisions and grammatical fragments, for example—he might have been more supportive of Bird's efforts. But tugging against Hemingway's urge to innovate was a conservative pull to be conventional, to be understood by the common reader as well as admired by the highbrow. Stein probably had this tendency in mind when she nastily called him "90% Rotarian." Certainly, this veering toward the conventional was evident when Hemingway removed some of the book's more radical elisions for the 1925 *In Our Time* (discussed in Chapter Five and the epilogue). Thus, it is not surprising in retrospect how quickly Hemingway disavowed the book's appearance when a critic complained about it—a critic he was assiduously courting at the time. Edmund Wilson concluded his review of *in our time* by objecting to the lowercase titles and names, which he considered a stale modernist device and "unsightly" to boot.[23] Hemingway replied:

> You are very right about the lack of capital letters—which seemed very silly and affected to me—but Bird had put them in and he was printing the *In Our Time* [sic] himself and that was all the fun he was getting out it[.] I thought he could go ahead and be a damn fool in his own way if it pleased him. So long as he did not fool with the text. (18 October 1924, *Selected Letters* 128).

By the end of December, the proofs were sent and corrected, the woodcut was done, and Bird claimed he was already starting the printing. But on a handpress the process took time, and he did not present the finished product until March 1924. Even then, a printing foul-up limited the run of 300 to 170 copies of Ernest Hemingway's most experimental writing. Although the book would have a small readership, Hemingway knew its importance at the time to his emerging style. Before it even appeared, he informed Edmund Wilson that "the *In Our Time* stuff in the *Little Review* . . . is where I think I have gotten hold of it" (25 Nov. 1923, *Selected Letters* 105).

Critical Response

Wilson, too, recognized the chapters' importance. He admired the ones in the *Little Review* and recommended them to Burton Rascoe, whose popular column in the *New York Tribune,* "A Bookman's Daybook," reached a large readership. Rascoe's note about this (21 October 1923) is interesting in showing how the limited publications of this unknown author were beginning to circulate and catch the eye of influential critics back in the States:

> [Edmund] Wilson called my attention to some amusing stuff by Ernest Hemingway in the new issue of the *Little Review.* [Lewis] Galantière sent me a copy of Hemingway's *Three Stories and Ten Poems,* which was published in Paris and said that I would find it interesting, but I have not yet got around to reading it. (Qtd. in "Emergence" 55)

When Hemingway read this mention in Canada, he immediately wrote to Wilson, introducing himself, enclosing a copy of *Three Stories & Ten Poems,* and asking if Wilson would consider reviewing it and *in our time* (which Hemingway expected in a few months). His letters to Wilson are, at once, obsequious (after Wilson agrees to review the books, Hemingway writes, "Thank you ever so much . . . It was awfully good of you"), chatty, and confidential in a "you and I understand" manner (*Selected Letters* 102–03, 104–06). Their "sucking up" tone expresses what Hemingway had bluntly confided to Edward O'Brien six months earlier: "I want, like hell, to get published" (*Selected Letters* 82). Hemingway was still an unknown. Wilson reviewed for a variety of magazines, including the prestigious *Dial,* and was fast becoming the most influential critic of his time, particularly for authors of his own generation. His opinion could help establish this young author's fledgling reputation—or shatter it.

Hemingway's efforts to court the powerful paid off richly in Wilson's review of the two books in the October 1924 *Dial.* Remarkably, this critic, known for measured and carefully qualified prose that made him appear older than his years, described Hemingway's achievement in superlatives: it was "prose of the first distinction." Although he perceptively linked Hemingway to Stein (*Three Lives*) and to Anderson in their ability to "convey profound emotions and complex states of mind" through "a naïveté of language," Wilson quickly added: "Not, however, that Mr. Hemingway is imitative. On the contrary, he is rather strikingly original, and in the dry compressed little vignettes of *In Our Time* [sic], has almost invented a form of his own." As other reviewers would, Wilson singled out chapter 6 (the cabinet ministers' execution) to show its author was

> remarkably successful in suggesting moral values by a series of simple statements. . . . [B]ehind [*in our time*'s] cool objective manner, it constitutes a harrowing record of the barbarities of the period in which we live . . . Mr. Hemingway is unperturbed as he tells us about these things: he is not a propagandist even for humanity.

"Dry" recurs in the review, as Wilson compares Hemingway's bullfight vignettes to "the dry sharpness of the bullfight lithographs of Goya. And like Goya, he is concerned first of all with making a fine picture" and with showing "what life is like." Wilson's title for the review, "Mr. Hemingway's Dry-Points," underscores this image of Hemingway as a miniaturist, an artist with words. The comparison is suggestive, for like the drypoint engraver's, Hemingway's "pencil" must be made of hard steel. Although Wilson ends the review rather weakly by criticizing the book's lowercase typography, his most powerful praise comes just before:

"I am inclined to think that his little book has more artistic dignity than anything else about the period of the war that has as yet been written by an American" (rpt. in *The Shores of Light* 119–22).

This review, as Jeffrey Meyers states, "was a great breakthrough for Hemingway and helped to establish his serious literary reputation" (*Critical Heritage* 12). Hemingway's response to Wilson continued the sycophantish tone of his earlier letters:

> I did appreciate the review. It was cool and clear minded and decent and impersonal and sympathetic. Christ how I hate this terrible personal stuff. Do you remember my writing from Toronto wanting some reviews and publicity? and then got some and it turned me sick.
>
> I think there's nothing more discouraging than unintelligent appreciation. Not really discouraging, but just driving something back inside of you. . . . You are the only man writing criticism who or whom I can read when the book being criticized is one I've read or know something about. . . . Intelligence is so damn rare. (18 Oct. 1924, *Selected Letters* 129).

Wilson's was not the first review of *in our time,* however. That honor went to M. R. (probably Ford Madox Ford) in the April 1924 issue of the *transatlantic review,* where Hemingway served as associate editor under Ford. Although brief, the review recognized qualities in Hemingway's prose that subsequent critics would echo and re-echo:

> He projects the moments when life is condensed and clean-cut and significant, presenting them in minute narratives that eliminate every useless word. Each tale is much longer than the measure of its lines.

Chapter 6, depicting the execution of the cabinet ministers, presented for this reviewer "the sort of detached circumstances that always penetrate deep into the consciousness in the wake of a bald and impressive fact." Similarly, chapter 4 (combat in a garden at Mons) "leaves a vivid impression of the scene. . . . The German somehow becomes more important and to be remembered than the hundreds of others who probably fell the same day" (1: 247–48).

"Vivid," "projects significant moments," "eliminates every useless word," "conveys more than it says"—these descriptions recur in virtually all reviews of the chapters either as *in our time* or within *In Our Time.* An unsigned review in Hemingway's alma mater, the *Kansas City Star* (20 Dec. 1924), praises the writing's descriptive selectivity "in picking out the essentials of an object or a person or an action in much the same way that contemporary painters are endeavoring to do; . . . " Noting Hemingway's history as a *Star* reporter, the reviewer not surprisingly lauds the writing's "superior objectivity . . . the best quality [of] modern journalism . . . , [which] he has carried . . . forward to a new point." The reviewer also singles out Hemingway's "fine unsentimental understanding" and, alluding to Sam Cardinella's execution, concludes: "it requires something approaching genius to present the actors' emotions accurately and keep the author and his opinions and emotions out" (*Critical Heritage* 65–66).

Not every critic admired the chapters, of course—indeed, unanimous praise would have cast doubt on their disturbing innovations. H. L. Mencken, for one, belittled them as "the sort of brave, bold stuff that all atheistic young newspaper reporters write. Jesus Christ in lower case. A hanging, carnal love, and two disembowelings" (*"Quackery"* 13).[24] And D. H. Lawrence, admiring the stories of *In Our Time* (which, like several reviewers, he called "sketches"), considered the "mottoes" in front of each story "a little affected" (*Critical Heritage* 73).

Like Lawrence, reviewers of the 1925 *In Our Time* saw the chapters in an entirely different setting, interspersed with fifteen short stories, an arrangement that changed the chapters' impact and led readers to wonder about their relationship to the stories as a whole and to the ones immediately bracketing them. Several reviewers of *In Our Time* considered it "an experiment in prose"—an impression to which the chapters surely contributed.[25] Scott Fitzgerald saw them almost as hors d'oeuvres for the stories:

> Anyone who first looks through the short interpolated sketches will hardly fail to read the stories themselves. The garden at Mons and The Barricade are profound essays upon the English officer, written on a postage stamp. The King of Greece's Tea Party, the Shooting of the Cabinet Ministers, and the Cigar-store Robbery particularly fascinated me, as they did when Edmund Wilson first showed them to me in an earlier pamphlet, over two years ago. (*Critical Heritage* 72)

Once again, Edmund Wilson had passed the word on Hemingway, and this time, Fitzgerald kept the ball rolling by alerting his editor at Scribner's, Max Perkins, to this new talent:

> This is to tell you about a young man named Ernest Hemmingway, who lives in Paris, (an American) writes for the transatlantic Review & has a brilliant future. Ezra Pound published a collection of his short pieces in Paris, at some place like the Egoist Press. I haven't it here now but it's remarkable & I'd look him up right away. He's the real thing. (c. 10 October 1924, *A Life in Letters* 82)

Taken together, the reviews of the chapters run counter to clichés of unrecognized genius and of artistic experiments waiting years to be appreciated. Hemingway's reviewers recognized instantly that this prose was something altogether new and powerful—not merely new in form but in its blend of style and voice, subject and tone—and the terms they chose to describe it show a remarkable consensus: "objective," "exact," "terse," "forceful," "abrupt," "brutal," "raw," "energ[etic]," "fresh and crisp," "unliterary," "powerfully good writing," "sordid," "hardboiled," "astringent," "like acid," "harsh," "bold," and "hard." Not all of the reviewers welcomed this "brutality," but all acknowledged its power and freshness. On the physically slender evidence of the *in our time* chapters and the *In Our Time* stories, several reviewers predicted that Hemingway would become a force to be reckoned with, and most agreed with Edmund Wilson that this was "prose of the first distinction."[26] "I know of no better among contemporary authors," the reviewer of the Cleveland *Plain Dealer* concluded.

The Chapters in the 1925 In Our Time

This chorus of affirmation was still in the future as the Hemingways had their first child in Toronto and waited for publication of *in our time.* In those dreary five months, Hemingway produced no new fiction, but ideas were accumulating while he churned out, with increasing distaste, feature stories for the *Toronto Star.* Moreover, another deus ex machina inspiration had occurred. Just as Pound's commission for "contemporary prose" helped spark the "unwritten stories," in November 1923 Edward O'Brien chose Hemingway's story "My Old Man" for inclusion in *Best Short Stories of 1923* and even planned to dedicate the volume to Hemingway. More important, Hemingway recounted, he asked "if I had enough stories for a Boni Liveright book." "How many stories would I need?" Hemingway wrote back.[27]

With his head now turned to short stories, Hemingway began writing at a white heat once he and Hadley returned to Paris at the end of January 1924. But he had not abandoned his creative experiments of the preceding year. By 12 September, he could offer O'Brien a remarkable progress report and a clear conception of his next book:

> I have written 14 stories and have a book ready to publish. It is to be called In Our Time and one of the chapters of the *In Our Time* [sic] I sent you comes in between each story. That was what I originally wrote them for, chapter headings. . . . [I]n between [the stories] comes bang! the In Our Time [chapters]. It should be awfully good, I think. I've tried to do it so you get the close up very quietly but absolutely solid and the real thing but very close, and then through it all between every story comes the rhythm of the in our time chapters. (*Selected Letters* 123)

A letter to Edmund Wilson the following month somewhat clarifies the intended effect of this arrangement:

> Finished the book of 14 stories with a chapter on *In Our Time* [sic] between each story—that is the way they were meant to go—to give the picture of the whole between examining it in detail. Like looking with your eyes at something, say a passing coast line, and then looking at it with 15X binoculars. Or rather, maybe looking at it and then going in and living in it—and then coming out and looking at it again. (*Selected Letters* 128)

These two descriptions both clarify and obscure the status of the chapters. Together, the chapters are intended "to give the picture of the whole"—the macrocosmic compressed into microcosmic glimpses—as opposed to the close-up "living in it" experience of the individual stories. The "rhythm" is thus one of alternation and jarring juxtaposition between the "quiet" stories and the "bang!" of the chapters. But Hemingway obviously rewrites the history of the chapters when he claims that they were originally written to be "chapter headings" for stories he had not even conceived in 1923. One rather unaesthetic reason he included the chapters was to serve as additional material—filler—to help bring the manuscript to book length. For the same reason, he included the stories he had already published in *Three Stories & Ten Poems.*[28] Fortunately, however, Hemingway was able to meld these disparate parts and achieve the powerful rhythmic juxtapositions and contrasting perspectives between chapters and stories that he described in his letters.

But the chapters' original integrity was lost in the 1925 *In Our Time:* two chapters, 10 and 11, had become stories: "A Very Short Story" and "The Revolutionist" respectively. The final chapter acquired a title, "L'Envoi," and dropped its number. The remaining chapters were separated, alternating with the short stories. For the first Scribner's edition in 1930, Hemingway added an "Introduction," later entitled "On the Quai at Smyrna," which was narrated in a British voice reminiscent of, but different from, the narrators of chapters 4 (combat in a garden at Mons) and 5 (the perfect barricade) and which anticipated the chapters' themes of brutality and civilian suffering following the Greco-Turkish War. In this form, that is, interspersed with the *In Our Time* stories, the chapters have appeared in all subsequent commercial reprintings and collections.[29]

While crucial to the avant-garde form of *In Our Time,* this interspersed presentation vitiates the cumulative impact of the chapters themselves as they originally appeared in *in our time.* Inevitably, the stories surrounding them—more conventional structurally and meatier in plot—are more approachable and thus tend to overshadow the chapters for both readers and scholars. (There have been several scholarly books on *In Our Time;* the present study is the first on *in our time.*) More important, the intensity of Hemingway's early experiments in compressed renderings of violent subject matter, experiments in narrative, in point of view, and in style, cannot be fully appreciated until the chapters again appear side by side without the "relief" provided by the stories. The 1924 *in our time* deserves to be reprinted as a trade publication and join the Hemingway collection.

PART 2
EXPERIMENTS

3
Narrative Modes

They are remarkably short, most just a paragraph. A few, like chapter 4 (combat in a garden at Mons), are not even one hundred words. The longest, chapters 10 (the recovering soldier and Ag) and 11 (the revolutionist) are two pages each, but they did not survive as chapters when *in our time* became *In Our Time* in 1925: Hemingway wanted to keep his new form brief. In the original edition, each is surrounded by expanses of white space, further emphasizing its brevity. Each appears on the page like a sudden illumination, like a camera flash—or an artillery burst—in the dark. This visual suddenness intensifies its narrative abruptness, heightens the shock of violence and the chillingly matter-of-fact tone in so many of them. The whole book—only thirty-one pages—has an unconventional look: its title is lowercase, as are the chapter headings and names on the title page, including the author's. Dialogue lacks quotation marks and is separated sometimes by jaunty dashes (chapters 9, 11), sometimes just by new paragraphs (16), sometimes by neither (18). And in a gesture certain to offend, "jesus christ" appears uncapitalized, in the praying soldier's monologue (8). The combined effect is startling, disturbing, compelling.

Arguably, the brevity of this form is its most radical feature, one that may well have inspired other techniques, such as beginning in the middle and not identifying narrators. Hemingway himself recognized his achievement when he showed Morley Callaghan the proofs, declaring: "I've discovered a new form" (Baker, *A Life Story* 121). Critics tend to trace its origins in the context of Hemingway's development—as a logical outgrowth of the "Paris 1922" sentences or, reaching further back, of the "Cross Roads" sketches he composed in 1919.[1] But these lineages overstress Hemingway as a solitary innovator and ignore practical exigencies and contemporaneous influences. Pound wanted the books of his *Inquest* series to be short. He called them "book*lets*" and envisioned their length at about fifty pages.[2] To be sure, Hemingway could have used short stories, or mixed stories and poems, to fill up his booklet, but by late spring he had promised Robert McAlmon all his extant stories for *Three Stories & Ten Poems.* And, besides, both the *Inquest* series and the *Little Review* issue were seeking "contemporary prose"—*modern* writing. Stein had predicted to him that "he might be a good writer of some new kind" (Fenton 126). *She* was, after all. Most of the abstract "descriptions" she called *Tender Buttons* were aphoristically short, no longer than a paragraph.

Pound, too, stressed radical compression in his two-line Imagist poems, his "ideogrammic method," his urging (in *Gaudier-Brzeska*) that a spatial, dynamic conception of poetic form should supplant traditional time-bound linearity. Modernist innovation, generally, tended to condense and compress, even if the final result occupied much time and space. Cézanne's reduction of complex forms into planes, the Cubists' compression of three-dimensional illusory space, modern composers' preference for creating brief "pieces" rather than longer, conventional forms all seemed to verify Stein's dictum that modern composition had dispensed with "beginning, middle, and end," had stopped organizing components around a unifying center. Freed of subservience to a whole, the individual fragment became self-sufficient.

These ideas were certainly not new in 1923, but they had only begun to be applied to the conservative medium of prose narrative—Joyce's *Ulysses* in book form was less than a year old. Although Hemingway's rejected subtitle disingenuously claimed "I am not interested in artists," he was astute enough to realize that any rethinking of prose narrative—any creating of a new form—must address how it unfolds in time and space and must take account of restructurings in the other arts. Necessity and influence both, then, pointed in the same direction: to pieces, not stories; fragments, not "finished" work; disjunctive order rather than consecutive sequence; instantaneity, not narrative development.

When the pieces first appeared together in *in our time,* no stories provided psychic relief (or as Hemingway described it, "the quiet close up"[3]) from the "bang!" of the chapters, as the stories of all later editions of *In Our Time* would do. The reader encounters just a series of paragraphs, each titled only as a "chapter" and numbered consecutively. But the chapters do not form a continuous narrative. Their subjects—war, politics, crime, bullfighting—keep shifting back and forth. The voices that narrate them, likewise, are diverse and barely identified. The point of view and tone of each chapter vary, the style and sentence structure likewise. Again, the cumulative effect of these discontinuous elements is jarring, restless. We never quite know where we are. But we know *when* we are: we are in our time.

What Should We Call Them?

Critics and scholars have been as uncertain as the book's initial readers and reviewers about what to call these chapters. Vignettes (the most popular choice)? Miniatures? Sketches? Impressions? Experiments? "Cameo stories"? "Stylistic exercises"? "Tools of self-instruction"? "Five-finger exercises"? The author's "honor's thesis" ending "his period of tutelage"?[4] Hemingway once titled a draft of chapter 14 "episode 14" (KL 94a)—but an episode of what? Any of the labels above might generally describe the chapters (except perhaps for "sketches" and "impressions," which connote improvisation). But all of these tags subtly impute to these chapters a generic consistency they do not possess as a group. Hemingway avoided this labeling problem by simply using the noncommittal "chapters" after he had toyed with heavily ironic, topical titles for the middle chapters ("Religion," "Love," and so on). In so doing, he left the pieces unencumbered, rather than forcing them into a generic mold. "The chapters are to be considered as separate entities," Louis Cohn noted after conferring with Hemingway over Cohn's 1931 bibliography of his work.[5] The advice is sound. Thus, besides sidestepping the reductive tags above, this study emphasizes the generic diversity of these chapters, beginning with their narrative modes. If nothing else, this diversity reveals a writer still exploring the possibilities of his craft, trying out a variety of narrative approaches within the self-imposed discipline of extreme brevity.

It may seem counterproductive to impose categories on this experimental variety of narrative techniques, but certain chapters generically resemble each other enough to justify grouping them, not only to analyze their common features, but to recognize how each varies from its generic composite. Four such narrative modes can be distinguished: (1) quasi-journalistic, (2) parodic, (3) experiential, and (4) descriptive (studies of character, action, or scene); in addition, some chapters mix genres. Self-evidently, these modes are not neatly parallel for they depend upon differing literary elements. The journalistic derives from tone and style, as does the parodic, which, as the name implies, plays off of an extant genre. The experiential, on the other hand, relies primarily on narrative voice, perspective, and especially on proximity to the action, while the descriptive implies distance or detachment from it. Lacking parallelism, these genres are not watertight categories, and a single chapter can encompass several. For example, chapters that are journalistic in style may also describe scenes (for instance, the civilian retreat in chapter 3), or create characters (Drevitts and Boyle in chapter 9) or depict actions (the gored horse in 12). Chapter 6 (the cabinet ministers' execution), for example, is journalistic in style; but is it primarily a depiction of a scene (the courtyard, hospital wall, windows with shut-tight shutters, rain, puddles, pools of water, wet dead leaves) or of an action (the execution)? Of course, it is both: one is inseparable from the other. Rather than consider these groupings as categories, therefore, we should see them as narrative tendencies that can easily fulfill more than one role.

Quasi-Journalistic Narratives

Not surprisingly for a writer who, in 1923, still earned his bread as a journalist, Hemingway built on his professional experience to fashion narratives that give the *feel* of journalistic reporting, but are not. Their sentences state facts without inflection and seem to avoid emotive rhetoric—"objective" devices that in fact exceeded journalistic norms of the time. Except in chapter 12 (the gored horse), however, this narrative mode does not continue through an entire chapter, but yields to modernist techniques or introduces fictive elements such as dialogue and action—journalistic means, in short, to achieve literary ends. Thus, chapters 3 (the civilian retreat), 6 (cabinet ministers' execution), the beginning of 9 (Drevitts and Boyle), 12 (the gored horse), and parts of 17 (Sam Cardinella's execution) are not simply "journalistic": indeed, in their willful avoidance of journalistic conventions, none would ever have gotten by a copy editor. But their *quasi*-journalistic style is immediately recognizable and powerfully effective—arguably, Hemingway's most potent style in *in our time,* especially when harnessed to violent and disturbing events.

To illustrate these borrowings and transformations, compare how two versions of the retreat from Adrianopole begin—his *Toronto Star* dispatch of 22 October 1922 and chapter 3:

> In a never-ending, staggering march, the Christian population of Eastern Thrace is jamming the roads toward Macedonia. The main column crossing the Maritza River at Adrianople is twenty miles

> long. Twenty miles of carts drawn by cows, bullocks and muddy-flanked water buffalo, with exhausted, staggering men, women and children, blankets over their heads, walking blindly along in the rain beside their worldly goods. ("A Silent, Ghastly Procession" 232)

> Minarets stuck up in the rain out of Adrianople. The carts were jammed for thirty miles along the Karagatch road. Water buffalo and cattle were hauling carts through the mud. No end and no beginning. Just carts loaded with everything they owned. The old men and women, soaked through, walked along keeping the cattle moving. (chapter 3)

"A Silent, Ghastly Procession" immediately establishes the factual "who-what-when-where" in a moderately lengthy sentence. Paragraph 2 supplies the why. By contrast, a tight, simple sentence launches chapter 3 with a powerful, assonant image: minarets "stuck up" in the rain. Geographical location here resides in concrete place-names—Adrianople, the Karagatch road.[6] The facts that matter here are images: the rain, the "jammed" carts, the "hauling" and walking with "no end and no beginning." As will be shown in Chapter Six, the narrative places the reader in the middle of the jam without the comforting overview conveyed by words like "procession" and "march." Pound taught Hemingway to convey through images; journalism taught him how to present them as facts. What may seem surprising is that the journalistic version is not only looser and wordier, padding the processional by enumerating its participants, but also more emotionally loaded in its diction: "staggering," which appears twice; walking "blindly" along; even "beside their worldly goods"—all intended to evoke sympathy for the evacuees.

Now compare their endings:

> There was a woman having a kid with a young girl holding a blanket over her and crying. Scared sick looking at it. It rained all through the evacuation. (chapter 3)

> Nearly half a million refugees are in Macedonia now. How they are to be fed nobody knows, but in the next month all the Christian world will hear the cry: Come over into Macedonia and help us! ("Silent, Ghastly Procession")

The chapter builds emotively to powerful images of agony and fear—a woman in labor with no midwife and no anesthetics, a crying "kid" "scared sick looking at it"—then falls back to a flat statement, an imagistic repetition of the opening that brings the narrative full circle—and the procession nowhere. The dispatch ends with an appeal to the Christian world for help. Such editorializing has no place in the "presentational" style of chapter 3, but artistic shaping does.

The same quasi-journalistic pattern informs chapter 6. It opens with an "establishing" sentence that *appears* journalistic in its factuality: "They shot the six cabinet ministers at half-past six in the morning against the wall of a hospital." But the sentence teases us with the unexplained: Who are "they"? "[T]he" cabinet ministers presumes that we know their nationality. Which hospital? Where? Most important, why? These ambiguities force the reader's attention to the facts that *are* provided: the political status of those shot, the precise time, the physical place. Two of these facts are ironic: the time is stated with the formality of an invitation, and the place is not where we expect to witness an execution. In sum, the opening conveys only the factual aura and dispassionate tone of journalism but at the same time exploits modernist devices of ambiguity and beginning in the middle of the action.

The mysterious "they" opens other quasi-journalistic chapters:

> They whack whacked the white horse on the legs and he knee-ed himself up. (12)

> They hanged Sam Cardinella at six o'clock in the morning in the corridor of the county jail. (17)

Chapter 9 presents a more precise variation of the factual opening, the crime-blotter report:

> At two o'clock in the morning two Hungarians got into a cigar store at Fifteenth Street and Grand Avenue. Drevitts and Boyle drove up from the Fifteenth Street police station in a Ford.

Like the other crime chapter (Sam Cardinella's execution), this one glides smoothly into narrative action and dialogue: Boyle shoots the two robbers, then the two policemen discuss whether he should have done it. Alternatively, Hemingway develops the quasi-journalistic mode imagistically. Rain heightens the misery of the evacuees in chapter 3 and foreshadows the imminent death of the cabinet ministers in chapter 6:

> There were pools of water in the courtyard. There were wet dead leaves on the paving of the courtyard. It rained hard.

As they often begin in the middle, so these chapters end without the comforting closure of journalism and conventional storytelling. The version in the *Chicago Tribune Paris Edition* states that the bodies of the cabinet ministers "were buried immediately near those of their relatives in the First cemetery. All six of the men executed today . . . will be regretted by a large part of the population of Greece."[7] By contrast, Hemingway's chapter ends with us looking at the sick cabinet minister at the moment the rifles fire: "When they fired the first volley he was sitting down in the water with his head on his knees." Not even the execution itself has ended ("*first* volley"). As the chapter denies us their past—their nationality and reasons why they were shot—it also precludes their future (burial and remembrance), leaving only the present action of unexplained and botched violence.

Chapter 12 (the goring of the horse) presents the purest example of Hemingway's journalistic mode: it both begins and ends in medias res and does not evolve into either dialogue or symbolic imagism. As we realize by the third sentence ("The horse's entrails hung down") why the horse is being whacked and must knee himself up, the vivid verbs and modifiers—"cantered jerkily," "stopped stiff," "nervously wobbly"—build tension of his impending and final collapse. But the chapter simply stops before it occurs. We do not even know whether the indecisive bull will charge again.

It is no coincidence that all but one of these quasi-journalistic chapters (chapter 3) address violent actions that have just occurred (a horse already gored), or are occurring (a policeman shoots two robbers), or are just about to occur (the two executions).[8] Their phlegmatic tone and factuality heighten the tension and the shock of the violence in complementary ways. First, they strip the reader of psychological buffers against violence that conventional treatments provide through sentimentality, clichés, euphemisms, explanations, and indirect reference. Here again, actual journalism is more likely to soften the presentation, for example in the shooting of the cabinet ministers. The anonymous *New York Times* account of the execution dramatizes the ministers' bravery with colorful gestures:

> Leaders Meet Death Jauntily
>
> The Cabinet Ministers . . . went courageously, even jauntily, to their deaths. [Three] wore their monocles as they took their places in the little line before the firing squads. All removed their hats except Gounaris, who stood[?] with his hands in his pockets.
>
> Stratos smilingly lit a cigarette as he took his place. Then he handed the silver case to the officer in charge of the execution as a sign of his appreciation of the latter's courtesy and tact in the exercise of a painful duty.
>
> Theotokis and Baltazzis chatted gayly with Gounaris as the brief final arrangements were made. Protopapadakis was silent and General Hadjanestis wore his usual air of nervousness and restlessness. . . .
>
> The condemned men were immaculately dressed and they showed no emotion as they alighted from the motor cars and walked to the square formed by the waiting troops. They took places at equal intervals, each man facing his own firing squad of twelve men, and refused to be blindfolded.
>
> When the order to fire rang out all fell simultaneously and physicians said that death in each case had come instantly. ("Greeks Take Steps to Arraign Prince" 1)

Several details in this account are virtual clichés of firing-squad bravery: refusing the blindfold, "smilingly" lighting the last cigarette and presenting the case to the presiding officer, "gayly" chatting with each other while waiting. For this reason, and because the account substantially disagrees with the terser version in the *Chicago Tribune Paris Edition,* its authenticity is questionable. Clearly, however, its emphasis on the ministers' "jaunty" courage defuses the execution's capacity to disturb the reader.

The version in the *Chicago Tribune Paris Edition* (the one Hemingway most likely read) is much shorter and lacks the Hollywood effects:

> They died silently, refusing to answer when they were asked to express their last wishes. ("Greeks Execute Six" 1)

Briefest and least clichéd of all is Hemingway's version in chapter 6:

> The other five stood very quietly against the wall.

As it avoids hackneyed gestures, Hemingway's chapter also avoids euphemisms and circumlocutions that mute the episode's violence and sordidness. Compare:

> It was said though that former Premier Gounaris, who had been ill with typhoid fever, was carried from *his sick bed* to *the place of execution*.
>
> The executions were swift and dramatic . . . the six doomed men received communion in the Averoff prison. From there they were taken to Goudi square outside Athens and *put to death* at 11.30 A.M. ("Greeks Execute Six," emphasis mine)

versus:

> One of the ministers was sick with typhoid. Two soldiers carried him downstairs and out into the rain. They tried to hold him up against the wall but he sat down in a puddle of water. . . . When they fired the first volley he was sitting down in the water with his head on his knees.

Rejecting the cliché "sick bed" and the vague "place of execution," Hemingway makes the reader see the action in detail—the soldiers carrying the minister downstairs and trying to hold him up against the wall, his sitting with his head on his knees when they fire—and feel it imagistically: "into the rain," "in a puddle of water," "in the water." Similarly, "fired the first volley" sharpens the newspaper's euphemistic "put to death," and the chapter's last image compels the reader to visualize with sickening clarity precisely where the bullets will strike the minister ("his head on his knees").

This forcing the reader to see violent or sordid actions through direct statement or sensory detail marks the second way that this quasi-journalistic style heightens tension or shock effect. It was a technique Hemingway carefully calculated and quickly became known for. He writes in *Death in the Afternoon:*

> I had read many books in which, when the author tried to convey [violent death], he only produced a blur, and I decided that this was because either the author had never seen it clearly or at the moment of it, he had physically or mentally shut his eyes. . . . [I]f these very simple things were to be made permanent, as, say, Goya

> tried to make them in *Los Desastros de la Guerra,* it could not be done with any shutting of the eyes. (2–3)

In forcing us to look, the narrative's unblinking stare goes far beyond journalistic standards or literary conventions to achieve a brutal candor that seemed altogether new:

> The horse's entrails hung down in a blue bunch and swung backward and forward as he began to canter, . . . (chapter 12)

> When they came toward him with the cap to go over his head Sam Cardinella lost control of his sphincter muscle. (chapter 17)

As much as they depict actual violence, these journalistic chapters also build tension through imminent violence: the cabinet ministers and Sam Cardinella are not executed until the last sentence, and even then the focus and sentence structure subordinates the act of execution to something else: the sick minister's sitting position, the priest's "skipping" back onto the scaffold. Similarly, the horse hovers on the brink of collapse, "nervously wobbly"; the bull may or may not charge again. As Hemingway recognized (in the passage from *Death in the Afternoon* quoted above), the "about to be" can be the true literary climax of a violent scene, while the actual act becomes anticlimax (3).[9] Finally, in both actual and imminent violence, Hemingway realized that, regarding emotion, less is more: the less emotive the prose, the greater the tension, as the reader's imagination supplies the unstated dread.

Parodies

The most atypical of Hemingway's genres appears in chapter 10 (the recovering soldier and Ag) and chapter 18 (the king in the garden), which parody genres from children's literature: the fairy tale (10) and the nursery rhyme with a touch of *Alice in Wonderland* in the concluding chapter. In both cases, the parodies are heavily ironic. As Chapter Six will discuss, the "Once upon a time" storytelling narrative of chapter 10 updates the typical love story of fairy tales (lovers who overcome separation and blocking characters to marry and live happily every after). In this modern version, the lovers, Ag and "he," are first together, then separated with fairy tale-like tasks *he* must fulfill, then break up via the mail to live unhappily ever after (for Ag's Italian romance) and painfully in the present (for him). "True love" does not prevail. Marriage becomes only a way of announcing and legally solidifying what the couple already achieves outside of marriage: "They wanted to get married. . . . They felt as though they were married, but they wanted everyone to know about it, and to make it so they could not lose it."

In place of love and marriage, sex begins and ends these relationships. The story begins with the couple sleeping together: "Ag sat on the bed. She was cool and fresh in the hot night." It ends with Ag's infidelity ("she had never known Italians before") and, in response to her Dear John letter, his having sex with a sales girl in a taxicab. The settings of modern love are also contemporary—sterile, public, impersonal: the antiseptic hospital room, a taxicab, the mail. In between the sexual endpoints, the fairy tale conventions of love and marriage take a beating. Their love, Ag hurtfully claims in her Dear John letter, was nothing more than "a boy and girl affair." The obstacles their love must overcome—separation, difficult tasks, temptation—instead overcome their love. The tasks are manifestly one-sided (all his) and absurd (for instance, giving up his friends), and Ag cannot keep the faith during their separation. Self-evidently, the story is a bitter parody of love "in our time," and Hemingway could not have chosen a more apt model than the fairy tale. Its resonance implies that "ever after" romantic love has itself become a fairy tale in the postwar world.

Like chapter 10, chapter 18 plays off of genres of children's literature: the nursery rhyme and the fantasy. This concluding chapter describes the narrator's social call on a king and queen—Greek King George and his wife—who have hastily replaced the abdicating King Constantine, only to be placed under house arrest by the new revolutionary government of General Plastiris. That these characters were contemporaneous figures, familiar to Hemingway's readers (at least those who followed international politics), only heightens his parodic treatment of them. The opening sentence,

> The king was working in the garden.

immediately summons up the nursery rhyme:

> The king was in his counting house counting all his money. The queen was in the parlor eating bread and honey.

The chapter's opening sentences have a "through the looking-glass" oddness to them. We are not told why the king is doing manual labor or why he is glad to see the narrator. His introduction of the queen is disarmingly informal and direct:

> This is the queen, he said. She was clipping a rose bush. Oh how do you do, she said.

Although she is merely "clipping a rosebush," not having it painted, her fantastic forebear in *Alice in Wonderland* lurks in the line.[10] This disparity between their royal titles and common behavior and speech—by the end of the chapter, the king is just "like all Greeks"—already gives a satiric edge to this modern fairy tale. But only as the chapter unfolds do readers discover that the royal couple has been placed under house arrest by a regime that has already executed the previous king's cabinet ministers. Thus, as the new king sagely confides to the narrator, "the great thing in this sort of an affair is not to be shot oneself!"

Hemingway's parody here is double-edged. It satirizes "the king business" (as he called the same situation in his *Toronto Star* story of 15 September 1923) and underscores royalty's vestigial irrelevance "in our time." By emotive contrast, the echoes of nursery rhyme and children's tale heighten the chapter's underlying tension: all is "jolly" within the garden, but the couple themselves may be clipped if they cross its boundary.

Romantic love and marriage in wartime and royalty in an age of political revolutions thus share a single quality: they are both superannuated notions in an age that undermines both relationships and governments. Hemingway's parodic style stresses this obsolescence by using literary models furthest removed from contemporary realities—the fairy tale, the nursery rhyme, the child's fantasy.

Experiential Narratives

A sizable number of chapters in *in our time*—1, 4, 5, 7, 8, and 16—present experiences of a protagonist, usually a young soldier. The narrators of these chapters are close to the action, often at the center of it, as the protagonist. All but one of these chapters are (or originally were) narrated in first person.[11] Nearly all deal with war experience, and some of those experiences—being under shellfire, being wounded—have autobiographical origins. Unlike most of the bullfight chapters, which position readers as spectators observing the action and central character from the outside, these experiential chapters present a protagonist's consciousness from the inside looking out.[12]

Thus, what matters here is not so much the event itself as the protagonist experiencing and responding to it. A young kitchen corporal recounts a bizarre, drunken night march en route to, but still safely distanced from, the Champagne battlefront (1). Two distinctly British officers describe with almost antithetical degrees of affect, different episodes of combat at Mons: the unexpected shooting of Germans coming over a garden wall (4) and the "absolutely perfect barricade" the British jam across a bridge (5). On the Italian front, chapter 7 narrates in third person Nick's reaction to being wounded, while in the next chapter, a peripheral narrator contrasts a fellow soldier's behavior under shellfire and in subsequent safety. Finally, the concluding bullfight chapter that depicts Maera's death (16) is perhaps the most purely experiential of the book since Maera's sensations and perceptions filter nearly all the action.

Some of these chapters—for example, 4 (combat in a garden at Mons), 5 (the perfect barricade), and 8 (the praying soldier)—could also be considered character studies (a type discussed below). They are grouped here as "experiential" narratives because they do not so much develop a character as his response to a particular situation or moment. Mortal danger colors many of these moments in red—being gored repeatedly by the bull, wounded by machine-gun fire, subjected to intense artillery shelling. But other moments portray strange and unpredictable episodes in wartime: the drunken night march, the unexpected combat, the perfect small action within a crumbling larger situation. These currents of violence—sometimes subliminal, sometimes blatant—circulate in jarring opposites of danger and drudgery (marching, repairing the trench), fear and relief, anticipation and forgetting.[13] The protagonist's responses to these situations—his sensations, perceptions, actions, and states of mind—are comparably diverse and yield both parallels and contrasts. The first British officer's numb recounting in halting sentences (chapter 4) sharply contrasts his compatriot's hyperbolic, almost manic, enthusiasm in chapter 5—even though for both the encounters have gone well. Nick's relief and sardonic humor about having made "a separate peace" (chapter 7) directly oppose the terror of a soldier still very much in it and his subsequent, self-protective forgetting (chapter 8). The kitchen corporal's sense of disorienting strangeness when nothing happens (chapter 1) ironically parallels the first British officer's reaction to unexpected combat and oddly anticipates Maera's disoriented final sensations.

The range and diversity of these experiential moments oppose the single protagonist's evolution in the bildungsroman. Among his modernist forebears, Hemingway had several precedents for this development of the single protagonist: Joyce's *A Portrait of the Artist as a Young Man,* Flaubert's *Sentimental Education,* Stein's "Melanctha," and, perhaps closest to his interest, Anderson's *Winesburg, Ohio.* A year later, he would follow their example in the Nick Adams stories he created for the enlarged *In Our Time.*[14] But these 1923 pieces resist monolithic progression of experience, just as they resist chronological ordering. They represent, particularly the war chapters, a kind of collage of moments, all roughly contemporaneous but otherwise difficult to type. This resistance to stereotype becomes in itself a metacommentary on the nature of violent experience "in our time." If "war is hell" for the praying soldier under shellfire, it ceases to be hell once the shelling stops. War is bizarre for the kitchen corporal, great sport for one British officer, and disorienting and numbing for another. No single experience is paradigmatic; it is only provisionally true for that particular character at that moment. Freed from subordination to a grand design (because the grand design itself is absent), each experience projects its own intensity, its own distinct strangeness—an echo of the modernist reality that Stein described: "each thing was as important as any other thing" (*Picasso* 37–38). Heightened by a corresponding diversity of protagonists, narrative voices, and styles, this distinctiveness accounts for much of the freshness of these pieces. Later, Hemingway would select from them the experiences and character responses he would develop into the progression of Nick Adams stories and into his early first-person novels.[15] For now, however, each of these experiences posited its own validity.

Descriptive Studies

All the *in our time* chapters depict an action, portray a character, and evoke a scene, but some chapters seem chiefly devoted to describing these elements. What distinguishes this descriptive mode from the experiential is essentially distance and perspective. In the experiential mode, the narrative voice and point of view are usually the protagonist's and close to the action. Even when the protagonist does not narrate the episode himself, the point of view stays close to him, for example, Nick in chapter 7. The soldier-narrator of chapter 8 is close enough to his comrade to see him as he "lay very flat and sweated" and to hear his desperate prayers. The descriptive chapters, conversely, presume narrative distance and emotive detachment. We observe more than experience the action. We are in the stands watching Villalta, "the kid," the bad bullfighter, or the gored horse's wobbly steps; we are part of the crowd, but we also observe the crowd. We see the wet, dead leaves on the paving of the courtyard, but we do not experience the execution from the cabinet ministers' point of view. We hear conversations between Boyle and Drevitts (chapter 9), between the young revolutionist and the older narrator (10), between the narrator-bullfighter and Maera (15). But we are essentially outside of their consciousness. This externality applies even to chapters 11 (the revolutionist), 13 (the bad bullfighter), and 15 (the drunken bullfighter), which have first-person narrators; for in each case, the narrator's role is secondary to a study of another character (the revolutionist, the failed bullfighter, and Luis and Maera, respectively). As detached observations these chapters are direct descendents—and expansions—of the experimental "I have seen" sentences of "Paris 1922" that Hemingway rewrote just before starting the *in our time* chapters.

A few descriptive chapters are purely of one type, for instance, the character study of the Hungarian revolutionary (11). For many others, however, it is difficult—and unnecessary—to determine whether description focuses primarily on action, character, or scene. Henry James's epigram is apposite here: "What is character but the determination of incident? What is incident but the illustration of character?"[16] Sam Cardinella's execution (17) is a perfect example. Action, character, and scene are balanced and inseparable: Sam reveals his abject fear through actions (being carried, messing his pants). But the chapter is finally not about Sam; it is about his execution as a scenic process—a staged event with actors (priests, executioners, victim), ritual (the processional, the last rites), and audience (the intimidated inmates of death row). And as each component of the scene goes awry, the drama becomes farce. Even as action, character, and setting interweave, however, one element is sometimes more equal than others. In chapter 14, for example, Villalta's superb performance obviously reflects his courageous and skillful character. Yet, Hemingway is concerned with showing us *how* Villalta dominates and kills the bull: it is his performance—the action—that matters most. Allowing, therefore, for the ambiguous and multiple identities of these descriptive narratives, we might still identify the three dominant orientations as follows.

Character Studies

As noted above, chapter eleven's depiction of the Hungarian revolutionary is a character study par excellence but also something of a rarity in its de-emphasis of present-time action. Having covered international political conferences and followed the Bolshevik and fascist revolutions as a journalist, Hemingway here constructs a political type: the revolutionary absolutist who permits neither imprisonment, physical torture, nor a discouraging political outlook to deter his religious faith in world revolution. As in the "experiential" chapters, however, it is not conflict per se, but the character's psychology that matters, in this case how the revolutionary handles the almost continuous discouragement and resistance to his cause. The very qualities that make him a sympathetic protagonist—the older and skeptical narrator describes him somewhat condescendingly as "a very nice boy and very shy"—also underscore his unworldliness and naiveté. Confronted with the narrator's bleak assessment of Italy's ripeness for revolution, he can only retreat into his preconceived beliefs that Italy "is the one country that everyone is sure of. It will be the starting point of everything." In sum, this is a study of ideological blindness coupled with a will to martyrdom in a world where such devotions (echoing those of the martyred saints the boy admires in painting) have little relevance.

The other character studies also present the mentalities of people in extreme situations, where death looms nearby. Boyle is a Kansas City cop who shoots first and rationalizes later (chapter 9). In contrast to his partner's skittishness, he has the opaque confidence of a murderous bigot, who knows that brutality against the despised Italians will go unpunished but is too thick to realize that he has misidentified the thieves' ethnicity. Along with his victims' actual nationality, Boyle's blindness links him to the Hungarian revolutionary's brittle worldview.

Chapter 15 is an interesting anomaly. Although narrated in first person, the bullfighter-narrator is ancillary to the chapter's contrast between the irresponsible Luis, whose drunken revels with the *riau-riau* dancers ensure that he will be in no shape to fight bulls, and the fatalistic Maera, who realizes that he and the narrator will face the nearly impossible task of killing Maera's bulls as well as their own. Although the chapter is dramatic in its portrayal of the "good" bullfighters' efforts to retrieve the errant Luis, its real focus is to contrast unspoken motives and attitudes toward mortal danger: Luis's drunken irresponsibility surely derives from fear and, if he is the same bullfighter described in chapter 13, incompetence. Maera's resigned fatalism steeps in foreboding:

> Yes, we, said Maera. We kills the savages' bulls, and the drunkards' bulls, and the *riau-riau* dancers' bulls. Yes. We kill them. We kill them all right. Yes. Yes. Yes.

The *yes*es are bitterly ironic and do not conceal Maera's recognition of the slim odds of his surviving the next *corrida*.

Action Studies

The preponderance of action in these chapters shows where Hemingway's narrative interests truly lay. "[T]o put down what really happened in action" was "the greatest difficulty"—and thus the greatest challenge—of his early writing (*Death in the Afternoon* 2). Accordingly, the chapters devote much of their brief narratives to capturing "the sequence of motion and fact" and to studying its psychological impact on individuals.

As readers quickly discover, most of this action is violent. Hemingway recalls in *Death in the Afternoon:* "I was trying to learn to write [in 1923], commencing with the simplest things, and one of the simplest things of all and the most fundamental is violent death" (2). Three of the book's subjects—war, crime, and the bullfight—are inherently violent, and of the fourth, politics, he examines its most violent aspects: political torture, execution, and atrocities, both actual and anticipated. Whether dominating the foreground or lurking ominously in shadows as memory or anticipation, violence is the common denominator of these chapters:

chapter	*type of violence*	*actions, reactions*
1	combat, anticipation of	getting drunk, fear
2	bullfight	being gored, killing several bulls
3	Turkish atrocities, anticipation of	fear, fleeing on foot
4	combat	shooting German soldiers
4	combat	shooting German soldiers
6	political execution	shooting of six cabinet ministers
7	combat	being wounded by machine-gun fire, relief

8	combat	being shelled, fear (vs. safety, forgetting)
9	crime	shooting two robbers
10	combat, past (implied)	recovering from wounds in hospital
11	political torture, past	becoming absolutist, repressing facts
12	bullfight	bleeding, tottering of gored horse
13	bullfight	botched killing of bull
14	bullfight	Villalta preparing and killing bull
15	bullfight	Luis's fear, revelry, Maera's fatalism
16	bullfight	repeated goring and death of Maera
17	crime	hanging of Sam Cardinella
18	political execution, danger of	royal couple's fear, restraint

Tellingly, the danger often lurks at or just beyond the temporal edge of the narrative: the drunken French soldiers march *to* the battlefield (1); the Greek civilians flee from Turkish brutality (3); the Greek cabinet ministers and Sam Cardinella each face imminent execution that does not occur until the final sentence of each chapter (6, 17); the praying soldier seems about to be blown to pieces (8); the responsible bullfighters know what they will face at their next *corrida* (15); and the Greek royal couple under house arrest live with the possibility of being shot (18). In a few cases, violence precedes the narrative: Nick has just been wounded when chapter 7 opens; the soldier recovering in a hospital (10) has also presumably been wounded; and the revolutionist (11) has been tortured before coming to Italy.

More than dramatizing the danger itself, these chapters study the ways that individuals—soldiers and civilians, criminals and policemen, politicians and bullfighters—respond to it. The action is as much psychological as physical, implied as much as stated. It is the anticipation or recollection of violence, the sense of imminent danger or the haunting memory of recent pain, that determines these characters' responses. Even when violent action is central to the narrative, still the characters' responses to it are what seem to matter most: the officer-narrator in chapter 4 numbly recalls combat at a garden wall, while his counterpart in chapter 5 ebulliently describes a perfect barricade. When the anticipated violence finally occurs—when the cabinet ministers are shot or Sam Cardinella hanged—the action seems anticlimactic and indirect, muted in subordinate clauses.

Of the potential responses to violence, fear and its rarer complement, courage, are what most interest Hemingway—fear triumphant in Sam Cardinella's befouling himself (17) and in the praying soldier's desperate promise to "jesus" (8); fear rigorously contained by the cabinet ministers standing "very quietly against the wall" (6) and in Villalta's performance (14); fear transmuted into Luis's drunken dancing (15) or exaggerated in the French adjutant's absurd cautions (1); and fear looked at steadily in Maera's resigned fatalism (15). Lines from *The Waste Land* seem to echo through these studies:

> There is shadow under this red rock,
> (Come in under the shadow of this red rock),
> And I will show you something different from either
> Your shadow at morning striding behind you
> Or your shadow at evening rising to meet you;
> I will show you fear in a handful of dust.
>
> (I, 25–30)

Other responses to violence relieve this pervasive dialectic of fear and courage: Boyle's crude self-confidence (9), the retreating Greek Christians' silent suffering and stoicism (3); Nick's relief at being out of combat and his private joke about making "a separate peace" (7); the praying soldier's rapid forgetting (once he is safe) of his promise to Jesus as he chooses prostitutes over proselytizing (8); the simultaneously gruesome and grotesquely comic aspect of the gored horse's cantering as his entrails "swung backward and forward" (12).[17] These varied and nuanced responses to mortal danger are what make Hemingway's action studies so powerful, so much more than just kinesthetic scene-painting. His imaginative capacity here, deriving from fascination with the subject, careful study (regarding the bullfight), and firsthand experience, distinguishes his work from his contemporaries.[18] No one else at the time made the study of contemporary violence his or her particular métier. Hemingway had the field to himself.

Scenic Studies

In a very few cases, a chapter's mise-en-scène makes as deep an impression as its characters or action: the rose garden in which the king and queen have their jolly chat with the narrator (18); the hospital courtyard with its driving rain, standing puddles, wet dead leaves, and nailed-shut shutters (6); the muddy, rain-soaked evacuation of Greek civilians (3). Our memory of these settings attest to their imagistic power.

In all cases, scenic description furthers the chapter's thematic aim. In chapter 3, for example, the recurring images of rain—"mud flats," "water buffalo," "mud," "soaked through," the Maritza "running yellow almost up to the bridge"—relentlessly drive home the misery of the cattlelike civilians in their seemingly endless march ("no end and no beginning") away from the Turks. Similarly, the rain and water images framing the execution of the cabinet ministers underscore their helplessness. Nature has made their final moments even more miserable—

> Two soldiers carried [the minister sick with typhoid] downstairs and out into the rain. They tried to hold him up against the wall but he sat down in a puddle of water.

—and leaves them utterly forlorn: "All the shutters of the hospital were nailed shut." In both scenes, this physical misery underscores the characters' endurance and courage:

> The other five stood very quietly against the wall. (6)

> The old men and women, soaked through, walked along keeping the cattle moving. (chapter 3)

Conversely, fear governs the scenic prelude to Sam Cardinella's execution, as the executioner intended it to. Because "the corridor" where he is to be hanged "is high and narrow with tiers of cells on either side," the men in the surrounding cells are not only forced to watch but are extremely close to the action. This proximity enables Hemingway to examine their fearful responses. The closing scene also contrasts images of fear. With his entourage safely on the scaffolding, Sam, like the cabinet ministers, is forlorn: "When they all stepped back on the scaffolding back of the drop, . . . Sam Cardinella was *left* sitting there strapped tight . . . " (emphasis mine). In comic contrast, "The priest skipped back onto the scaffolding just before the drop fell." Such contrasts point up the ironic function of settings, as does the dissonance between tranquil settings (garden, hospital, church) and brutal acts.

But beyond using setting to further theme, Hemingway also shapes these scenic chapters as imagistic tours de force. The narrative describing the Greek evacuation begins in rain—"Minarets stuck up in the rain out of Adrianople across the mud flats"—and ends in rain: "It rained all through the evacuation." The water images of chapter 6—the "pools of water" and "wet dead leaves"—anticipate the pools of blood, and wet, dead bodies "on the paving of the courtyard" and culminate in the final image of vulnerability and watery death: the sick minister "sitting down in the water with his head on his knees."

Within eighteen short chapters, Hemingway's variety of narrative modes is impressive: sober quasi-journalistic reporting interchanges with mock fairy tales. Some actions are experienced close-up (the drunken night march); others are described from a distance (the bad bullfighter). Narratives of interior consciousness (Maera's) follow objective narratives in an anonymous voice (the gored horse). While threads of violence and irony weave through these modes, their restless diversity remains their overriding impression. They show a young writer still determining his fictional technique, trying out narrative strategies not so much to see which are congenial to his talents, but to discover what his talents really are by understanding how these narratives work.

4
Voices

As both journalist and fledgling fiction writer, Hemingway knew that voice is a crucial and complex aspect of narrative. Encompassing diction, grammar, tone, and emotion (or the lack of it), voice characterizes, creates verisimilitude, and suggests theme. As substance intertwines with vacancy in the visual arts, voice interacts with silence. What the voice tells us and what it does not or cannot say both signify, likewise what it quietly understates or hyperbolically overstates. The voice that narrates a story is particularly important since it bends that narrative as a lens does light. Textbooks on fiction usually relegate narrative voice to "point of view," but voice determines more than just the perspective or angle from which the story is told. Even when it belongs to an anonymous narrator, the voice possesses a distinct identity in its rhythms and texture.

Aware of this complexity, Hemingway used these brief narratives to explore and develop his vocal range. The chapters of *in our time* are a medley of voices: voices that tell a story, voices that dramatize themselves, voices that comment on and often undercut other voices, voices that are conspicuously silent.

Characters' Voices

The vocal range and diversity in these eighteen chapters are remarkable. Apart from the voices of anonymous third-person narrators and of the crowd in the bullfight chapters, at least twenty-six distinct characters and narrators speak.[1] Equally important are characters whose silence distinguishes them: Rinaldi and Maera are too badly wounded to speak; Sam Cardinella, too frightened; the cabinet ministers, too proud—or despairing. Table 1 is a list of speakers, grouped by occupation, with chapter numbers in parentheses (an asterisk denotes narrator).

Recalling the social juxtapositions of Mark Twain and O. Henry, the

Table 1.

Speakers Soldiers	Politicos	Bullfighters	Cops	Other
*kitchen corporal (1)	revolutionist (11)	bad bullfighter (13)	Drevitts (9)	*anon. bullfight observer (2)
French lieutenant (1)	*older comrade (11)	Villalta (14)	Boyle (9)	
French adjutant (1)	King (18)	Luis (15)	Guard (17)	Ag (10)
*Brit. officer (4)	Queen (18)	Maera (15)	Will (17)	*bullfight fan (13)
*Brit. officer (5)		*anon. bullfighter(15)		priest (17)
Nick (7)		[crowd (2, 13, 14, 16)]		*visitor to King & Queen (18)
praying soldier (8)				
*fellow soldier (8)				
Totals: 8	4	5 [9]	4	5 = 26
Silent characters				
cabinet ministers (6)				
Rinaldi (7)				
"he" (10)				
Sam Cardinella (17)				
Maera (16)				
Total: 5				

voices of *in our time* span social classes and occupations even within the chapters' limited subject range. They belong to monarchs and revolutionaries, priests and cops, diverse bullfighters and assertively vocal crowds, and soldiers spanning three nationalities (four, if Nick in chapter 7 is Italian). Well-educated voices intersperse with the semiliterate; voices schooled at Sandhurst and Oxford mingle with voices at home in a boxing gym. With Europe as the locale of all but two chapters, French and Italian phrases ("mon vieux," "Senta") and British locutions ("potted," "young Buckley") season the predominantly American English of these voices. As Chapter Six will show in detail, this internationalism sometimes makes the speaker's nationality ambiguous: Is the kitchen corporal who speaks American English in a French unit (chapter 1) American or French? Is the wounded Nick who uses both American English and Italian in chapter 7 an Italian because he appears to be fighting in an Italian combat unit?[2] Soldiers' and bullfighters' voices dominate this mélange, but the variety within their ranks only underscores the larger vocal diversity. Here are some samples of this diversity:

He couldn't hardly lift his arm. (2)
I think he did the right though shooting those chaps. (18)
They're wops ain't they? Who the hell is going to make any trouble? (9)
It was funny going along that road. (1)
She loved him as always, but she realized now it was only a boy and girl love.(10)
oh jesus christ get me out of here. (8)
We were frightfully put out when we heard the flank had gone, and we had to fall back. (5)
Yes. We kill them. We kill them all right. Yes. Yes. Yes. (15)
We waited till he got one leg over and then potted him. (4)
Senta. You and me we've made a separate peace. (7)
Be a man, my son. (17)
I am not really a good bull fighter. (13)
You have everything here. It is the one country that everyone is sure of. It will be the starting point of everything. (11)
The bull looking at him straight in front, hating. (14)
I'm drunk, I tell you, mon vieux. Oh, I am so soused. (1)
The crowd shouted all the time and threw pieces of bread down into the ring, then cushions and leather wine bottles, keeping up whistling and yelling. (13)
There was a woman having a kid with a young girl holding a blanket over her and crying. Scared sick looking at it. (3)

Hemingway is especially good at capturing the voices of the demimonde—cops and tough guys—that he had heard firsthand covering the police and hospital beats for the *Kansas City Star.* The dialogue between Drevitts and Boyle in chapter 9 is especially convincing:

> Drevitts got frightened when he found they were both dead. Hell Jimmy, he said, you oughtn't to have done it. There's likely to be a hell of a lot of trouble.
> —They're crooks ain't they? said Boyle. They're wops ain't they? Who the hell is going to make any trouble?
> —That's all right maybe this time, said Drevitts, but how did you know they were wops when you bumped them?

Casual, ungrammatical ("ain't," "oughtn't"), slangy ("bumped them"—which Hemingway later made a little less slangy when he added "off" for the 1925 *In Our Time*)—their speech locates them in the same world as the criminals they shoot just as much as Boyle's murderousness and bigoted ignorance do. Similarly, hard-boiled narrative voices in other chapters use "kid" to refer to a young bullfighter (chapter 2), to children, and even to a baby being born (chapter 3). The latter usage—"There was a women having a kid"—so disturbed an editor at Scribner's that he summarily changed it to "baby" for Scribner's first edition.

Far fewer voices come from the upper classes, but one that does—the king's voice in chapter 18—shows that Hemingway's ear was just as finely tuned to that end of the social scale:

> Plastiras is a very good man I believe, he said, but frightfully difficult. I think he did right though shooting those chaps. If Kerensky had shot a few men things might have been altogether different. Of course the great thing in this sort of an affair is not to be shot oneself!

The British usages—"frightfully," "chaps"—show that this young Greek king was schooled in England (or had British tutors). Something of this elite education perhaps creeps into his elitist support of absolute power—shooting the cabinet ministers that his own predecessor had abandoned[3]—even when that power may very well be turned on him.

The emotional range of these voices is equally wide. The effusive English officer narrating chapter 5—

> It was a frightfully hot day. We'd jammed an absolutely perfect barricade across the bridge. It was simply priceless.

—sharply contrasts with his laconic counterpart (4) who pots Germans climbing over a garden wall:

> Then three more came over further down the wall. We shot them. They all came over just like that.

The narrator of the *corrida* in chapter 2 is breathlessly excited:

> The second matador slipped and the bull caught him through the belly and he hung on to the horn with one hand and held the other tight against the place, and the bull rammed him wham against the wall and the horn came out and. . . .

The observer of Villalta's technique in chapter 14 is coolly precise and a touch literary:

> when the bull charged he swung back firmly like an oak when the wind hits it, his legs tight together, the muleta trailing and the sword following the curve behind.

These emotive contrasts distinguish characters, such as the British narrators of chapters 4 and 5, who might otherwise be taken as one voice because of their similar dialects and idioms. Most critics, in fact, do treat the two voices as one.[4] But as Chapter Six will show, the voices of these two narrators employ sharply differing sentence structures and diction to suggest virtually antithetical states of affect. If the two voices do come from one speaker, then they point to a split personality or, at the very least, a manic-depressive narrator.

The very contrast of emotive states becomes, ipso facto, thematic, often ironic, especially when the speaker is a peripheral observer. Chapter 8, for example, begins with the desperate prayers of a terrified soldier under shellfire:

> While the bombardment was knocking the trench to pieces at Fossalta, he lay very flat and sweated and prayed oh jesus christ get me out of here. Christ please please please christ. . . .

The narrator separates himself from this fearful litany with a cheerful description of the next morning:

> We went to work on the trench and in the morning the sun came up and the day was hot and muggy and cheerful and quiet. (8)

Similarly, the narrator's refusal (in chapter 11) to respond to his younger comrade's blind optimism subverts the boy's naïveté with skeptical silence.

Silent Voices

Silence, in fact, performs its own array of thematic roles. The Greek cabinet ministers "stood very quietly" awaiting their execution in the rain and watching the farce of soldiers trying to make a very sick man stand up to be shot. A different author would have highlighted their heroic self-control, their contemptuous refusal of last words—as, in fact, one newspaper journalist did (discussed in Chapter Three). For Hemingway, one parsimoniously parceled out adverb—"very"—conveys their stoical courage. Conversely, another prisoner to be executed is silenced by all-consuming fear: facing the gallows, Sam Cardinella has lost control of his legs, his bowels, and his voice. His guards converse, one priest exhorts, the narrator reports, but Sam is silent. If Sam is too scared to speak, Rinaldi (in chapter 7) is too badly wounded. His "poor audience" thus makes Nick's remark about making "a separate peace" a private joke. Silence is especially powerful when a character has much to say. Chapter ten's story of broken promises and blighted romance renders this near quotation of Ag's voice in her Dear John letter in order to convey her unthinking cruelty:

> [She] finally wrote a letter to the States that theirs had been only a boy and girl affair. She was sorry, and she knew he would probably not be able to understand, but might some day forgive her, and be grateful to her, and she expected absolutely unexpectedly, to be married in the spring. She loved him as always, but she realized now it was only a boy and girl love. She hoped he would have a great career, and believed in him absolutely. She knew it was for the best.

Conspicuously, the narrative omits "his" verbal response: "Ag never got an answer to her letter to Chicago." But as critics have noted regarding the narrative's concealed first-person point of view, the entire chapter is "his" response to Ag's perfidy.[5]

The Narrator's Voice and Point of View

Constructing narrative voices was an especially important technique for Hemingway to master, and the chapters show how thoroughly he experimented with various possibilities. As with identities and emotive states, he tried out all the first- and third-person viewpoints and even began chapter 14 with a teasing touch of second person—"If it happened right down close in front of you, you could see Villalta"—before quickly settling into third person.[6] Each perspective enables particular narrative possibilities and closes off others as it focuses the reader's attention differently, and each point of view reveals or conceals the speaker to differing degrees. Table 2 lists the chapters by their point of view.

As this table shows, third-person omniscient was the point of view Hemingway favored least, for several reasons. First, its multiple perspectives can easily disunify a chapter, whose brevity in any case did not usually require a shift of perspective. Moreover, as the oldest point of view historically, emerging with the novel form itself, the omniscient recalls the era of intrusive authors whose freewheeling shifts from character to character assert the novel's artifice, its storytelling conventions. Although modernist innovators like Woolf and Joyce freely exploited the omniscient's capacity to jump among characters, Hemingway subscribed to Flaubert's realist credo that the author should be everywhere present but nowhere visible. The story, in brief, should give the illusion of telling itself. Accordingly, narrative perspective should not destroy verisimilitude by reminding the reader of an all-controlling author but should remain constant and limited—as it would be from the perspective of an actual person or from an on-the-scene narrator. Finally, the omniscient was, in a sense, too easy: it encouraged telling the reader what mattered beneath the dramatic surface. As virtually all commentators have observed, Hemingway's modernism, as well as his journalistic training, inclined him strongly toward showing through action and dialogue, leaving deeper meanings unstated and only hinted at through images, symbols, repetitions, and the like.

Only one chapter, 10, employs omniscient point of view as we are told what both lovers think or feel at various stages of their romance: "he thought about Luz in his bed. . . . They felt as though they were

Table 2. *Points of view in the chapters*
(chapter numbers in parentheses refer to drafts, in brackets to a substantial portion of chapter)

1st-person central	1st-per. peripheral	3rd-per. objective	3rd-per. limited omniscient	3rd-per. omni.
1	2	3	7	10
4	8	6	[8]	16?
5	11	9	16	
(8)	13	12		
(10)	15	14		
	18	17		
Totals: 3 (5)	6	6	2 (3)	1(2?)

married, . . . It was lonely and rainy there . . . and she had never known Italians before." Chapter 16 has been called omniscient,[7] but this identification is debatable. For nearly all of the chapter, Hemingway experiments with interior consciousness: the narrative voice limits itself to what the silent Maera can see, hear, feel, or infer—a limited-omniscient point of view. In a few instances, however, the narrative voice strays from Maera's consciousness. The first instance is questionable: "Someone had the bull by the tail. They were swearing at him and flopping the cape in his face. Then the bull was gone." Arguably, Maera, who lies face down in the sand, understands what is happening from the fact that the bull has stopped goring him and from his long experience in the ring. But he cannot see someone pulling the bull by the tail or flopping the cape in its face. He can only sense "the bull was gone"—a brilliantly restrictive sentence.[8] The second instance is definite: the perspective briefly shifts from Maera, lying on an infirmary cot, to the doctor, running from the corral and stopping to wash his hands before arriving at the infirmary. But these exceptions do not, I feel, represent a genuinely omniscient point of view; they are more like digressions from a point of view that otherwise limits itself rigorously to the sensations of a man being gored repeatedly and to his final, faltering perceptions.[9]

If he avoided the omniscient, Hemingway at first gravitated toward first-person central point of view, in which the narrator himself is the story's chief protagonist. Originally, in five of his eighteen chapters, the narrator was the central character. This perspective had several immediate attractions, especially for a novice writer. Unlike the omniscient, it creates unity through one consistent voice and focus. It also encourages the reader's identification with and empathy for the "I" narrator. Writing in first person, moreover, tempts an author to draw on personal experience—another facilitator since material is readily at hand. By yielding to this autobiographical urge, however, an author risks losing critical detachment from his material and revealing sides of himself he might prefer to remain private. These dangers, particularly the latter, prompted Hemingway to conceal the autobiographical origins of chapters 8 (the praying soldier) and 10 (the recovering soldier and Ag) in his revisions, shifting his first-person protagonist-narrators to a peripheral narrator in chapter 8 and to an anonymous narrator in chapter 10.

Significantly, both chapters 8 and 10 and the ones that remain in first-person central describe war situations that Hemingway either experienced himself, heard described by friends who had, or (in the case of chapter one) easily imagined himself experiencing. Except perhaps for the British officer-narrators of chapters 4 and 5,[10] the voices in these chapters are of young soldiers who describe events they have experienced firsthand and close-up. Yet, as I have argued in Chapter Three, the focus of these first-person chapters is not so much on action itself as on the narrator's psychological response to it: the kitchen corporal's sense of strangeness in the drunken night march (1); the British officer's comparable disorientation in suddenly encountering attacking Germans coming over a garden wall (4); and the panic of the praying soldier (who was originally the first-person narrator) in chapter 8.

Interestingly, Hemingway scants the point of view closest to first-person central, third-person limited-omniscient. Like first-person central, this perspective stays very close to the story's protagonist, describing what he thinks and feels but not ostensibly in his voice.[11] Only two chapters of *in our time* use a limited-omniscient perspective: chapter 7, which describes Nick's responses to being wounded, and nearly all of chapter 16, which clings closely to Maera's consciousness. This avoidance tells us something about how Hemingway conceived these chapters. Most stories and novels narrated in third person use the limited-omniscient to establish close rapport between reader and protagonist without limiting the narrative voice and perceptions to the protagonist's own. The narrative voice of chapter 7 *sounds* like a novelistic narrator as it follows Nick's perceptions, judgments, and expectations:

> Nick looked straight ahead brilliantly. The pink wall of the house opposite had fallen out from the roof, and an iron bedstead hung

> twisted toward the street. Two Austrian dead lay in the rubble in the shade of the house. Up the street were other dead. Things were getting forward in the town. It was going well. Stretcher bearers would be along any time now. Nick turned his head carefully.

Hemingway would use precisely this point of view in the Nick Adams stories he would write the following year—one reason that most critics assume (with questionable validity) that Nick in chapter 7 is Nick Adams. But the writer clearly did not intend the *in our time* chapters to be read merely as mini-short stories: their voices are too numerous, their experiences too fragmentary, their foci too much directed toward the particular moment to justify a point of view that encourages the ongoing development of *one* character's experience.

The two points of view Hemingway exploited brilliantly are perhaps the least common to fiction writers: first-person peripheral and third-person objective (or dramatic). Both tend to subordinate, even efface, the personality of the narrative voice. Although Scott Fitzgerald's superb handling of the peripheral point of view in *The Great Gatsby* was just over the horizon, Hemingway had no doubt studied Melville's use of it in *Moby Dick.* Having a peripheral character tell the story could be tricky in plausibly providing him or her access to key events; but it enables an author to combine the intimacy of first person—and the verisimilitude of a character's voice—with some of the detachment offered by third person. Directing our attention elsewhere, the peripheral voice seems almost disembodied. In chapter 2 ("the kid" kills five bulls), the voice is distinct enough for us to characterize the narrator as a graduate of the school of hard knocks: "and the bull rammed him wham against the wall . . . and then [he] got up like crazy drunk and tried to slug the men carrying him." Yet the narrator never once refers to himself; hence, the point of view is first-person solely by virtue of his diction and grammar.[12] In chapter 13 (the bad bullfighter), the peripheral narrator is scarcely more distinct even though he does mention himself:

> Afterwards, I saw him at the cafe. He was very short with a brown face and quite drunk and he said after all it has happened before like that. I am not really a good bull fighter.

The "eye" of what had been a third-person narrator now becomes an unidentified "I," enabling a previously impersonal and objective narrative voice to acquire intimacy with the subject. In chapter 8 (the praying soldier), we do not even realize that a different character narrates the terrified soldier's litany until two-thirds of the way through the chapter, when "he" becomes "we"—"We went to work on the trench and in the morning the sun came up and the day was hot and muggy and cheerful and quiet"—forcing us to reconsider not only the narrative's point of view but also the narrator's attitude toward the praying soldier.

Hemingway clearly recognized the ironic potential of this point of view. A peripheral narrator may share some of the protagonist's experiences but not necessarily his mentality. Thus, the narrator in chapter 8 undergoes the same shelling as the praying soldier and is even privy to that soldier's desperate prayers (just how we are not told), but he shows no empathy for that soldier's ordeal. His description of the "cheerful" morning after, in fact, pointedly excludes the praying soldier. And his summary of that soldier's reneging on his promise to Jesus— "The next night back at Mestre he did not tell the girl he went upstairs with at the Villa Rossa about Jesus. And he never told anybody"—is so emphatically dismissive that, as George Cheatham has observed, it poses a credibility problem: how could the narrator state with futuristic certainty that "he never told anybody"?[13] As Cheatham shows, in drafting this chapter Hemingway shifted a first-person, confessional narrative away from the praying soldier, presumably so as not to have that character's fear construed biographically. After rewriting the chapter in third person, he returned to first but used a different narrator. In so doing, he inadvertently created access problems for his new narrator.

Another example of peripheral undercutting occurs in the final chapter. The visitor to the king and queen is unnamed (in the 1925 *In Our Time,* he is ironically entitled "l'Envoi"), deflecting our attention to the royal couple's situation and speech in the garden setting. In the final paragraph, however, the speaker's condescension emerges: "It was all very jolly. We talked for a long time. Like all Greeks he wanted to go to America." The visit could be "very jolly" provided its fairy tale-like setting remains inviolate and the tension of possibly being "shot oneself" ignored. And the final line reduces the monarch to being "like all Greeks" in wanting "to go to America"—a belittling not only of the king but of Greek patriotism generally.

Tellingly, the point of view that appears most often in *in our time,* third-person objective or dramatic, is usually considered the most difficult to work in. Six chapters, 3, 6, 9, 12, 14, and 17, employ narrative voices remote from the characters' thoughts and feelings. As discussed in Chapter Three, these impersonal narrative voices sound journalistic as they narrate with a seemingly dispassionate objectivity action that is often violent: "They shot the six cabinet ministers at half past six in the morning against the wall of a hospital." Virtually transparent, these voices direct our attention to the scene and action. But their journalistic impassivity is a facade: beyond merely "reporting" the facts, they communicate emotion indirectly through artistic devices: images, symbols, dramatic irony, and so on:

> There were pools of water in the courtyard. There were wet dead leaves on the paving of the courtyard. It rained hard. All the shutters of the hospital were nailed shut. (6)

Innumerable critics have observed the symbolic power of "wet dead leaves" and "pools of water" in foreshadowing the blood soon to flow, the bodies to be strewn on the paving. Similarly, critics have noted the irony of this execution occurring against the wall of a hospital and the symbolism of the hospital windows nailed shut like eyes that do not want to see. Finally, the pervasive rain inverts traditional evocations of rebirth and fertility to convey misery, bleakness, and death, exactly as Hemingway will later use the symbol throughout *A Farewell to Arms.* All of these devices convey the scene with far more emotive power than merely "factual" reporting could do. Indeed, the combination of this seemingly objective narrative voice with powerfully emotive literary devices is arguably Hemingway's most effective use of narrative voice in the book.

Experiments with Narrative Voice and Point of View

As the chapters using peripheral and objective points of view suggest, Hemingway devised narrative voices that vary in their concealment and delineation. The peripheral narrator of chapter 13 (the bad bullfighter) is virtually anonymous. The most one can assume is that, in talking to the bullfighter in the café, he has more access to bullfighters than would the typical fan. The narrator may be a fellow torero (as in chapter 15), a newspaper critic, or an aficionado. The peripheral narrators of chapters 8 (the praying soldier), 11 (the revolutionist), and 15 (the drunken bullfighter) have somewhat clearer identities; they are colleagues of the central character: a fellow soldier, an older revolutionist, and a fellow matador, respectively. In the first two examples, they are—as Nick Carraway described himself in *The Great Gatsby*—"both within and without simultaneously," close enough to study the central character firsthand, distant enough to express reservations about his mentality. The fellow matador of chapter 15, conversely, assumes a "we're in this together" attitude with Maera regarding Luis's misbehavior; but the focus in the second half of the chapter is clearly on Maera's responses, an emphasis that the succeeding chapter intensifies by shifting the perspective to his interior consciousness.

Indistinct narrators parallel the ambiguous agents ("They shot. . . . ") discussed in Chapter Three. These effacements focus our attention on the action and catapult us into it:

We were in a Garden at Mons. Young Buckley came in.(4)
We'd jammed an absolutely perfect barricade across the bridge. (5)
I heard the drums coming down the street.(15)
The king was working in the garden. He seemed very glad to see me. (18)

Compacting the time and space necessary to identify the first-person pronouns, these narratives don't begin; they simply start. The narrators sound casual, matter-of-fact, as if we overhear their voices in midstory and already know the situation. Their ambiguity and abruptness affirm the chapters' experimental, open-ended nature as "untold stories."

Vocal ambiguity works quite differently in chapter 2. Here, a narrative voice that first appears to be in anonymous third person (it never refers to itself as "I") reveals itself as belonging to an unidentified character through its shaky grammar and breathless run-on sentences:

> The kid came out and had to kill five bulls because you can't have more than three matadors and the last bull he was so tired he couldn't get the sword in. He couldn't hardly lift his arm. He tried five times and the crowd was quiet because it was a good bull and it look like him or the bull and then he finally made it. He sat down in the sand and puked and they held a cape over him while the crowd hollered and threw things down into the bull ring.

If Hemingway had rewritten this narrative using "I" (for example, "Then I saw. . . . "), the effect would scarcely change, so sharply has he characterized this narrator with colloquial diction ("kid"), defective grammar ("couldn't hardly"), a vivid idiom ("puked"), and a childlike sentence structure (fused by *and*s) that conveys at once excitement and unsophistication. These qualities coalesce into the narrative identity of an active, excitable, shakily educated speaker, perhaps an athlete or even a tough. He is enthusiastic about the bullfight he narrates but not especially discerning, suggesting that he is a novice and a tourist. Along with the vocal crowd he describes so well, the narrator's voice is really at the center of this chapter; "the kid" in the ring, like his order among the matadors, is still in the number three position.

The demonstrative crowd also lends its voice to other bullfight chapters, but in contrast to the narrators, its voice hardly varies, regardless of whether it showers approval or scorn, flowers or wine bottles, on the matador in question:

the crowd hollered and threw things down into the bull ring. (2)
The crowd shouted all the time and threw pieces of bread down into the ring, then cushions and leather wine bottles, keeping up whistling and yelling. (13)
and each swing the crowd roaring . . . (14)
There was a great shouting going on in the grandstand overhead. (16)

Only when that voice is stilled—as when a hushed crowd waits to see whether it is "him or the bull" that prevails (2)—does this public monster show any capacity for variety. Hemingway probably did not intend a social comment here about crowd mentality—his interest was far more aesthetic and thematic in delineating through contrast the isolation of the performer.

One other experiment with voice deserves attention: chapter 16 (Maera's death), as noted above, might be considered omniscient, but its real achievement is to render the protagonist's unvocalized consciousness, a technique Joyce may well have inspired. It is ironic that Maera says nothing during these last minutes of his life, and that, even when he wants to, he "found he could not talk," for in no other chapter is the point of view narrated from so deeply within the character's consciousness. Yet, the narrative *voice* is not Maera's—the reader hears no Spanish phrases or idioms or characteristic usages such as his "Yes. Yes. Yes" of chapter 15. Instead, a detached narrator describes what Maera senses through a sequence of primarily simple sentences linked by repetitive *thens*:

> Maera felt everything getting larger and larger and then smaller and smaller. Then it got larger and larger and larger and then

> smaller and smaller. Then everything commenced to run faster and faster as when they speed up a cinematagraph film. Then he was dead.

The repetitive structure awkwardly calls attention to an external narrator and thus conflicts with the interiority of the point of view. By contrast, the opening sentences not only narrate from within Maera's consciousness but capture more convincingly *his* processing of these sensations:

> He felt warm and sticky from the bleeding. Each time he felt the horn coming. Sometimes the bull only bumped him with his head. Once the horn went all the way through him and he felt it go into the sand. Someone had the bull by the tail. They were swearing at him and flopping the cape in his face. Then the bull was gone.

Hemingway's attempt to narrate interior consciousness with predominantly simple sentences works better when the actions themselves are discrete, for instance, the separate thrusts of the bull's horns and the bull's sudden disappearance (from Maera's perspective). When the sensations run together, despite the cinematic simile, the closest he can come to emulating the process is by repeating, compounding, and elaborating the adjective strings ("larger and larger and then smaller and smaller").

Conclusion

The multiple voices of *in our time* show a young author developing his ability to characterize by imagining just how a character in a given situation would speak (or fail to). Eschewing regionalism, Hemingway's world was large and diverse: it was comfortable with the tough-guy, semi-educated characters of the demimonde—denizens of the gym and the racetrack, the police beat and the bullring—but could reach to the British educated upper classes. His voices speak colloquial American English mingled with Briticisms and European phrases, reflecting the cosmopolitan settings of his narratives: British, French, and Italian combat zones, the Spanish bullring, American jails, Greek palace gardens, the roads of Eastern Thrace.

Capturing with authenticity this geographical and social diversity of voices required more than miming idiom and phrasing. Hemingway also had to find the sentence rhythms to recreate this speech, convey the character's psychological state, and release the particular dynamism of that scene. If capturing these voices began with having a good ear—and fortunately Hemingway had an excellent one—it also required mastering stylistic devices—phrasing and diction, understatement and hyperbole, silence and repetition, and a gamut of sentence rhythms—to work those voices into a narrative.

Through these voices Hemingway addressed age-old narrational issues that were as relevant to his "untold stories" as to traditional narrative: Who should narrate? From what angle and proximity to the action? If he is a character himself, how close is he to the other characters (a colleague? a distant observer?), and what thematic possibilities does this relationship offer? To what degree should he be present or concealed? Should his voice call attention to himself, as the voice does in chapter 2 ("the kid" kills five bulls), or should it disappear in quasi-objective narrations? Can interior consciousness be rendered by an exterior narrator? Through his drafts and revisions, Hemingway discovered that his narrative answers to these questions opened and closed thematic as well as characterizing possibilities. Making the praying soldier the first-person narrator of chapter 8, as the first drafts had him, builds the reader's identification with the soldier's experience but inhibits critical distance between narrative and speaker and might be taken as autobiography. Placing the narrative in third person solves the objectivity problem but loses the immediacy of a first-person narrator. Creating a peripheral narrator—a fellow soldier—captures both intimacy and detachment but at the cost of some verisimilitude.

What the range and profusion of these voices and their multiple narrative angles finally demonstrate is a diligent craftsman exploring possibilities of voice and narrative rather than settling into a pattern. Because he was not constructing these narratives as conventional stories, he largely avoided the novelistic or short story point of view that follows a single protagonist, third-person limited-omniscient. For the same reason, he could chop off conventional openings and mask speakers, characters, and agents to drop us abruptly into the action and to create a tense fusion of ambiguity, violence, and dispassionately factual statements: "They whack whacked the white horse on the legs and he knee-ed himself up (12)."

In trying out so many voices, so many narrative angles, Hemingway may have already recognized his natural talent for characterizing through voice. He later boasted that if he had learned abstract relationships of words from Stein, he had taught her dialogue (*Selected Letters* 649). But the experiments in *in our time* first had to teach him the inextricable links between voice, narrative, and point of view—and, as the next chapter will explore, between voice, action and sentence rhythms.

5
Sentence Rhythms

From its very first sentence, *in our time* announces a radically new style. "Everybody was drunk" is a declarative sentence reduced to skeletal simplicity, but also a blunt, unmodified statement. Readers of 1924 were immediately put on notice that they were not reading Henry James, or Theodore Dreiser, or any other familiar stylist of the day. Readers today, encountering *In Our Time* for the first time, are nearly as startled by the radical simplicity of its prose. In the interval, generations of critics have assiduously demonstrated how deceptive this simplicity is: how it conceals linkages, submerges themes, denies explanations—in short, how it is a complex, modernist construction akin to the planar reduction of naturalistic form in a Cézanne, say, or to the sparse chords and minimalist motivic progressions of Webern.

Yet the image of Hemingway's style as a "Dick and Jane" sequence of simple sentences has stuck—a stereotype open to endless parody (for instance, E. B. White's unsubtle rendering in the *New Yorker*), scorn, admiration, and most of all, misunderstanding. At the center of this stylistic stereotype is the "Hemingway sentence," and critics typically credit the chapters of *in our time* with its formulation.[1]

There is considerable truth in the critical assumption that these chapters represent the distillation of a new style of simplified sentence structure and diction. The opening chapter, for example, consists of eleven sentences, of which five are obviously simple and two more essentially so. (For a tabulation of sentence structures for each chapter, see the appendix.) In total, *in our time* contains 280 sentences, of which 133—nearly 50 percent—are simple. Of the thirty-three more that are linguistically simple but may contain clauses, many have only a short subordinate clause, infinitive, or participle imbedded in an essentially simple structure, as in:

> The first German I saw climbed up over the garden wall (chapter 4).

> It was funny going along that road. (chapter 1)[2]

Yet if we look closely at the sentences of chapter 1, we note that several are compound, either completely:

> We were fifty kilometers from the front but the adjutant worried about the fire in my kitchen.

or in their predicates:

> The lieutenant kept riding his horse out into the field and saying to him . . .

or both:

> We went along the road all night in the dark and the adjutant kept riding up alongside my kitchen and saying . . .

Moreover, two technically simple sentences contain participles—present progressives that make the action ongoing, less clearly bounded in time: "The whole battery was drunk going along the road in the dark. . . . It was funny going along that road." Other sentences also use participles where they might have conveyed the narrative present in simple past tense, for example: "The lieutenant rode his horse out into the fields continuously." Finally, only one sentence is structurally complex, though its brevity scarcely makes it seem so: "That was when I was a kitchen corporal."

All of these sentence structures affect the reader's sense of how an action or a sequence unfolds in space and time and how it is logically related to, or separated from, the actions surrounding it. For example, Hemingway might have combined the opening sentences:

> The whole battery was drunk going along the road to the Champagne in the dark.

Instead, he constructs an intentionally repetitive and overlapping pattern:

> Everybody was **drunk.**
> The whole battery was **drunk going** along the road in the dark.
> We were **going** to the Champagne. (emphasis mine)

This plodding, incremental progression, in which a bit of new information intermingles with much repetition, emulates a slowly evolving movement—a march, with its repetitive "left-right-left" and its barely perceivable progress, kilometer by dusty kilometer. The participles—"going," "riding," "saying"—intensify this march rhythm by spanning past and present. The style thus recreates the march rather than summarizing it. Kinesthetic realism, however, becomes surreal as repetitive gestures—the lieutenant drunkenly talking to his horse, the adjutant warning of nonexistent dangers—acquire a ludicrous unreality appropriate to a drunken night march. The repetitive participles

> The lieutenant kept riding . . . and saying. . . .
> the adjutant kept riding . . . and saying . . .

are so highly stylized as to evoke the nightmarish effect of going through the same absurd experiences repeatedly. One other stylistic element is noteworthy: "We were fifty kilometers from the front but the adjutant worried about the fire in my kitchen." A compound structure typically excludes the explanatory causality of complex sentences. It tells the sequential order of events but not how to construe them. Had Hemingway constructed this as a complex sentence—"Although we were fifty kilometers from the front, the adjutant worried about the fire in my kitchen"—"although" would underscore the absurdity of the adjutant's fear. The compound structure only implies it and thus contributes to an evolving technique of understatement.

In sum, the seemingly naive simplicity of chapter 1 proves to be carefully crafted and highly stylized—simplified rather than simple—with verbs conveying particular sequences of events (incremental, repetitious, ongoing) in several structures. A glance at the other chapters shows comparable degrees of stylization but with sharply contrasting sentence structures and sequences. In chapter 2, for example, only one sentence is simple, and compound or compound-complex run-ons predominate. Chapter 3 uses three sentence fragments. Chapter 4 breaks up a string of very simple sentences with a triple compound predicate: "He had so much equipment on and looked awfully surprised and fell down into the garden." Chapter 14 mixes complex structures with participial fragments and with compounds:

> When he started to kill it was all in the same rush. The bull looking at him straight in front, hating. He drew the sword from the folds of the muleta and sighted with the same movement and called to the bull, Toro! Toro! and the bull charged and Villalta charged and just for a moment they became one.

In their relentless variety, the sentences refute the conventional view of the chapters as representing a finely honed synthetic style—*the* Hemingway style. Rather, they form a series of stylistic experiments to capture an array of effects—temporal, kinesthetic, thematic, and psychological—that Hemingway integrates with narrative techniques, voice, and thematic development in each chapter.[3]

Sentence Rhythms and Action

In *Death in the Afternoon,* Hemingway describes most incisively his early technique:

> I was trying to write then and I found the greatest difficulty . . . was to put down what really happened in action; what the actual things were which produced the emotion that you experienced. . . . the real thing, *the sequence of motion and fact which made the emotion.* (2, emphasis mine)

Two themes stand out here. First, emotion is a consequence, not a cause of these experiences. It is achieved indirectly, implied rather than stated, by reproducing the elements that "produced the emotion."[4] But what does he mean by "the sequence of motion and fact"? Clearly, it means more than finding the precise word to name the "fact" (itself predicated on a deep understanding of the subject) and more than describing events in motion. The key word is "sequence": the pattern or rhythm through which motion and fact combine to *reveal* a particular action and the particular voice describing or experiencing it. Sentence structure is crucial to these sequences of action, and in no other aspect of his craft does Hemingway experiment so relentlessly and so productively. Since most of *in our time*—fully fifteen of the eighteen chapters—reflects Hemingway's aim "to put down what really happened in action," and since action is central to his subsequent writing, understanding how sentences create the rhythmic sequences of action is vital to understanding Hemingway's emerging style.

Fragments

Arguably, the single most experimental structure in *in our time* is not even a sentence: "No end and no beginning" (3). Why didn't Hemingway write: "There was no end and no beginning"? His subsequent editors at Scribner's must have asked themselves this question because someone converted the fragment in the first Scribner's edition (1930). Indeed, nothing so testifies to the subversive power of these fragments—their jarring disruption of conventional prose—as the desire of subsequent editors (in some cases, with Hemingway's concurrence) to "correct" them into complete sentences in later editions. All the fragments and abbreviated phrases below suffered this fate:

No end and no beginning. (3)	There was no end and no beginning. (1930 *IOT*.)
Not patriots. (7)	We're not patriots. (1925 *IOT*)
bumped them (9)	bumped them off (1925 *IOT*)
and each swing the crowd roaring (14)	and at each swing the crowd roaring (1925 *IOT*)
The street full of them. (15)	The street was full of them. (*First 49 Stories*)[5]

No single strategy governs these fragments; the sequences they help form are objective and descriptive in some chapters, psychological and subjective in others. Chapter 3, for example, records an anonymous narrator's fragmented observations of the "never-ending" march of Greek families from Eastern Thrace. Following three simple sentences imaging the march, the prose breaks up into fragments: "No end and no beginning. Just carts loaded with everything they owned." One can well imagine Hemingway, who saw the retreat firsthand as a journalist, hurriedly jotting down his impressions, and, in fact, one surviving draft for chapter 3 is virtually all in fragmented impressions (discussed in Chapter One). But this aura of a journalist's hurried impressions is illusory, for Hemingway had already written his journalistic account of the retreat ("A Silent, Ghastly Procession") in complete sentences long before he started paring it down as chapter 3. Thus, he converted complete sentences back to their fragmented origins to capture the *effect* of on-the-spot journalism—"cablese" he called it—and the laconic, deadpan voice of a detached narrator. The fragments also efface weak "is" verbs: if the narrative successfully captures what "is," then "is" becomes superfluous.

Beyond capturing a journalistic aura, fragments serve thematic purposes. The fragment "No end and no beginning" grammatically replicates its meaning since it lacks both beginning and end. More important, it acts as a structural microcosm for the chapter that begins *in medias res* and presents a seemingly endless march in which the tired civilians (like the observer-narrator) can *see* no beginning and no end. By contrast, a subjective voice determines the fragment in chapter 15, a bullfighter-narrator's contemptuous description of drunken *riau-riau* dancers who have attracted his irresponsible colleague: "and then they came around the corner, all dancing. The street full of them." "Full of them," with its echo of "full of it," connotes the narrator's disgust, but so too does the paltry fragment he devotes to a presence he will not dignify with a complete sentence.

That Hemingway himself cautiously "corrected" some of these fragments for the 1925 Boni & Liveright edition of *In Our Time* says something about his rapidly changing sense of himself as a writer.[6] The avant-garde experimenter was yielding to the persona of popular writer. His work, he later predicted to Horace Liveright, "will be praised by highbrows and can be read by lowbrows. There is no writing in it [the 1925 *In Our Time*] that anybody with a high-school education cannot read."[7]

Simple Sequences

As noted above, Hemingway is best known for his simple, declarative sentences. But like the fragment, this structure varies in its uses even though the way it functions in time and space does not. Simple sentences typically retard a sequence. By focusing exclusively on a single event or condition, a simple sentence intensifies it and structurally implies that event is no less important than the one preceding or following it: "Both legs stuck out awkwardly. He had been hit in the spine. His face was sweaty and dirty. The sun shone on his face. The day was very hot" (7). Equally important, each simple statement requires the grammatical apparatus of any complete sentence: subject and predicate. Hence, no matter how simple the action or how logically related it might be to preceding and following actions, the simple statement creates the rhythmic effect of starting with a perceptible heave and closing down with a thud. This finite, self-contained quality puts distinct space and time between the simple sentence and the ones preceding and following it:

> Then three more came over further down the wall. We shot them. They all came over just like that. (4)

Spatial gaps, temporal pauses, and stops and starts fashion a rhythm that is inevitably halting, choppy, disjointed—precisely why students are taught to combine and subordinate their sentences in expository writing. But Hemingway found that this disjointedness fit sequences in which each event seems disconnected from the preceding one or when each stands out luminously: "Blood pumped regularly from between the horse's front legs. He was nervously wobbly. The bull could not make up his mind to charge" (12).

The three examples quoted above show how simple sequences produce disjointedness in quite different situations. In the first, Nick has just been wounded, dragged out of the line of fire, and now sits against the wall of a church. We share his first disjointed perceptions and sensations as the consciousness of being wounded and separated from combat begins to sink in. Hemingway could have combined the first two simple sentences variously:

> He was wounded in the spine, and his legs stuck out awkwardly.

or:

> Wounded in the spine, he sat with his legs sticking out awkwardly.

Both revisions relate the two facts: the first sequentially, the second with implied causality. But these linkages are not the way Nick takes in his world. We see—as he sees—his legs sticking out as a separate, powerful fact. The next sentence tells us why, but more important, it tells *Nick* why; the reason occurs after the perception. It takes a moment to settle in: he has been badly wounded, hit in the spine. Wrongly positioned, his legs look different to him now, and the world looks different—it has been transformed by his wounding. Each fact, sensation, perception—his face being sweaty, the sun shining on it, the day being hot—is new, individual, and no less important than any other. Thus, facts that could easily form one compound-complex sentence—"The day was very hot, and his face felt sweaty and dirty as the sun shone on it"—are separated to capture the rhythm of how Nick's mind processes these conditions.

The second example also captures the consciousness of a character, here, a British officer who encounters attacking German soldiers where his unit had not expected them—climbing over a garden wall—and where the Germans obviously had not expected to encounter the British. The disjointedness of the simple sentences recreates events that occur with a dreamlike slowness and magnification: "Then three more came over further down the wall. We shot them." The soldier's halting speech sounds dazed.

The final action (the gored horse and the bull) is equally disjointed but exterior to a character's consciousness. No other chapter in the book is so chillingly detached in its narration. The actions here are almost an interlude between what has preceded them—the bull tearing open the horse's entrails—and what will likely follow—the bull possibly charging again, the horse collapsing, dead. The very tension of this narrative derives from these uncertain but impending actions. In the meantime, the rhythm of action—and thus its sentence structure—is pointillistic, presenting the last jerky motions of the unsteady horse, the bull disengaged, uncertain whether to charge again. Just as the chapter has begun in the middle, so it ends in disjointed events lacking culmination.

Obviously, not all of the 133 simple sentences in *in our time* construct rhythms of action and consciousness identically. Context matters. But each, through its self-contained, edged discreteness, taps out staccato, stop-and-start rhythms and inserts pauses, brief silences, and negative spaces between positivistic assertions. This isolation eerily illuminates the factuality of that sentence, imbues the statement with what Harry Levin called a "special vividness" when for a "brief moment . . . it commands the reader's undivided attention" ("Observations" 80).

Compound Rhythms

When Hemingway joins related actions into one sentence, he especially favors compound structures, either as full compounds:

> They whack whacked the white horse on the legs and he knee-ed himself up. (12)

or as compound predicates:

> The picador twisted the stirrups straight and pulled and hauled up into the saddle.

This predilection is not accidental: as will be shown below, Hemingway composed naturally in compounds, then often revised them into simple or complex sentences to vary the sentence rhythms. Forty-nine sentences in *in our time* (out of 280) are fully compound (or 17.5 percent); seventeen, or 6.1 percent, have only compound predicates; and seven more are fusions of compound and complex structures (2.5 percent). In all, compounds account for all or part of 73 sentences—a quarter of the total. With their unobtrusive "ands" and equally weighted components, compound structures build a rolling, sometimes hypnotically regular prose rhythm. Yet, as noted above, these structures limit the logical relationship of actions to temporal sequences. By not subordinating one action to the other, the compound structure not only balances their importance but precludes causality—the explanatory function of subordinating conjunctions:

> They tried to hold him up against the wall but he sat down in a puddle of water. (6)

Subordinating the first action to the second would have diminished the former's importance and, in this case, made its irony more obvious:

> Although they tried to hold him up against the wall, he sat down in a puddle of water.

In this complex structure, his sitting down assumes more importance and thus makes the soldiers' attempt to force the execution into a traditional mold more ludicrous. The compound structure, in equalizing the two actions, is more closemouthed and denies the reader a structural frame for interpreting the events.

Hemingway found the sequential logic of compounds especially apt for describing a sequence of actions that occur in such quick succession that the narrator cannot—or will not—sort them into the hierarchies of complex sentences. To construct these hierarchies would rob the sequence of its speed. In some of these sequences, particularly in chapter 2, the narrator's palpable excitement is inseparable from the rapid action, and the conjunctive *ands* capture both. In the example that follows, a boldfaced and underlined **and** identifies a full compound (subject and predicate), while boldface alone marks a compound predicate:

> The second matador slipped **and** the bull caught him through the belly **and** he hung on to the horn with one hand **and** held the other tight against the place, **and** the bull rammed him wham against the wall **and** the horn came out, **and** he lay in the sand, **and** then got up like crazy drunk **and** tried to slug the men carrying him away **and** yelled for his sword **but** he fainted. (2)

Seven complete sentences and four additional predicates—seventy-four words—are here fused into one remarkable run-on that barrels forward, scarcely impeded by commas, and permits neither speaker nor reader time to pause until the entire sequence is finished.[8] The same bullfight locale also inspires this compound run-on:

> The crowd came over the barrera and around the torero **and** two men grabbed him **and** held him **and** some one cut off his pigtail **and** was waving it **and** a kid grabbed it **and** ran away with it. (13)

Another breathless rush of actions, but this one shows careful structuring as compounds and compound predicates alternate in balanced symmetry.

Complex Structures

If simple sentences slow narratives by isolating actions, and compounds accelerate them by joining and equalizing actions, complex structures arrange action into hierarchies of importance and emphasis. Although decoding these structures requires more cognitive time than compounds demand (especially if the architect is a James or Faulkner), complex sentences are the most efficient structure for conveying large amounts of information and for disclosing their internal relationships. This clarifying function, especially as it explains causality and motivation, runs counter to Hemingway's aesthetic of understatement and showing rather than telling. Not surprisingly, then, complex structures account for the fewest sentences of the three major types: eighteen, or 6.4 percent; seven complex-compound sentences raise the total to twenty-five, or 9 percent. Yet Hemingway did not shy from subordinate clauses when he needed to summarize facts, to provide historical background, or to delineate how several facets of a complex action cohere. Numerous sentences in *in our time* that are not technically complex contain dependent clauses, participles, or infinitive phrases. Although classified as subcategories of simple or compound (see appendix for rationale), these forty-four sentences amount to almost 16 percent, bringing the total of sentences using subordinate clauses to more than sixty-nine, or about 25 percent.

This high percentage is skewed, however, by the atypical chapter 10, a narrative that summarizes a blighted love affair between a recovering soldier and his nurse. The chapter relies heavily on dependent clauses and complex structures to combine facts efficiently: of its forty sentences, eight fall into one of the complex categories, while another fifteen contain dependent clauses, infinitives, or participles. To break up these complexes into simple statements would create a maddeningly slow pace:

> After he got on crutches he used to take the temperatures so Ag would not have to get up from the bed.
>
> > [Eventually,] he got on crutches. [Then] he used to take the temperatures. Ag would [then] not have to get up from the bed.
>
> They felt as though they were married, but they wanted everyone to know about it, and to make it so they could not lose it.
>
> > They felt as though they were married. But they wanted everyone to know about it. They wanted to make it so they could not lose it.
> >
> > [Even this revision cannot avoid adverbial clauses in sentences 1 and 3.]

As noted, subordinate clauses defer to main clauses in importance, but Hemingway sometimes reverses the hierarchy for thematic effect, as in chapter 17:

> When they all stepped back on the scaffolding back of the drop, which was very heavy, built of oak and steel and swung on ball bearings, Sam Cardinella was left sitting there strapped tight, the younger of the two priests kneeling beside the chair.

At the penultimate moment of Sam's execution, the sentence suddenly becomes very interested in the construction of the scaffold and drop, distracting us from Sam and subtly positioning us with his safe entourage. No sooner does the sentence finally light on Sam than it shifts to the kneeling priest. This positioning, in turn, sets up the concluding satiric sentence about the priest "skipping" back to the safety of the scaffold.

Matching Sentence Rhythm to Action

Nothing better demonstrates Hemingway's concern for "the sequence of motion and fact" than the care he took in finding the right sentence rhythms to express a particular action or state of mind. Categorically, the subjects of *in our time* gravitate to particular structures. The war chapters—1, 4, 5, 7, and 8—rely heavily on simple sentences—57 percent of their sixty-one sentences.[9] By contrast, simple sentences make up only 33 percent of the bullfight chapters (2 and 12–16). Here, the compound sentence's fluid, sequential structure is especially effective in recreating the rush of actions. Narrative perspective bears on this difference. The war chapters are essentially experiential, and the protagonist's consciousness is often the true subject. The bullfights are mostly described, observed from the stands, where the narrator attempts to convey the action in the ring and the crowd's response. When the perspective shifts to the bullfighter's consciousness—Maera's in chapter 16—the percentage of simple sentences rises accordingly.

Searching for the right rhythms, Hemingway mixed his sentences not only to realize different types of action, but to manipulate our sense of how they unfold in time and space. For example, as he acquired an insider's appreciation of the corrida, as expressed in chapter 14 (Villalta), the sequential run-ons of chapters 2 ("the kid" kills five bulls) and 13 (the bad bullfighter) were insufficient to convey the simultaneous and overlapping actions of bull, torero, and audience. Just so, the excited, impressionistic narrator must yield to a discerning aficionado, the distant, naive view to the close-up and knowledgeable. A tour de force, chapter 14 employs a dazzling mixture of complex and compound sentences and participial fragments. Notable by their absence are simple sentences, making this chapter an excellent rebuttal to the stereotype that Hemingway wrote in nothing else. The entire second paragraph will be analyzed in Chapter Six, so the analysis here will be limited mostly to the first paragraph. The opening sentence, a fifty-two-word whopper, is a long complex-compound-participial structure:

> If it happened right down close in front of you, you could see Villalta snarl at the bull and curse him, and when the bull charged he

> swung back firmly like an oak when the wind hits it, his legs tight together, the muleta trailing and the sword following the curve behind.

For this anonymous narrator, being "close in front" becomes a spatial metaphor for having a close-up understanding of what is happening. Note the conditional "If"; only if "you" have this close-up discernment can you see as the narrator himself sees: "you could see Villalta snarl at the bull and curse him." Following the opening dependent clause, the sentence shifts to compound actions—"snarl" and "curse"—then shifts again to the compound-complex: "and when the bull charged." As noted above, dependent clauses usually diminish their subject matter, and in this one the bull practically disappears. The main clause overwhelms it, first by depicting Villalta's motion ("swung back firmly"), then elaborating it into a simile ("like an oak")—the only simile in the book—and finally by modifying it with three nearly parallel constructions:

> his legs tight together,
> the muleta trailing
> and the sword following the curve behind.

As parallelism aligns the components, the participles ("trailing," "following") make their actions simultaneous and ongoing. In sum, the structure is complex (dependent clause, main clause with compound predicates) and compound-complex (dependent clause, main clause, simile with dependent clause, adjectival phrase, and parallel participial phrases). Not so bad for a "dumb ox."[10]

The second sentence repeats several components and actions of the first: "Then he cursed the bull, flopped the muleta at him, and swung back from the charge, his feet firm, the muleta curving and each swing the crowd roaring." This time, a triple compound predicate precedes exactly the same modifying sequence—an adjective phrase and two participles—that use almost the same language as sentence 1:

sentence 1	*sentence 2*
swung back firmly	swung back
his legs tight together	his feet firm
the muleta trailing	the muleta curving
the sword following the curve	the crowd roaring

Note that the last participial—"and each swing the crowd roaring"—daringly elides the preposition "at." (The more cautious 1925 *In Our Time* would restore it.) In an especially brilliant stroke, Hemingway transfers the crowd "roaring" (paragraph 1) to the bull "roaring blood" (paragraph 2), thus implying without stating the crowd's roaring delight at the kill.

The participles of paragraph 1—"the muleta trailing," "the sword following," "the muleta curving," "the crowd roaring"—are crucial in their capacity to continue an action as Hemingway superimposes another onto it. By paragraph 2, their importance supercedes grammatical correctness: "The bull looking at him straight in front, hating." Critics sometimes describe these participials as freezing the moment, giving Villalta's triumph the timelessness that Keats's Grecian urn imparts to its lovers. Michael Reynolds, for example, eloquently writes:

> he got it down on paper the hard line of it forever so that years later when Villalta was as dead as that afternoon bull, it was still there fresh as always, happening now. Sentence fragments and present participles keep it alive . . . not letting the blood stop or the bull die. No matter the years in between, the reader would have it happening in his own present time. (*The Paris Years* 139)

All of these actions are happening and continue to happen as the chapter ends. Hemingway's dazzling diversity in mixing, merging, and shifting his sentence structures in this chapter thus provides the perfect stylistic analog to Villalta's consummate skill in the bullring. Each artist demonstrates his mastery in a public display of adroit moves grounded by cool control over the pace and sequence of the action.

Beginnings and Endings

As these "unwritten stories" emphasize momentary experience, they posed problems of how to construct sentences that begin and end them. The most radical beginnings are those that don't seem to begin at all: the chapters simply start matter-of-factly in medias res:

> They whack whacked the white horse on the legs and he knee-ed himself up. (12)
> The king was working in the garden. (18)

> The crowd shouted all the time and threw pieces of bread down into the ring. . . . (13)
> Everybody was drunk. (1)
> Maera lay still, his head on his arms, his face in the sand. (16)

Conversely, several quasi-journalistic openings begin with "establishing" sentences that locate the place and time of an action in a phrase-laden sentence.

> At two o'clock in the morning two Hungarians got into a cigar store at Fifteenth Street and Grand Avenue. (9)
> In 1919 he was travelling on the railroads in Italy carrying a square of oilcloth from the headquarters of the party. . . . (11)
> They hanged Sam Cardinella at six o'clock in the morning in the corridor of the county jail. (17)

When these factual details combine with ambiguous agents (such as the unidentified "They"), the result is a particularly unsettling tension, ominous because the agents of violence are masked, and as unstable as a Cézanne that is at once figurative and abstract in its intentionally unfinished images.

A few chapters substitute images for conventional referents: "I heard the drums coming down the street and then the fifes and the pipes and then they came around the corner, all dancing" (15). We don't know where we are, who "I" or "they" are, but we do hear the music and see the dancing.[11]

The openers Hemingway least resorted to were those that sounded most like fictional first lines, either by conveying a definite beginning to a story:

> One hot evening in Milan they carried him up onto the roof and he could look out over the top of the town. (10)

or by following the sequential experiences of one protagonist:

> Nick sat against the wall of the church where they had dragged him to be clear of machine gun fire in the street. (7)

Ending sentences raise the analogous question of closure: Should there be one? How definite? What type? Logically, if a chapter begins in the middle, it should end there, without a wrap-up sentence; indeed, many Hemingway critics assume this technique prevails in *in our time.*[12] But Hemingway usually defied this logic, and only one chapter simply stops: "The bull could not make up its mind to charge" (12). Another chapter abruptly stops a sequence of *thens*, but with an obviously thematic closure: "Then he was dead" (16). A few sentences at or near a chapter's end provide maximal, even implausible, storytelling closure by projecting into the future:

> And he never told anybody. (8)
> The Major did not marry her in the spring, or any other time. (10)

And some closures reverse this time leap by revealing that the entire narrative has been retrospective:

> That was when I was a kitchen corporal. (1)
> They all came over just like that. (4)
> We were frightfully put out when we heard the flank had gone, and we had to fall back. (5)[13]

Several closing lines are short, usually simple sentences that evoke "a dying fall" to deflate the mood or intensity, often ironically:

> Rinaldi was a disappointing audience. (7)
> Wops, said Boyle, I can tell wops a mile off. (9)
> The last I heard of him the Swiss had him in jail near Sion. (11)
> I'm not really a good bull fighter. (13)
> Like all Greeks he wanted to go to America. (18)

These deflating closers most closely resemble the pure in medias res ending of chapter 12.

The most self-consciously "artistic" closer brings the narrative imagistically full circle: "Minarets stuck up in the rain out of Adrianople across the mud flats. . . . It rained all through the evacuation" (3). In sum, no single pattern of beginnings and endings prevails in these chapters. As with the other literary elements, Hemingway tries out several types to explore the narrative and emotive effects of each.

Highlighting Themes and Climaxes

The radical form of these chapters raises another question: Can such brief narratives develop, reach a climax, and suggest themes as conventional narratives do? Logically, these attributes of a linear plot might seem irrelevant to such truncated forms. Yet Hemingway's retention of endings shows that strict logic does not govern his decisions. Even narratives confined to a few paragraphs can still develop thematically. Readers, at least, are still prone to *discern* thematic development in a fragmented narrative. That Hemingway consciously retains these narrative elements appears in the care he took in signaling themes and climaxes through sentence structure. In all, fourteen of the eighteen chapters signal either a narrative climax or thematic center, or both, through a sharp contrast of sentence structure, sentence length, or narrative voice. For example, in chapter 2, the sentence that most dramatizes "the kid"'s exhaustion—"He couldn't hardly lift his arm"—is a simple sentence sandwiched between long compounds of thirty-two and twenty-nine words each. This short sentence largely repeats "he couldn't get the sword in," but its contrasting brevity and simplicity makes this image of exhaustion stand out and marks the sentence as the dramatic center of the narrative. Chapter 14 (Villalta's bullfight) similarly makes the climactic sentence overlap the crucial moment of the preceding sentence while sharply contrasting it in length and structure:

> He drew out the sword from the folds of his muleta and sighted with the same movement and called to the bull, Toro! Toro! and the bull charged and Villalta charged and just for a moment they became one. Villalta became one with the bull and then it was over.

Conversely, in chapter 4, a narrative of mostly simple sentences, the fifth sentence—"He had so much equipment on and looked awfully surprised and fell down into the garden"—stands out as the one comparatively long compound. It is also the chapter's thematic center and climax as it combines the overburdened German's surprise at encountering the enemy, the unlikely garden setting for his death, and the uncanny ease of "potting" him. Similarly, the succeeding Mons chapter (5) makes the only complex sentence in the narrative, the concluding one, the ironic turning point, announcing how uncontrollable factors in the larger battle ("the flank had gone") end this perfect little encounter. But in a chapter where complex and compound sentences predominate (10), the one fragment—"Only to get a job and be married"—epitomizes how radically (and unfairly) "he" has constricted his future life in order to meet Ag's conditions for marriage.

In some chapters a sequence of sentences stands out grammatically as the climax or thematic center. In the evacuation of Adrianople (3), the two shortest sentences, both fragments, embody the chapter's theme: "No end and no beginning. . . . Scared sick looking at it" (sentences 4 and 12). The latter sentence immediately follows the chapter's longest and most involved: "There was a woman having a kid with a young girl holding a blanket over her head and crying" (sentence 11). Together, sentences 11 and 12 form a climax within the seemingly endless suffering of this evacuation: a mother gives birth with scarcely any assistance and under conditions of extreme discomfort; her daughter (or perhaps the narrator?) is terrified by what she witnesses. The imagistic closure—"It rained all through the evacuation"—then falls away from this intense moment.

The introduction of a new narrative voice in a contrasting style can also signal a climactic or thematic turning point. The praying soldier under shellfire, for example, dominates the first half of chapter 8 with his desperate litany—a monologue comprised of repetitive fragments and complex-compound structures. The narrative voice and style shift, however, with the sentence "The shelling moved further up the line." Lacking any causal connection to the prayers, the simple statement is factual and uninflected, suggesting both the narrator's emotive distance from the frantic soldier and the fact's unrelatedness to his prayers.

Perhaps the subtlest signal of thematic climax is not just contrast, but the complete absence of a statement where it might be expected—an early example of Hemingway's technique of omission. In chapter 11, the revolutionist ignores his older comrade's gloomy assessment of political conditions in Italy and insists that the movement "will go better. . . . You have everything here. It is the one country that everyone is sure of. It will be the starting point of everything." The narrative then begins a new paragraph and subject, pointedly omitting the narrator's response. The more cautious 1925 *In Our Time* backs away from this bold stroke by adding: "I did not say anything," leaving no doubt as to the narrator's disbelief.

Repetition

If structural contrast highlights themes and climaxes through difference, repetition emphasizes through sameness. But not just theme—repetition can also characterize, establish a scene, and create aural rhythms for their own sake. Hemingway acknowledged learning this technique from Stein, and he uses it extensively in *in our time.* Virtually every chapter employs some form of repetition, and their varieties show how assiduously he explored its possibilities.

Imagistic repetition is perhaps the most obvious, for it appears within chapters and links chapters of otherwise different subjects and themes. Among the key images that recur in the book are walls and gardens, both providing the ironical context for grim actions: a bullfighter is rammed against a wall (2); German soldiers are shot climbing over a garden wall (4); Greek ministers are shot against a hospital wall (6); and a Greek king *might* be shot if he ventures outside the garden wall (18). Rain also cuts across chapters 3 and 6 to provide a setting of dreariness and misery, intensifying the suffering of the refugees, symbolizing the death of the cabinet ministers. Here, Hemingway exploits near repetition by using numerous related images: mud, water buffalo, being "soaked through," and the Maritza River running yellow in chapter 3; pools of water and wet dead leaves in chapter 6.

Imagistic actions are also repeated and varied: the gored horse in chapter 12 is "whacked"—three times—and canters "jerkily" with "wobbly" legs. Nick's disabling wound (7) appears in variants of physical stiffness and limited movement: legs sticking out "awkwardly," head turning "carefully," while wounded Rinaldi breathes "with difficulty." The bullfight crowd expresses itself—whether in approval or anger—by shouting, whistling, yelling, and throwing things into the arena (2, 13). "Dancing" and related acts—crouching, jumping—guide chapter 15, while variants of shooting (potting, being shot, shooting others, machine-gun fire) recur in chapters 4, 5, 6, 7, and 18. Finally, perceptual repetition of everything becoming "larger and larger and larger and then smaller and smaller" expresses the distortions of Maera's fading consciousness in chapter 16.

One of the most interesting imagistic patterns occurs in the Villalta chapter (14), which repeats curves and angles that Hemingway actually drew at the bottom of one draft (see Chapter Six). Thus, the bull's straight-line charge complements Villalta's swinging back "firmly" and contrasts the curving sweep of the muleta (each mentioned twice). At the crucial moment when the two become one, a draft and drawing describe Villalta "folded over" the bull. But in the following moment of separation, repeated verticals prevail: Villalta is "standing straight" while the red hilt of the sword is "sticking out" and the bull is "caving."

As repetitions can generate a rhythm, so they can halt it: "the bull charged and Villalta charged and just for a moment they became one. Villalta became one with the bull and then it was over (14)." Like a freeze-frame in film, the repeated "became one" momentarily stops the action at the moment of deadly fusion between the two killers, man and bull. This repetition bridges the two sentences' structural contrast (noted above) while it affirms this symbolically sexual union.

Recurring words become thematic shorthand in several chapters. They condense, for example, the heavily narrated story in chapter 10. Thus, "bed," "married," "agreed," "understood," "come," "rainy," "lonely," "boy and girl [affair]," "expected unexpectedly," "absolutely," and "not/any/never" (in the last paragraph) codify the thematic development. Some of these repetitions in Ag's voice develop her flighty character, a technique Hemingway uses often: Boyle, the Irish cop, insists that his killing "wops" will not arouse any "trouble" (9). The British officer's hyberbole in chapter 5—especially "absolutely"—conveys his almost manic enthusiasm. And "tell" becomes a key repetition in chapter 8, as the terrified solider first promises to "tell everyone in the world" about Jesus, then (when he's safe) neglects to "tell" the prostitute the next night, and finally "never told anybody."

A particularly effective repetition explains the prisoners' behavior in chapter 17:

> They *hanged* Sam Cardinella at six 'o'clock in the morning in the corridor of the county jail. The corridor was high and narrow with tiers of cells on either side. All the cells were occupied. The men had been brought in for the *hanging.* Five men sentenced *to be hanged* were in the five top cells. Three of the men *to be hanged* were negroes. They were very frightened. One of the white men sat on his cot with his head in his hands. The other lay flat on his cot with a blanket wrapped around his head. (emphasis mine)

Just as the jailers have sadistically brought in the condemned men to watch the hanging, the repetitions of "hanged" verbally represent the scene's impact on their fearful minds.

One especially curious repetition Hemingway experiments with is numerical. One might dismiss as coincidence chapter 6 beginning "They shot the six cabinet ministers at half-past six in the morning."[14] But three other instances suggest the repetitions were intentional:

he had to kill five bulls. . . . He tried five times [to get the sword in].(2)

At two o'clock in the morning two Hungarians got into a cigar store at Fifteenth Street and Grand Avenue. Drevitts and Boyle drove up from the Fifteenth Street police station.(9)

Five men sentenced to be hanged were in the five top cells. (17)

These Steinian repetitions impart an eerie, almost incantatory quality to otherwise matter-of-fact statements.

Finally, aural repetition can be heard in several chapters of *in our time.* Two critics, Matthew Stewart and Wendolyn Tetlow, each have called attention to these poetic qualities. Stewart writes of chapter 14:

> The first paragraph emphasizes Villalta's mastery and determination by using words which concentrate the *l, f, s* and *w* sounds: "Villalta," "snarl," "bull," "firmly," "following," "feet firm," "when," "wind," "swing," and "swung." In the second paragraph, *l* continues to carry this sense: "Villalta," "kill," "called," "bull," and, as Wendolyn Tetlow has pointed out, *f* and *s* sounds "give the prose a movement like the smoothness of the bullfighter's movements": "front," "from," "folds," and "sword," "sighted," and "same" (42). In each paragraph alliterated pairs emphasize Villalta's will to dominate: "feet firmly," "standing straight," and his eventual success: "sword sticking." . . . The final sentence . . . uses variations on the *o* vowel as well as the consonant *l* to emphasize the bull's defeat: "Villalta, his hand up at the crowd and the bull roaring blood, looking straight at Villalta and his legs caving."[15]

This sound play raises an interesting question about genre: should the chapters in *in our time* be considered prose poems? The answer depends on which literary elements one chooses to emphasize. Figurative language (of which there is little), aural rhythms, and sound play indicate poetry; narrative, characterization, and dramatic action point to prose fiction. Biographical and historical evidence do not tilt the scales either way. Although Hemingway originally called these pieces "unwritten stories" and moved on to write short stories and novels in the years following, he had not yet abandoned an identity as poet. Moreover, when he chose to intersperse his stories with these chapters for the 1925 *In Our Time,* he could be said to have juxtaposed narrative and lyrical modes. Nevertheless, the narrative and dramatic elements of these chapters seem to be their most compelling features: in a variety of narrative voices, they create distinct characters and place them in highly dramatic situations. The poetic qualities of the prose ultimately strengthen, rather than pull against, these microdramas, as Stewart has demonstrated. But the aural repetitions and rhythms also affirm the chapters as carefully crafted objects, recognizable as, yet in many ways abstracted from, realistic narrative. If, as Archibald MacLeish asserts, "a poem should not mean but be," then the self-sufficiency of these constructions might indeed make them prose poems. But at the same time, each chapter is more than just an arrangement of pleasing sounds and images on the page: it does tell a story, even if the terms of its storytelling have been thoroughly redefined.

From Draft to Text: Revising Sentences

The drafts of the *in our time* chapters reveal a curious fact about Hemingway's compositional practice: contrary to his reputed preference for simple sentences, Hemingway's first and most natural tendency was to compose in compounds. Numerous sentences begin that way in the drafts, only to be revised into other structures, for example:

Draft	*Revision*
(chapter 1)	
I remember riding along in the dark and the the whole battery was drunk. (KL 92)	The whole battery was drunk going along the road in the dark.
I was a kitchen corporal then and we were going to entrain for the Champagne. (KL 92)	That was when I was a kitchen corporal.
(chapter 2)	
Bull got the first matador through [. . .]	
The ~~first matador got the horn through the hand~~ and the crowd hooted him out and the second matador slipped and the bull caught him. . . . (KL 92)	The first matador got the horn through his sword hand and the crowd hooted him out. The second matador slipped and the bull . . .

(chapter 4) Young Simmons came in with his patrol from across the river ~~and said they xxx~~ [illeg.]. (KL 94a)	Young Buckley came in with his patrol from across the river.
(chapter 8) They shelled further up the line and There was xxxxx no attack. and We went to work on the trench in the morning the sun came up. . . . and the day was. . . . (KL 94a)	The shelling moved further up the line. We went to work on the trench and in the morning the sun came up and the day was. . . .
(chapter 10) The major never married her and I got ~~didn't marry her after all. In the meantime I got~~ a dose of clap from a girl in Chicago riding in a yellow taxi. (KL 633)	The major did not marry her in the spring or at any other time. Ag never got an answer. . . . A short time after he contracted gonorrhea. . . .
(chapter 13) Afterwards I saw him at the cafe sitting alone and he was very short with a brown face and quite drunk and he said. . . . (KL 94a)	Afterwards I saw him at the café. He was very short with a brown face and quite drunk and he said. . . .
(chapter 14) ~~There was one great killer and that was~~ Villalta. (KL 94a)	[deleted]
(chapter 15) For Christ sake you've got bulls this afternoon. And he didn't listen to me he was listening so hard for the music to start (KL 94a)	For Christ sake you've got bulls this afternoon. He didn't listen to me, he was listening so hard for the music to start.

Not all of Hemingway's revisions follow this pattern, of course. Some sentences move away from complex structures:

Draft	*Revision*
(chapter 9) Drevitts and Boyle drove up in a ford car from the Fifteenth Street police station as they [the Hungarians] were backing the wagon out of an alley. (KL 94a)	Drevitts and Boyle drove . . . up in a Ford. The Hungarians were backing their wagon out of an alley.
(chapter 12) Blood pumped regularly from the horses forelegs as he lay on the sand with his legs up ~~where~~ The bull had gored him after he was lifted over and ripped by the charge. He was bleeding so regularly they were worried and were trying to get him out so the bull would charge him again before he keeled over. He cantered jerkily. (KL 94a)	Blood pumped regularly from between the horse's front legs. He was nervously wobbly.

As discussed above, each structure unfolds differently in time and space. Thus, in shifting from compound to simple sentences, Hemingway was slowing the pace and isolating, hence emphasizing, a particular statement: "The shelling moved further up the line" acquires more weight by itself. Sometimes, the revised simple sentences are intended to provide rhythmic contrast, breaking up the rolling, potentially monotonous rhythms of compounds, as in chapter 13, where the sentence—"Afterwards I saw him at the café"—breaks up a predominantly compound style. In removing complex sentences, Hemingway was also removing logical and causal connectives. In the "Drevitts and Boyle" example above, this change affects the pace and narrative tone: deleting "as" makes the sequence of events choppier, the tone more a bland listing of facts, like a police report. The large deletion in chapter 12 (shown above) removes past and future contexts that explain the horse's condition: how it was gored and what may happen. Without these contexts, the revision gives the horse's condition in radically present time.

From Draft to Text: Honing Phrases, Polishing Diction

Like any good writer, Hemingway worked over his chapters, searching for the most effective phrasing and *le mot juste.* This polishing in itself is unremarkable, but several of his revisions are interesting for what they reveal about his aesthetics or about the theme or characters of a particular chapter.

In the opening sentence of chapter 8, for example, he struggled to find the right focus:

> While we were lying in the sunken road at Fossalta during the bombardment . . .
>
> While the trench was going to pieces under the bombardment at Fossalta I lay very flat.
>
> While the bombardment was knocking the trench to pieces at Fossalta, I lay very flat. (qtd. in Reynolds, *The Paris Years* 124)

Shifting "bombardment" to the subject makes it the powerful agent that is "knocking" the trench to pieces—the vivid and necessary cause of the narrator's fear. In the second version, the trench at first appears to go to pieces of its own accord.

Some revisions sharpen characterization. The excited narrator of chapter 2 originally said: " . . . and the last bull he killed he was so tired he couldn't get the sword in" (KL 92). Hemingway then omitted the clarifying "he killed" to dramatize how the narrator's excitement muddles his sentence: " . . . and the last bull he was so tired he couldn't get the sword in" (KL 94a). Boyle, the policeman in chapter 9, originally had more of a clue about the Hungarians he shoots: "They're crooks ain't they? . . . They're hunkies or wops ain't they?" (KL 94a). In cutting "hunkies," Hemingway made him more ignorant and bigoted. A revision in chapter 10 shades the lovers' relationship to show how the burden of obligations falls unfairly on the man. Originally, the sentence in question read: "After the armistice I went home to get a job so we could get married." (KL 633 ms.) Two revisions later, the man's voluntary action ("went home") becomes the couple's agreement that the man must find work before they can marry: "After the armistice they agreed he should go home to get a job so they might be married" (chapter 10). Two decide, but only one must act, and the goal, marriage, now appears more provisional in the subjunctive: "might be married."[16]

Although Hemingway typically pruned his prose, he also recognized passages that needed more detail.[17] Sometimes, just a word sufficed; thus, the terrified soldier under shellfire first says "I lay very flat and prayed." (KL 94a). But one additional verb achieves verisimilitude: "I lay very flat and sweated and prayed." (KL 94a). The gored horse in chapter 12 "stopped" in one draft (KL 94a) but "stopped stiff" in a revision, anticipating his soon-to-be state of rigor mortis. Other passages required more. Paul Smith shows how the revisions of chapter 10 gradually emphasize how the young man is abused (*Reader's Guide* 25–26). One addition, however, sympathetically and rhythmically develops the factors that lead to Ag's infidelity. The drafts evolve thus:

> It was lonely there and there was a battalion of Arditi quartered in the town. ~~She didn't marry the Major so she wrote me after a while.~~ (KL 633 ms.)
>
> It was lonely and rainy there and there was a battalion of arditi quartered in the town. The major made love to her and she had never known Italians before and finally wrote to the States . . . (KL 94a).
>
> It was lonely and rainy there, and there was a battalion of *arditi* quartered in the town. Living in the muddy, rainy town in the winter the major of the battalion made love to Ag, and she had never known Italians before, and finally wrote a letter to the States. (chapter 10)

The weather grows steadily drearier; hence, the temptation for Ag to relieve her boredom increases and becomes more understandable.

At times, the revisions search for the right level of diction. In chapter 7, the self-consciously foreign "two Austrian *cadavre*" lying in the rubble first become "two Austrian corpses," then the plainer "two Austrian dead" (Derounian 72). Similarly, Hemingway vacillated between "abdomen" and "belly" in chapter 2, "intestines" and "belly" in a rejected draft of chapter 16. Finding the right level of diction was especially important when he knew the language would offend readers. Thus, he rewrote the controversial conclusion of chapter 10 three ways, first in the colloquialism true to the soldier-narrator's voice and the chapter's cynical ending:

> I got a dose of clap from a girl in Chicago riding in a yellow taxi. (KL 633)

Then, when "I" became "he," the statement reverts to the other extreme, polite euphemism:

> he ~~got a dose of the clap~~
> he had gotten sick from a girl riding in a taxicab through Lincoln Park. (KL 94a)

Finally, Hemingway settles on formal medical diction:

> he contracted gonorrhea from a sales girl from the Fair riding in a taxicab.(10)

Even this compromise, however, offended Dr. Clarence Hemingway, who allegedly told his son that such subjects were not to be discussed outside a doctor's office (Sanford 218–19).

Many changes strive for greater precision. Thus, "He had so much stuff on" becomes "He had so much equipment on" (4). "Then they raised hell" becomes "the crowd hollered and threw things" (2). Other revisions find a stronger word: the little girl "scared to death" in chapter 3 becomes, alliteratively, "scared sick." "We put up an absolutely perfect barricade" (KL 94a) improves with "We jammed an absolutely perfect barricade" (chapter 5). And the final image of chapter 14, showing the dying bull, gains immeasurably when Hemingway substitutes for "his legs going" the vivid "his legs caving" (KL 94a).

As might be expected, Hemingway frequently compressed a phrase ("rode herd on" becomes "herded" in chapter 3) or cut an inessential image. An excellent example appears in the Villalta chapter when he deletes a powerful simile at the conclusion that describes the bull "roaring blood like a hydrant" (KL 94a). He had already used an elaborate simile in the same chapter, comparing Villalta's swinging back with feet firmly planted to "an oak when the wind hits it." Perhaps the second simile made the passage seem too literary and distracted attention away from the triumphant Villalta. At times, Hemingway cut several lines from these already short vignettes, as when the narrator of chapter 18 originally tells the king how the military situation looks and receives the king's prediction that the war will soon resume.

In only a few instances do these revisions seem to obscure or weaken their subjects. One obscuring was intentional: one of Sam Cardinella's hangmen, identified in a draft as a deputy sheriff (KL 94a), now becomes the Eliotic "man in a derby hat." In the same chapter 17, however, the convicts in the top row of cells "sentenced to be hanged" were originally—and more clearly—"waiting to be hanged" (KL 94a): their proximity to the rope in the first version better explains their dreadful responses that morning. Also, the severity of Nick's wounding in chapter 8 seems more clearly conveyed when his legs stick out "rigidly" (KL 94a) rather than "awkwardly," as Hemingway amended the phrase.

Conclusion

Hemingway's experiments with sentences in this book are not those of a polished stylist but of a conscientious craftsman striving to become one. His sentence structures are remarkably fluid, shifting among compounds, simple sentences, fragments, complex structures, participles, and combinations of these. What Hemingway taught himself in composing and reconfiguring these structures was how they *move,* how they enable, impede, and alter various rhythms: in rolling and lulling compounds; in halting, choppy, simple sentences and in harshly abrupt fragments; in efficiently compressed, yet sometimes overly explanatory complex structures; and in the ongoing motions of participles. He discovered, further, that rhythm is not an isolated consideration, determined apart from the chapter's other elements—the very same recognition Pound had driven home in Imagist poetry. "Rhythm MUST have meaning," Pound declared to Harriet Monroe in 1915 (*Selected Letters of Ezra Pound* 49). Pound's protégé took the lesson to heart. His rhythms shape voice, reveal character, delineate action. To capture in a linear sequence the particular *kind* of action and the quality of voice meant constructing the right rhythm, the right sequence of sentences. The analyses above show that, while Hemingway did draw heavily on simple sentences to break up rhythms and highlight a momentary action or condition, he composed more naturally in compounds and employed complex sentences and dependent clauses when he needed to summarize facts efficiently or to show a hierarchy of actions hinging on each other. Equally important, he experimented freely with elisions, participles, and fragments, sometimes sacrificing grammatical correctness for the fuller impact of a participle's ongoingness, a fragment's compelling abruptness: "Scared sick looking at it." Seldom in his future career was Hemingway so willing to take chances, to overturn convention for a particular rhythmic effect. Composing these chapters, he learned to write sentences that begin a narrative without appearing to, that end it with an ironic fall rather than a flourish, and that suggest themes and hint at climaxes through structural contrast or repetition of key images and phrases.

The stories he would write the following year for the 1925 *In Our Time*—and for the rest of his career—would smooth out some of these rough edges, conventionalize the ungrammatical rhythms, modify some extremes. But they would adopt, as well as adapt, the rhythmic discoveries he made in *in our time.* In constructing these rhythms, Hemingway was discovering not only how these sentences worked, but how they worked for him, how their collaborations with voice, point of view, character development, and action could be shaped into a style of his own.

PART 3
TEXTS

6
The Chapters

Thus far, the *in our time* chapters have been analyzed collectively by how they employ narrative mode, voice, and sentence structure. This section studies each chapter individually, attending closely to its historical context, its thematic content, and its origins and drafts to show how it evolved, and, most important, the particular configuration of diction and sentence rhythms that express its action and affect. The schematic categories used in this chapter—"Background," "Content," "Style," and "Drafts"—are never wholly separable, and where appropriate they are discussed together. Where chapters lack drafts that differ from their first printing, this section is omitted.

chapter 1 (the kitchen corporal)

Background

Of *in our time*'s eighteen chapters, one-third deal with World War I: chapters 1, 4 (combat in a garden at Mons) and 5 (the perfect barricade) are set on the Western Front, while chapters 7 (Nick wounded), 8 (the praying soldier), and 10 (the recovering soldier and Ag) describe actions on or behind the Italian-Austrian front. In addition, two chapters that I have labeled "political," 3 (the civilian retreat) and 6 (the cabinet ministers' execution), describe events in 1922 that resulted from the Greco-Turkish War. Hemingway got his Western Front material secondhand in stories from his friend, Eric Dorman-Smith, or he invented it as in this chapter; his Italian material (being shelled, wounded, and recovering in the hospital) he drew and extrapolated from his own experience.

The immediate source of chapter 1 is unknown, and precisely when and where the action occurs is not certain. Since the men march "to the Champagne," E. R. Hagemann identifies the time as September–December 1915, the date of a major Franco-German battle there.[1] But the French fought several battles in this area, so the time cannot be precisely determined. Moreover, in the draft (KL 92), the men march *away* from "the front" in order to entrain for the Champagne, suggesting they might still be a long distance from that battle area. By removing those details in the published version, Hemingway brought them closer, within fifty kilometers.

Content

The ambiguity of the opening sentence—Who is "everybody"? Where are they? When? Why are they drunk (and why are there no exceptions)?—clarifies only gradually and incrementally. The second sentence establishes the military setting with "battery"; the third locates country, *approximate* time, and situation: the speaker is a member of an artillery unit, marching to a battlefield in France. Further on, we learn the speaker is a kitchen corporal, the battery's cook. But ambiguities and tensions remain. Some are thematic and intentional: the battery marches, drunk, in the dark—a disorienting experience, surely, reinforced by bizarrely comical, drunken episodes: the lieutenant talks repeatedly to his horse, calls him "mon vieux." The adjutant nervously warns the kitchen corporal that his fire will be spotted by an enemy fifty kilometers away. Little wonder that the speaker describes the experience as "funny" with its colloquial meaning of "strange" or "odd."[2] Precisely this sense of strangeness dominates the chapter's ethos: "drunk," or its slangy equivalent, "soused," appears four times in these eleven sentences, twice in the speaker's own voice. Also, in 1924, describing "everybody" in the battery as "drunk" could still shock those readers who clung to idealized conceptions of the soldier.[3]

Other tensions arise from what is not stated: though the battery is *now* safe from combat, the Champagne battlefield they march toward was notoriously bloody. That they march all night suggests they are being brought up for a battle. If the adjutant is inexperienced enough to ludicrously misjudge danger, possibly the whole battery is. All of these conditions make the comic strangeness of the present-time narrative collide with our *retrospective* awareness of the scene's grim context: they are in for a bad time and soon.[4] The last sentence reinforces this temporal ambiguity: "That was when" jerks us out of the narrative's present time and into retrospective; the narrator has survived the battle that he has not yet even joined and has eventually changed jobs. A Conradian touch, this retrospective revises our sense of the previous action, which first seems to occur in the fictional present, then resides in the narrator's recollection.

These implied facts only reinforce the speaker's ambiguous status. As noted in Chapter Four, he is one of several narrators whose national status is unclear. Clearly in a French detachment, he speaks in idiomatic and colloquial American English ("soused," "funny"). Even his title, "kitchen corporal," sounds more American than French. If, as seems likely, Hemingway was "translating" a French cook's experience into the American vernacular, suggesting the universality of such experience, why didn't he make the unit American in the first place?[5]

Stranger still is the subdued emotion of the narrative's conclusion. Following the punch-line climax of the adjutant's fear of being seen fifty kilometers from the front, the ambiguous "funny" deflates the scene's comic potential. And the retrospective concluding sentence, in excluding "big picture" facts—the battle, the fate of the battery—seems almost irrelevant and trivializing as it breaks away from present-time action and dates it only by the narrator's job at the time. Overall, the chapter presents soldiers in a familiar condition—drunk—which causes another familiar condition—marching—to become "funny" and disorienting in its nighttime antics. Beneath these antics and charging this mundane, antiheroic vignette of soldierly life lies the tension of their bloody destination—a retrospective knowledge shared by reader and narrator but only sensed by the soldiers who march blindly in the dark, en route to where "ignorant armies clash by night."

Style

In addition to the incremental style of the opening sentences, the chapter's most telling feature is its repetition of participial verbs: "going," (3 times), "riding" (2), "saying" (2). Hemingway even added "going" to sentence two after the chapter's original publication in the *Little Review.* As noted in Chapter One, both techniques derive directly from Gertrude Stein's "beginning again" and, less directly, from Flaubert's fondness for the imperfect tense. Here, the ongoing action of repeated participles recreates the continuous marching of the soldiers, repetitive and monotonous, but it also emphasizes the continuing strangeness of this drunken night in which the lieutenant "*kept* rid*ing* his horse out into the fields and saying . . . " and the adjutant "*kept* rid*ing* . . . and say*ing*"

The chapter's form is almost symmetrical. Sentences 2 and 10 are strikingly similar:

> The whole battery was drunk going along the road in the dark. (2)
> It was funny going along that road. (10)

The opening and closing sentences are quite short, while the longest sentence setting up the chapter's climax (the only one in which the narrator is directly addressed) comes exactly at the middle. The one notable asymmetry occurs in the abrupt time jump ("That was when") of the concluding sentence.

Sentence structure and sequence (*thematic center; **climax)[6]		*Word Count*
	1. simple	03
	2. simple	12
	3. simple	06
monologue a	4. compound predicate-compound (f-s)	21
"	5. simple	05
monologue b	6. compound-compound predicate-compound (f-s)	26
"	7. simple	03
"	8. simple	04
	**9. compound	17
	*10. simple‡ (participle)	07
	11. complex	08
	Total	112

Drafts

The one substantially different draft of this chapter (KL 92) shows two ways that Hemingway strengthened its style. Originally, the chapter applied incremental repetition more loosely:

> Unwritten Stories
>
> I remember riding along in the dark and the whole battery was drunk.
>
> Everybody was drunk going along xxxxxxxxxx the road in the dark.

"I remember" recalls the "I have seen" sentences of "Paris 1922," but it also echoes an elegiac voice in *The Waste Land:*

> I remember
> Those are pearls that were his eyes.

While the draft establishes from the outset the chapter's retrospective view, it loses the immediacy and bluntness of "Everybody was drunk."

The second change shows Hemingway gauging sentence rhythms. Compare:

> We went along the road all night in the dark and the adjutant was very drunk and I had a fire in my kitchen and he kept riding alongside and saying, "You must put it out." (KL 92)

with:

> We went along the road all night in the dark and the adjutant kept riding up alongside my kitchen and saying, "You must put it out!" (chapter 1)

The *and*s of the draft anticipate the run-on structure of the next chapter. There, however, the run-ons characterize the speaker's excitement and how the headlong rush of action appears to his undiscriminating eye. Here, the style seems out of place: too callow for this bemused narrator-soldier, too effusive for his understated emotion.

chapter 2 ("the kid" kills five bulls)

Background

The first of six chapters devoted to the bullfight, this one stands apart from the others spatially, stylistically, and in its compositional history. Placed second in the *Little Review* sequence,

> the kitchen corporal
> "the kid" kills five bulls
> the civilian retreat
> combat in a garden at Mons
> "MONS 2" (the perfect barricade)
> the cabinet ministers' execution

it was the only bullfight piece in that collection, and it retains that position in the Paris sequence, well separated from the other bullfight pieces, chapters 12–16.[7]

Significantly, Hemingway composed this chapter before he ever saw a bullfight. Gertrude Stein and Mike Strater had urged him to see one, and he may well have heard "the kid"'s story from one of them. Or, he may have invented it from whole cloth.[8] Curiously, after he did see his first bullfights in the summer of 1923, he later described them in his *Toronto Star Weekly* dispatches (20, 27 October 1923) using details similar to this invented chapter. The first dispatch refers often to a bullfighter named Chicuelo (and to other bullfighters) as the "kid." In the 27 October article, Algabeno faces nearly the same situation as the kid in chapter 2: he has to kill all six bulls after the other two bullfighters are injured. And the injured Maera kills his bull much as the kid precariously kills his last bull:

> With his wrist sprained . . . Maera *tried again and again* to make his death thrust. He lost his sword again and again, picked it up with his left hand from the mud floor of the arena and transferred it to the right for the thrust. *Finally he made it* and the bull went over. (*Dateline: Toronto* 353, emphasis mine)

> . . . the last bull he was so tired he couldn't get the sword in. He couldn't hardly lift his arm. He tried five times. . . . and then he finally made it. (chapter 2)

So life imitates art.

Content and Style

That Hemingway did not witness the events described here may help explain the narrator's distinctive voice, distance, and perspective. His obvious excitement, his boxing-ring argot and colloquial, colorful speech, his poor grammar, and his need to explain basic rules of the bullfight ("because you can't have more than three matadors") identify the narrator not as a professional journalist and certainly not as a native aficionado, but as a semi-educated tourist enthusiastically relating his first experience. If Hemingway was projecting himself as speaker (accurately anticipating his own lifelong enthusiasm for the corrida), it was as the same rough-and-tumble persona who appears in "Today is Friday" as the Roman soldier who praises Christ's conduct during the crucifixion in sports language: "he was pretty good in there today."[9]

The speaker's inexperience and distance from the action (compare the close-up, informed perspective in chapter 14) express themselves in two distinct features of this narrative: his undifferentiated excitement about *all* of the events, related in the same style—an anticipation of the "bullfight as spectacle" discussion in *The Sun Also Rises*—and his distracted awareness of the crowd as an active participant. In sharp contrast to the kid's singularity, the crowd is crudely collective; its contempt when it "hooted . . . out" the first failed bullfighter is scarcely distinguishable from its approval of the kid's success: "the crowd hollered and threw things down into the bull ring." Finally, just as the drunken antics in chapter I function antiheroically, so the kid's puking (while the crowd hollers) deflates romantic heroism with ugly and mundane realism and prevents the chapter from lapsing into a Frank Merriwell ending.

Style

More than in any other chapter, narrative style determines character here. The narrator's breathless run-on sentences convey his rampant excitement: the second sentence alone (longest in the book) fuses eleven separate actions with ten conjunctions:

> The second matador slipped and the bull caught him through the belly and he hung on to the horn with one hand and held the other tight against the place, and the bull rammed him wham against the wall and the horn came out, and he lay in the sand, and then got up like crazy drunk and tried to slug the men carrying him away and yelled for his sword but he fainted.

In compound structure, moreover, the actions seem to run together in an undifferentiated, cinematic stream. Linked sequentially by *and*s, "he lay in the sand" becomes just as important as "the horn came out." The narrator, in short, tries to convey these actions as quickly as they happen, but without the sophistication that subordinates lesser details to the crucial ones. Similarly, the narrative's proportion is skewed. The speaker's detailed attention to the second bullfighter's goring forces him to summarize and radically compress the kid's achievement: "The kid came out and had to kill five bulls . . . and the last bull." If the narrative rides on the speaker's excitement and surges with a vivid detail ("He sat down in the sand and puked and they held a cape over him"), it also falters on his cliché—"it looked like either him or the bull"—and vagueness: "then he finally made it."

As noted above, the narrator's fumbling but colorful English sharply characterizes him. Solecisms proliferate: "like crazy drunk," the casual "you can't have," the marvelous elision and comical ambiguity of "the last bull he was so tired he couldn't get the sword in," and, most egregiously (since it stands apart, implying the speaker took more time to form it): "He couldn't hardly lift his arm."[10]. But these gaffes are inseparable from his colorful colloquialisms: "puked," "slugged," and the onomatopoeic "rammed him wham."

Stylizing the narrative voice so severely enabled Hemingway to screen action he had not yet seen firsthand by deflecting our attention to the speaker and crowd. In so doing, he implies that action—at least, in this instance—is inseparable from the character who perceives it, the voice that narrates it. This radical subjectivity marks one extreme in his study of how voice conveys psychological states as well as action.

Sentence structure and sequence (*thematic center; **climax)	*Word count*
1. compound	16
2. run-on: multiple compounds (7)-compound predicates (4)	74
3. run-on: compound predicate-complex-simple‡	32
*4. simple	06
**5. run-on: multiple compounds (5)-complex	29
6. run-on: compound predicate-compound-complex	27
Total	184

Drafts

Of the two drafts of chapter 2, one (KL 94a) is nearly identical to the first published version in the *Little Review.* But both it and the *Little Review* version have one significant detail that Hemingway subsequently dropped: following the kid's triumph, the crowd does not simply holler and "throw things down into the bull ring"; instead, "The crowd come down the barrera into the bull ring" (*Little Review*). This addition makes the crowd's approval virtually indistinguishable from its hostility (see chapter 13); perhaps for this reason, Hemingway deleted the action in chapter 2. In KL 94a, the English is standard: "came down *over* the barrera." Here, as in the "couldn't hardly lift his arm" and "the last bull he was so tired" constructions, Hemingway's revisions made the sentence ungrammatical to emphasize the speaker's poor education.[11]

The other draft (KL 92) is much worked over and, interestingly, shows Hemingway rejecting a version of sentence 1 he was later to restore:

Unwritten Stories

Bull got the first matador through the sword hand

The ~~first matador got the horn through the hand~~ and the crowd

out T

hooted him ~~and~~ the second matador slipped and the bull caught him.[12]

The draft also shows how the author could make a vivid action even more striking. Originally, part of sentence 2 read:

> wildeyed
> he lay in the sand and then got up / and slugged the men that tried to carry him away.

The final version appears as:

> he lay in the sand, and then got up like crazy drunk and tried to slug the men carrying him away.

"Like crazy drunk" is at once more colorful and truer to the speaker's ungrammatical English, while "*tried* to slug" seems more apt for a badly gored bullfighter about to faint.

Not all of Hemingway's revisions were better, however. Compare the draft version of the climactic action:

> H
> ~~he~~ tried five times and finally got it through and the
> was quiet all the time waiting and never razzed him.
> crowd ~~didn't say a word each time he missed.~~
>
> Then they raised hell when he finally put it through and the bull went down. (KL 92)

with the published version:

> He tried five times and the crowd was quiet because it was a good bull and it looked like him or the bull and then he finally made it. He sat down in the sand and puked and they held a cape over him while the crowd hollered and threw things down into the bull ring. (chapter 2)

Without doubt, Hemingway improved the published version when he added the unromantic puking and sharpened the draft's trite "the crowd raised hell" into "hollered" and "threw things." But the cliché "it looked like him or the bull" is distinctly inferior to the ominousness of the crowd "waiting" (to see the outcome or to see this bullfighter gored like his predecessors?) Similarly, the clichéd "he finally made it" blurs the more precise "when he finally put it through and the bull went down."

chapter 3 (the civilian retreat)

Background

This is the first of three chapters that portray scenes following the Greco-Turkish War that ended in disaster for Greece in 1922.[13] All three depict the geopolitical consequences for civilians: the evacuation of Greek Christians through Eastern Thrace (3), the execution of six cabinet ministers of King Constantine (6), and the house arrest of his successor, King George II (18). Turkey's gain of Eastern Thrace from the war's settlement compelled hundreds of thousands of Greek Christians, fearing persecution, to evacuate to Western Thrace and on to Greece itself. Hemingway, on assignment from the *Toronto Star,* arrived too late to cover the war, but he witnessed part of this civilian retreat through Adrianople along the road to Karagatch.

More than any other chapter, this one derives from previous texts, namely the two news dispatches Hemingway wrote for the *Star.* Nearly the entire chapter comes from "A Silent, Ghastly Procession" (20 October 1922), supplemented by a few details from the 14 November dispatch, "Refugees from Thrace" (*Dateline: Toronto* 232, 249–52). This chapter is also one of the few whose events Hemingway experienced firsthand. "Refugees from Thrace" describes his experiences getting to the scene and "walk[ing] five miles with the refugee procession." A few years later, in a deleted stream-of-consciousness section of "Big Two-Hearted River," he attributed to his protagonist, Nick Adams, the experience of witnessing the childbirth described in both "A Silent, Ghastly Procession" and chapter 3: "Of course he'd never seen an Indian woman having a baby. . . . He'd seen a woman have a baby on the road to Karagatch and tried to help her" ("On Writing" 238).

Even with a ready-made text, Hemingway completely reworked his *Star* material, cutting almost two-thirds of "Procession"'s 348 words, rearranging and compressing details, and shaping the whole into a miniature masterpiece. Examining differences between these two texts reveals much about his technique and aesthetic priorities. Essentially, the changes fall into three categories: (1) cutting explanatory or hortatory sections; (2) cutting colorful details that Hemingway deemed inessential; and (3) changing and rearranging imagistic details for thematic emphasis. Major cuts in the first two paragraphs of "Procession" omit much of the journalistic "who?-what?-where?-when?" opener: the chapter does not locate Adrianople in Eastern Thrace, nor identify the evacuees as Christians, nor tell us they are headed "towards Macedonia." Nor does the chapter answer the more important "why?": the Christians evacuate, the dispatch tells us, "when they heard the Turk was coming." Another wholesale cut—the entire last paragraph of the dispatch—describes the inadequate relief available to the evacuees, provides more context ("250,000 Christian refugees"), and projects their cry for help: "in the next month all the Christian world will hear the cry: 'Come over into Macedonia and help us!'" (Acts 16.9), reflecting the thoroughness of Grace Hemingway's Christian upbringing of her children.

The cutting of colorful details demonstrates Hemingway's art of compression, of letting the single image stand for a plethora. In the dispatch, for example, the simile "mud-splashed Greek cavalry herd them along like cow-punchers driving steers" becomes in the chapter "Greek cavalry herded along the procession." "Herded" already reduces the refugees to cattle, obviating the simile. Also superfluous are other colorful details, such as the chickens dangling from the carts and the old man "bent under a young pig, a scythe and a gun."

Content

As it deletes the dispatch's geopolitical context, its moralizing conclusion, and its adjectival padding, the chapter emphasizes the here-and-now actuality—miserable and muddy—of the marchers. It lengthens the procession by ten miles, stresses the near gridlock of carts by repeating "jammed" (a condition Hemingway would return to in the Caporetto retreat of *A Farewell to Arms*), and reinforces the continuous rain by adding imagistic sentences about minarets sticking up in the rain and (altering a detail from "Refugees from Thrace") the Maritza "running yellow almost up to the bridge." A clichéd detail, the "never-ending" march of the dispatch, expands to: "No end and no beginning." The fragment vivifies the abstract "endless" by assuming a perspective from somewhere within the march, with only the moving procession as far as one's eye can see in both directions, hence, the profound despair of having no way out, of having no sense of where or when the misery will end. The truncated fragment literally embodies "no end and no beginning," all of which makes us *feel* in the chapter what the dispatch must explain: "They don't know where they are going." Framing this immediacy, the opening and closing sentences provide more distant perspective. The first two are spatial, presenting the distant view of

Adrianople's minarets and the totality of the jam-up ("thirty miles"), while the last sentence is temporal: "It rained all through the evacuation."[14] All three sentences underscore the prevailing misery. Finally, the chapter develops the marchers' sense of helplessness by sharpening the childbirth scene. But it does so without resorting to the dispatch's sentimentality:

> A husband spreads a blanket over a woman in labor in one of the carts to keep off the driving rain. She is the only person making a sound. Her little daughter looks at her in horror and begins to cry. ("A Silent, Ghastly Procession")

> There was a woman having a kid with a young girl holding a blanket over her and crying. Scared sick looking at it. (chapter 3)

Forty-one words become twenty-three; three sentences contract to one sentence and a fragment; three characters diminish to the essential two; the formal "in labor" toughens to the hard-boiled "having a kid"; the syrupy "her little daughter" becomes the deadpan "young girl"; the stock phrase "in horror" turns into the powerful, colloquial, and alliterative "scared sick." This dramatic climax develops the helplessness of "Women and kids were in the carts crouched with mattresses" into something worse: stark fear. It also establishes a major theme of *in our time* when the young girl (or is it the speaker?) is "scared sick looking at it." Repeatedly, the characters in these vignettes must look at something horrible, and so must the reader. There is no turning away through euphemism or softened diction, and Hemingway carefully records the responses of his characters.

Style

As the setting of chapter 3 is new to *in our time,* so is its narrative voice and style. Gone is the fumbling excitement of the bullfight narrator, the subdued emotion of the kitchen corporal. This narrator is observant but laconic, impassive, tough—and anonymous. He may borrow the colloquial looseness of the speaker in chapter 2 ("having a kid"), but his emotion is anything but enthusiastic. And just as the run-ons of chapter 2 convey that speaker's indiscriminate excitement, here the staccato rhythms of simple sentences and fragments (nine of the thirteen sentences) evoke this speaker's impassivity, his reportorial neutrality and emotive detachment. Images prevail; emotion is understated; yet, the misery comes through in sharply etched details like "soaked through."

In one notable respect, however, this chapter recalls chapter 1: both use participial verbs to convey the ongoingness of a procession. Thus, the cattle "were hauling"; the old men and women were "keeping the cattle moving"; "The Maritza was running"; the camels were "bobbing"; a woman was "having a kid" while the little girl is "holding a blanket and crying." Even simple past-tense sentences lack finite action: "carts were jammed" (twice), "cavalry herded *along* the procession," "old men and women . . . walked *along*" (emphasis mine).

More than most chapters, this one shows careful and more traditional shaping: opening and closing sentences establish the controlling image of rain, which appears six other times in various guises. The opener—"Minarets stuck up in the rain out of Adrianople across the mud flats"—is especially remarkable in the way it contrasts vertical and horizontal images. "Minarets stuck up" links a sharp image to a harshly assonant but powerful action verb (compare a more literary alternative such as "thrust"). "Stuck up" also evokes an abrupt, kinesthetic verticality, only to yield to an increasingly horizontal view as the perspective pulls back to see the minarets distantly ("out of Adrianople") and from "across the mud flats." This horizontal perspective—the procession with no end and no beginning—dominates the remainder. In contrast to the abrupt, dynamic opener, the closing sentence ("It rained all through the evacuation"), immediately following the childbirth climax, effects the same dying fall that we noted in the closer of chapter 1. Though it unifies the narrative imagistically, it offers no thematic resolution of the refugees' suffering and need to get somewhere.

Sentence Structure and Sequence (*thematic center; **climax)	*Word Count*
1. simple	13
2. simple	11
3. simple	10
*4. fragment	05
5. fragment	07
6. simple‡ (participle)	13
7. simple	10
8. simple‡ (participle)	13
9. simple	06
10. simple‡ (adverbial past participle)	14
**11. simple‡ (3 participles)	18
**12. fragment	05
13. simple	06
Total	131

Drafts

Of the two drafts of this chapter, one (KL 94a) is virtually identical with the *Little Review* version. The other (KL 693) presents nearly the same images but in participial fragments, as if Hemingway intended to capture in "cablese" the verismo of on-the-scene reporting that permits no time for complete sentences:

> Carts ~~were~~ jammed for thirty miles on the Karagatch road. Rain coming down. Mud splashed water buffalo and cattle hauling carts. No end and no beginning.

Significantly, his final version stays close to this emphasis on fragments, participles, and simple sentences. The deletion of this draft's final sentence—"That was the beginning of the retreat" (KL 693)—keeps the entire experience in the narrative present, rather than suddenly jerking it into the retrospective past, as chapter 1 does.

The "Helene" draft

One version of this retreat, entitled "Exodus," adopts the perspective of a nauseous woman, "Helene," riding in a cart—almost certainly the woman whom the other versions describe in childbirth. Unlike the detached perspective of the published chapter and newspaper dispatch, the reader is in the cart with her, experiencing its jarring progress. The opening paragraph describes what she sees, looking straight ahead, most of it devoted to the bobbing, manure-matted rump of the camel, which "swung slowly up and down, the tail twitching" as it pulls the cart. Only the last sentence of this paragraph refers to the cart's driver

> on the front seat / hunched ~~over,~~ the rain dripping.

The sight (and, presumably, the smell) of the camel's backside and the motions ("bobbing rump" and bumping ride) are nauseating. But Helene is also in pain—obviously, labor pains strong enough to make her grip the side of the cart—and dizzy as well (the ground was "whirling"). With the same unblinking stare at the sordid that runs through the book, the narrative does not just tell us that Helene vomited, but describes the act:

> The vomit belched and then dribbled away slowly. xxxxx It spilled
> wheel revolved,
> onto the / hub ~~spoke wheel~~ and the wheel slowly xxxxxxx . chunks
> in a rain washed glaze sticking to the hub and revolving.

Momentarily relieved, she settles back against the grain sacks and looks at an old man walking alongside the cart carrying a chicken. The draft, here handwritten, ends as

> Helene watched the old man's[?] wet back, the open bore of
> the gun barrel and the draggle feathered chicken spinning from the
> as the pain came again
> scythe crook. She shut her eyes/ and pressed her feet against the
> ~~iron~~ base of the table piled in the cart in front of her. (KL 701)

Hemingway probably wrote this version while he was in Thrace because the reverse side of the draft contains notes on the political conference and on some of its participants (Kemal Pasha, Harrington), as well as snappy lines he planned to use in his dispatches, for instance,

> Greece by the folly of her government has lost all that was given her—
>
> —If it took 10 days to come to Mauldania [sic] settlement it will take 30 years for a peace conference at Smyrna—

If he composed this draft at the time, he may have had less reason to empathize with the problem of pregnancy since Hadley was not yet pregnant. Yet, difficult childbirths would appear often in his early work. The son of a doctor who had specialized in obstetrics intuitively recognized the fictional potential of this life-and-death subject.[15] Moreover, he had already written a short story partially from a woman's point of view—Liz Coates's in "Up in Michigan"—and in both cases the women suffer physical and psychological pain from intercourse or its consequences. In this version, we do not stare *at* the women in childbirth ("scared sick looking at it"); we see and feel as she does. Yet, although the perspective is more personal than the other versions of the Greek evacuation, several elements point up the author's allegorical intentions: the biblical title, the woman's name representing the Hellenic people, and perhaps even her resemblance to Mary, journeying to avoid the Romans. Had he finished and used this version, it would have provided a significant counterbalance to the male perspectives in the other chapters, but the allegorical mode would clearly have jarred.

chapter 4 (combat in a garden at Mons)

Background

Chapters 4 and 5 both narrate incidents occurring during the Anglo-German battle of Mons (August 1914).[16] In fact, chapter 5 was originally entitled "MONS (Two)" in the *Little Review* version. Hemingway also composed a "MONS (Three)" vignette (KL 94a, discussed in Chapter Two) but chose not to publish it. Critics nearly always link chapters 4 and 5 because they describe events from the same battle, because the narrators' voices are British, and because Hemingway got the stories from his British friend, Captain Eric Dorman-Smith. Most critics go further, however, and assert that the narrator is the same in both chapters, and some critics assume the same voice narrates the unpublished "MONS (Three)" and "On the Quai at Smyrna," the introduction Hemingway added in 1930.[17] But as I argue in the "Voices" chapter, this assumption overlooks major stylistic and expressive differences among the British voices—differences that suggest sharply contrasting psychological and emotive states in the narrators. Each chapter deserves to be studied as a separate entity.

Content

Like chapter 1, this war episode bristles with incongruities that remove the experience from stereotyped "over the top" combat and imbue it with a feeling of strangeness. The setting seems more appropriate for a garden party, the Germans "dropping in" for tea like uninvited guests. There is no mention of an expected attack. Young Buckley's patrol might have been a routine action and, in any case, it does not announce (does not even detect!) the advancing Germans—an astounding blunder. "We" are "in" a garden, but the narrator does not refer to being dug in or entrenched. Nor does he tell us whether these Germans are the spearhead of an attack (unlikely, since he does not mention a preliminary bombardment) or a raiding party. Neither case would explain why these Germans are overloaded. Like the French troops in chapter 1, the matadors in chapter 2, and the refugees in chapter 3, "we"—both characters and readers—begin in the middle with no explanatory context.

If the speaker's side is surprised by these enemy troops (but not *too* surprised since they quickly pot them), the advancing Germans are even more so: why else would they be climbing blindly over a wall, with "so much equipment on," without knowing what was on the other side? That the "first German" was "awfully surprised" at being shot is almost redundant in this context. The contextual gaps in this narrative are wide enough for a battalion to pass through: *When* did Young Buckley's patrol come in? How was that event related, in time, space, or causality, to the first German appearing? Was the "first German I saw" the first of this encounter, of this battle, or the first the narrator has ever seen in combat? The self-contained simple sentences provide no links.

In any case, the combat is ridiculously easy—just as it will be in chapter 5. Struggling over a wall—just as they will labor to get past "an absolutely perfect barricade" in chapter 5—the Germans are sitting ducks to be "potted" (not just "shot") by the narrator and his men. The dreamlike ease of this combat—a soldier's dream of shooting safely at easy targets—thus reinforces the overall strangeness of the encounter.[18] And, in slowing down the action to emphasize its strangeness, the short, declarative sentences (all lacking causal connections) seem to emulate separate shots. The closing sentence—"They all came just like that"—seems redundant but reasserts the strange actuality of the experience. Although vague ("just like what?"), it is both convincing as spoken language and reiterates the speaker's own sense of the encounter's improbability, as if to affirm it to a skeptical listener. Ultimately, the speaker's sense of the experience is the strangest aspect of the encounter.

Style

Like chapter 1, very short, simple sentences, virtually shorn of modifiers, predominate here. Two sentences have short dependent clauses—"that I saw" and "till he got one leg over"—but these clauses scarcely complicate the structures. One sentence is of such textbook simplicity—"We shot them"—that it reminds us why Hemingway is popular with readers learning English. The one exception to these patterns—in length, structure, and modifiers—stands out as the dramatic climax: "He had so much equipment on and looked awfully surprised and fell down into the garden."

This radically simple structure, as noted above, leaves contextual gaps by not linking events causally. The reader has no explanations, only individual actions. But the style does more: narrated in first person, it conveys the speaker's psychological state during the combat and as he recalls it. With its numerous stops and starts—its spaces, hence pauses, between sentences—the style is not merely British understatement. It deflates emotion. It suggests a speaker who is psychologically detached—emotionally drained, perhaps stunned, possibly even shell-shocked. The bizarre conditions of this encounter partially explain this affect: its unlikely setting, its unexpected spontaneity, its comic aspect in the surprised, overloaded German falling off the wall like Humpty Dumpty. But if the uncanny simplicity of this combat anticipates the potting in chapter 5, it also recalls the disorienting strangeness in chapter 1 where "everyone was drunk" and acting "funny" marching in the dark. This encounter with the Germans is strangely dreamlike, and the soldier's voice, too, has a disembodied somnambulism in its halting, simple sentences. Once again, combat "in our time" resists stereotype; the experience seems altogether strange, and the narrative voice is startlingly free of affect, except for a kind of dazed wonderment: "They all came over just like that."

Sentence Structure and Sequences (*thematic center **climax)	*Word Count*
1. simple	07
2. simple	11
3. simple‡ (adjective clause)	11
4. complex + compound predicate	12
**5. compound predicate (3)	16
6. simple	09
*7. simple	03
8. simple	06
Total	75

Drafts

Two drafts of this chapter reveal very little of its composition. One (KL 94a) is identical to the *Little Review* version and differs from the *in our time* version only in not capitalizing "German." The other, KL 821 (typed just below the text for chapter 5), has more cross-outs and two differences from the *in our time* text. "Young Buckley" is "Young Simmons" here; more important, he was going to state the result of his patrol: "Young Simmons came in with his patrol from across the river ~~and said theyxxxxxxxxxxxxx~~ [illeg.]" (KL 94a). In removing this temporal link between the patrol and the "first German," Hemingway strengthened the disjointed strangeness of the narrative.

chapter 5 (the perfect barricade)

Background

Unlike chapter 4, where the combat at the garden wall has not been noted in the Mons battle history, this narrative describes a recorded battle between the British Expeditionary Force and the attacking Germans at the Mons-Condé Canal on 23 August 1914.[19] Hemingway's source, his friend "Chink" Dorman-Smith, commanded a battalion defending the Mariette Bridge over the canal. The barricade that the British jammed across the bridge, their easy combat and the large German losses that resulted, and the larger British retreat that ended the battalion's stand at this "absolutely perfect barricade" have been documented. What Hemingway has added is the particular character of the speaker's voice.

Content and Style

If the narrative voice of this chapter is indeed the same as in chapter 4, as so many critics assume, then the speaker must be bipolar, for this voice brims with emotion precisely to the extent that the previous voice lacks it.[20] The speaker narrates the "absolutely perfect barricade" he and his men have constructed with the enthusiasm of a hunter recalling a perfect blind. His hyperbolic speech brims with British superlatives: "absolutely," "simply priceless," "absolutely topping," "absolutely perfect." Even the weather is "frightfully" hot. And like a sportsman, the speaker admires quality in his opponents: "Their officers were very fine."

This hyperbole cannot be written off simply as a British mannerism: its insistence (to use Gertrude Stein's word) conveys a psychological state of almost manic euphoria. The proximate reason for his enthusiasm is not mysterious: in the chaotic and unpredictable nature of combat, such ideal conditions—when soldiers can shoot close-up at the enemy without the corresponding danger of being shot at—are exceedingly rare: "you could shoot through [the barricade] and they would have to climb over it." The moment cannot last, of course, and succumbs to the larger, uncontrollable forces of battle: "We were frightfully put out when we heard the flank had gone, and we had to fall back." Tellingly, even this ironically deflating conclusion is hyperbolic, suggesting that the hyperbole derives not simply from the situation but from the speaker's psychological condition. In "A Way You'll Never Be" (1932), Hemingway develops this effusiveness into a neurotic combat condition, in which a psychically damaged soldier cannot stop babbling.

Although the prevalence of simple sentences and fragments somewhat recalls the style of chapter 4, significant differences remain, reflecting the two speakers' contrasting mental states. First, even though the simple sentences and fragments in chapter 5 are formally disjunctive, the separate units form a cohesive narrative describing the perfect barricade: where "we" jammed it, what it consisted of, its weight and density ("you could shoot through it"), the problem it posed the Germans, their responses, and the British actions ("We potted them from forty yards"). Moreover, several simple sentences and fragments merely repeat in slight variants the barricade's perfection, again denoting the speaker's enthusiasm. The cohesiveness of this perfect little moment thus complements the sense of disconnection in chapter 4.

Hemingway got the material for chapters 4 and 5 (as well that of "MONS (Three)"[21]) secondhand, but he has shaped the affect of the narrative voices through sentence structure and diction. Once again, it is not so much the action itself that matters as how a particular participant responds to it: his perceptions, sensations, and psychic state, conveyed through voice and determined by style, are Hemingway's real focus.

Sentence Structure and Sequence (*thematic center **climax)	*Word Count*
1. simple	06
2. simple	09
3. simple	04
4. fragment	12
*5. triple compound (including elliptical fragment)	18
6. simple	04
7. compound	13
8. compound	12
9. simple	06
10. simple	05
**11. complex	18
Total	107

chapter 6 (the cabinet ministers' execution)

Background

When King Constantine of Greece abdicated to England in the summer of 1922, following the Turkish rout of his army, he left behind the cabinet ministers and generals who had originally brought him out of exile. This group, including the premier and the military commander closest to Constantine, faced the retribution of the military junta that overthrew the Constantine government. Charged with high treason for the military debacle, they were court-martialed, found guilty, and executed by firing squad on 28 November 1922.

The execution caused an international flap. Britain, a major player in the region, had urged clemency during the trial and now broke relations with the junta. The *New York Times* compared the shootings to the Reign of Terror of the French Revolution (29 Nov. 1922, p. 2). The story made the front page of the *Times* and of the Paris edition of the *Chicago Tribune,* where Hemingway almost certainly read it.

Curiously, the newspapers' accounts of the execution differ markedly. The *New York Times* story of 29 November provides few details: the military commander, Hadjianestes, was "solemnly degraded" and "Communion was administered to all the men before they were shot." The *Times* story two days later is far more colorful. As quoted in Chapter Three, it shows the ministers going "courageously, even jauntily to their deaths" as a few "chatted gayly" and one "smilingly" had a last cigarette before giving the silver case to his executioner. In contrast to Hemingway's more gruesome version, "death in each case had come instantly" with the volley.

The Paris *Tribune* version lacks these Hollywood heroics. While it mentions the military degrading and the communion, it states that the ministers "died silently, refusing to answer when they were asked to express their last wishes." Without question, this was the version Hemingway read, for it mentions that "former Premier Gounaris, who had been ill with typhoid fever, was carried from his sick bed to the place of execution." And it refers to the "deaths of the six men against the wall."

Hemingway's chapter obviously takes these images from the Paris *Tribune* account. But the chapter excludes all political context that would identify the ministers, their executioners, and the reason for the shooting. It also omits any linkage to the evacuation of Greek Christians in chapter 3. Yet, in describing to Pound how the chapters "all hook up," Hemingway writes: "The refugees leave Thrace, due to the Greek ministers, who are shot" (*Selected Letters* 91). Perceptive readers might note that the two chapters share a third-person perspective and the cool, factual, uninflected voice of Hemingway's quasi-journalistic mode. But separated from the evacuation by two World War I chapters, this execution exudes an eerie anonymity: "They" could be anyone; the shooting might have occurred anywhere and for any reason. Like the war shootings, this one is simply another form of violence "in our time."

Content

Shorn of historical context and causality, chapter 6 nonetheless begins with a journalistic "establishing" sentence fixing time and place: "They shot the six cabinet ministers at half-past six in the morning against the wall of a hospital."[22] But the narrative immediately shifts to scene and action. As in the evacuation chapter, rain presages human suffering, and also like that chapter, this one finds several imagistic ways of conveying "It rained hard": pools of water, wet dead leaves, shutters nailed shut against the storm, "into the rain," "sat in a puddle of water," and "sitting in the water." In fact, rain might be said to be the real subject of the chapter—rain as a symbol, not just of misery as in chapter 3, but of death. Numerous critics have observed how "pools of water" anticipates the undescribed "pools of blood"; how "wet dead leaves" foreshadows the undescribed dead cabinet ministers lying in the courtyard; how the hospital ironically serves as a backdrop of killing, its shutters nailed shut like closed eyes unwilling to witness (or intervene in) the grisly scene.

But if Hemingway's suggestive images here owe much to Pound's Imagism and Eliot's objective correlative, his techniques of omission and understatement are original. One sentence in particular brilliantly fuses these qualities:

> The other five stood very quietly against the wall.

Here, Hemingway compresses two imagistic statements of the *Chicago Tribune* story that must have impressed him: "They died silently, refusing to answer when they were asked to express their last wishes" and "The deaths of the six men against the wall today. . . . " Permitting himself only an uncharacteristic "very" to emphasize their bravery, his understatement is terser, less emotive than actual journalism. No final cigarette, no offer or refusal of blindfolds, no brave last words or refusal to speak them. Yet the ministers' dignity in their final moments is unmistakable—an example of *in our time*'s study of how people respond under life-and-death conditions.

What contrasts and thus intensifies the ministers' courage is the execution's messy, antiromantic quality—another idiomatic theme in Hemingway's mature work. Significantly, half the chapter is devoted to the sick minister. In the first place, shooting a man so ill that he must be carried seems particularly brutal. Forcing him to stand with the others makes a travesty of execution rituals, while the soldiers' failure to make him stand and his sitting down in a puddle of water turns travesty into pathetic farce. But the worst is still to come. The last sentence is gruesome in its implications: "When they fired the first volley he was sitting down in the water with his head on his knees." His head would thus become the executioners' target, and "*first* volley" indicates that there was another. From virtually every standpoint, then—the miserable weather, the shooting of the sick victim, the failure to make him conform to execution ritual, and the requirement of a second volley—this botched execution undermines romantic stereotypes (the *New York Times* version). Only the quiet bravery of the other ministers offsets the brutal farce of their execution.

Style

The opening string of five simple sentences powerfully establishes the dreary scene and the factual, unemotive tone. As these simple sentences resist the explanatory linkage of subordination, they each focus our attention wholly on their minute actuality. We *see* the "pools of water in the courtyard" because the sentence allows us to focus on nothing else. Sound patterns also slow and thus intensify our perceptions: the repeated sixes (including the chapter number) in the first sentence, the assonance of "wet dead leaves" and repetition of "shutters" and "shut." And the repeated "s" throughout the chapter evokes the hiss of the driving rain.

Only when description turns to narrative action (beginning with sentence 7) does the structure change to accommodate sequential and causal actions. Sentence 8, a comparatively long compound—"They tried to hold him up against the wall but he sat down in a puddle of water"—marks both the chapter's stylistic turn and thematic center: the botched execution. In this second context of compound and complex action sentences, the simple sentence 9—"The other five stood very quietly against the wall"—stands out grammatically and thematically as it counterpoints the ministers' courage to their executioners' bungling. By contrast, the most conventionally complex sentence, the last, provides the climax of that bungling.

Hemingway must surely have recognized the strength of this vignette in choosing it to close his *Little Review* collection. Critics have confirmed his judgment. Early reviews of the chapters quoted it often to illustrate the powerful impact and artistic control of Hemingway's writing. Edmund Wilson's comments are typical:

> in the dry compressed little vignettes of *In Our Time* [he] has almost invented a form of his own: [quotes chapter 6 in its entirety]. Mr. Hemingway is remarkably successful in suggesting moral values by a series of simple statements of this sort. ("Dry Points" 121–22)

Subsequent critics have celebrated this chapter as an example, par excellence, of Hemingway's mature technique of understating themes through images and symbols. Arguably, it is the best chapter of *in our time.*

Sentence Structure, Sequence (*thematic center, **climax)	*Word Count*
1. simple (with 4 prepositional phrases)	19
2. simple	08
3. simple	11
4. simple	03
5. simple	09
6. simple	08
7. simple	10
*8. compound	18
*9. simple	09
10. simple‡ (object clause)	16
**11. complex	19
Total	130

Drafts

The one extant draft of this chapter (KL 94a) is virtually identical to the published version in its bottom half (sentences 6–11), but its first half is much revised. Hemingway played with variant sentence structures to combine, separate, or move the key facts of the setting:

They shot the six cabinet ministers at half past six in the morning against the wall of a hospital. There were ~~wet~~ pools of
stone paving   water in the courtyard . ~~There were~~ wet ~~dead~~ leaves ~~on~~ the/ stones
T was full. was ing
~~of th~~e courtyard /. It / rained hard. All the shutters of the hospital were nailed shut/

Based on these changes, a revised paragraph might have looked like this:

> There were pools of water in the courtyard [and] wet leaves ~~on~~ the stone[s / stone paving]. The courtyard was full. All the shutters of the hospital were nailed shut. It was raining hard.[23]

Gaining nothing from the ambiguous sentence "The courtyard was full," the draft also loses the grim, staccato sequence of seven simple sentences by joining "pools of water" and "wet leaves" into a single sentence. Hemingway considered this structural economy, then wisely returned to the emphatic simple sentences and repetitions of "There were" and "courtyard" that he began with. Returning "It rained hard" to its original place recaptures its menace—both symbolic and structural—in closing these repetitions with ominous brevity:

> There were pools of water in the courtyard.
> There were wet, dead leaves on the paving of the courtyard.
> It rained hard.

chapter 7 (Nick wounded)

Background and Drafts

Chapters 7 and 8 return the action to World War I but now shift the front to Italy, where Hemingway drove a Red Cross ambulance and then ran a frontline canteen until he was wounded. Unlike the earlier war chapters in first person, chapter 7 is narrated in third person and introduces us, for the first and only time in the book, to "Nick" as the point-of-view character. If third-person narration seems to impart a more objective tone here, it nonetheless leaves several ambiguities unresolved. As in chapter 1, the protagonist's nationality is uncertain, and the army is not American: the Italian "*Senta*" that Nick uses to address Rinaldi tells us that. Scholars have usually assumed that Nick is the Nick Adams of the stories Hemingway began writing in 1924.[24] But if so, why is this American fighting in the Italian army? Or is he an Italian whose speech is rendered mostly into American English, as seems likely for the French kitchen corporal in chapter 1? Or is he an Italian-American modeled on someone Hemingway knew in Chicago, as Michael Reynolds argues?[25]

Hemingway himself may have been uncertain about Nick's nationality. In the first draft of this chapter (KL 94a), Nick says, "*You're* no patriot Rinaldo" (emphasis mine), leaving open the possibility that Nick is American or Italian-American. The next draft substitutes "We're not patriots. . . . " Then, the declaration drops out altogether in the third draft but reappears in the final version, sans pronoun, in the breathless fragment "Not patriots." For the 1925 *In Our Time,* the complete sentence, "We're not patriots" is restored. The plurality of "patriots" in the published chapter 7 makes clear that Nick includes himself in the depiction. Would he have referred to himself this way, that is, fighting for his homeland, if he were *not* Italian? After the war the noncombatant

Hemingway boasted of having fought alongside the Italian Arditi that he so much admired. Nick's placement may well represent Hemingway's fictional self-projection, but how his American manqué comes to fight for the Italians is never explained.

Further problems arise if we assume Nick begins a unified Nick Adams experience, continued and developed in the stories. Here, Nick is wounded in the spine. In "Cross-Country Snow," he has a bum leg, presumably from a war wound. "Big Two-Hearted River," where he hikes briskly shouldering a heavy pack, makes no reference to a physical wound at all but hints strongly of a mental one. We have, therefore, not one Nick Adams experience, but rather variations on a theme of wounding.[26] One ambiguity in this chapter is typical of most chapters: the name, date, and locale of the battle in which Nick is wounded is never specified.[27]

Content

What is clear in this chapter is that Nick has been badly wounded during an Italian attack on an Austrian-held town. To be hit in the spine is no superficial wound: the narrative images the likely paralysis to follow as "Both his legs stuck out awkwardly" (originally: "rigidly") and, again, when Nick must turn his head "carefully" to speak to Rinaldi.[28] This central fact would seem to render ironic the bland statement that the attack "was going well"—not very well for Nick, it would seem. Yet, both the chapter's drafts and the final version in *in our time* convey Nick's "smiling sweatily" and laughing (in the first draft) at his own "good joke" (in the second draft). Indeed, this chapter was originally entitled "Humour."

The joke, however, is sardonic and a tad ambiguous. Nick informs the badly wounded, perhaps dying Rinaldi that "You and me we've made a separate peace. . . . Not patriots." *Nations* make a separate peace, as Russia did with the Central Powers in 1917; now, Nick ironically applies this grand language to his and Rinaldi's minuscule fate, just as Frederic Henry would later use it—with less irony—to describe his desertion. The woundings mean they are now out of combat, out of further danger, ultimately out of the army.[29] They no longer have to be—pretend to be?—patriots. But these are hardly "million dollar wounds" (as noncrippling wounds that sent a soldier home were called in the next great war), and Nick's joy at being freed—so contrary to the stereotypical loyalty depicted in propagandistic war literature—suggests how deeply he must have hated the war, how desperately he wanted out, even at the cost of being invalided out. Is Nick, then, smiling only at his verbal inflation, or laughing with relief that he and Rinaldi are now out of the battle, or both?

Or is he merely striking a pose? He requires an "audience" for his remarks, chooses a poor one in the badly wounded Rinaldi, who, lying facedown and "breathing with difficulty," is scarcely capable of responding or even listening, and feels "disappointed" when Rinaldi shows no sign of having heard these grandiose declarations. As in other war vignettes, communication is essentially one-way: the protagonist expresses feelings no one else seems to hear, or, as in chapter 1, the protagonist does not respond verbally when someone else speaks to him. Nick must enjoy his bitter joke by himself. Similarly, the soldier in chapter 8 "never told anybody" about Jesus, breaking a vow made under shellfire ostensibly to Jesus but really to himself.

Like the humor, the chapter's symbolism is as much ambivalent as ironic. Critics have long noted Hemingway's penchant for placing despairing characters "against the wall" (like the cabinet ministers in chapter 6), or having them turn toward it, like the Indian father in "Indian Camp" and Ole Andreson in "The Killers," as they confront situations with no way out. The symbol turns ironic when those walls belong to churches and hospitals, institutions that should provide spiritual comfort and physical healing. Hemingway no doubt intended the irony here when in an early draft he changed the wall of "a house" the wounded Nick sits against to the wall of "the church."[30] But the church wall *does* provide Nick at least the physical shelter that may have saved his life. Moreover, the sentence further on—"The sun shone on his face"—also has positive religious connotations that have eluded critical comment.[31]

Style

Unlike the preceding chapters, this one narrows its third-person perspective to the consciousness and actions of a single protagonist. This point of view and the chapter's greater length and number of sentences give it a more fictional feel. Beginning in medias res, the chapter sounds as if it were excerpted from a larger narrative. Within this limited perspective, Hemingway employs the modernist technique of merging objective narration and subjective perception.[32] The passage—"His face was sweaty and dirty. The sun shone on his face. The day was very hot"—encompasses both realms: the statements could be objective facts presented by a detached narrator or conditions Nick subjectively senses. The chapter's concluding sentence, lacking a "he thought" tag, also merges subjective and objective: "Rinaldi was a disappointing audience." Moreover, as Kathryn Derounian observes, the limited-omniscient point of view rigorously restricts details to what Nick can see, looking "forward":

> We see in detail Nick's view of the exact damage to the house opposite; we follow his glance down to the two dead Austrians lying in the rubble; we watch him shift his gaze ahead, beyond the house, and up the street; and finally, we move back with him as he carefully tries to look at his friend Rinaldi, lying nearby. (64)[33]

For all of its verisimilitude in narrative and perspective, however, the chapter is artfully shaped. Dramatically, it peaks with Nick's "smiling sweatily" at his own joke, then falls with "Rinaldi was a disappointing audience." Structurally, it balances parallel images: the wounded Nick and Rinaldi offset the two dead Austrians; Nick's wounding, causing his legs to stick out awkwardly, parallels the house's mutilation: "an iron bedstead hung twisted toward the street."

After the relatively long sentence that sets the scene with three actions, the sentences that follow are predominantly simple and short with only one longer compound in the middle ("The pink wall") for rhythmic contrast. This apparent sameness, however, does not prevent Hemingway from structurally highlighting his most important sentences. Arguably, the ironic sentence 13 ("It was going well") acts as one of the chapter's two thematic centers and is also the shortest complete sentence. Similarly, "Not patriots" expresses part of the key theme (Nick's relief in being out of future combat) in its most abbreviated, fragmented form.[34]

Sentence Structure and Sequence (*thematic center, **climax)	*Word Count*
1. simple‡ (adverb clause)	23
2. simple	05
3. simple	07
4. simple	06
5. simple	06
6. simple	05
7. simple	12
8. simple	05
9. compound	22

	10. simple	13
	11. simple	06
	12. simple	07
	★13. simple	04
	14. simple	08
	15. compound predicate	10
monologue	16. simple (imperative)	02
"	17. simple (imperative)	01
"	★18. simple	08
	19. simple‡ (participle)	09
monologue	★20. fragment	02
	★★21. simple‡ (participle)	08
	22. simple	05
	Total	174

chapter 8 (the praying soldier)

Background

The setting here is more definite than in chapter 7, since "Fossalta" identifies a place on the Piave River, where, on 16 June 1918, the Italians had halted the Austrian offensive.[35] On the Piave, in a forward observation post, the eighteen-year-old Hemingway was badly wounded by an Austrian trench mortar on the night of 8 July 1918.

Content

Chapter 8 abandons Nick and the limited-omniscient point of view of the preceding chapter and returns to the semi-anonymous character-narrators of the other war chapters (1, 4, and 5). The point of view here is shifting and ambiguous, with problems Hemingway did not fully resolve. The chapter appears to begin in third person, focusing on the praying soldier (identified only as "he"). The soldier's desperate litany, however, which occupies almost half the chapter and is not set off by quotation marks, repeats "I" or "me" enough to establish a first-person presence. The voice in "The shelling moved further up the line" could belong to either the praying soldier or the anonymous narrator of sentence 1; but the next sentence ("We went to work on the trench. . . .") introduces a new pronoun and a new character, a comrade of the praying soldier, whose peripheral point of view, we discover, has governed the narrative all along.

This point-of-view ambiguity continues in the concluding sentence:

"And he never told anybody." As George Cheatham notes, first-person peripheral point of view renders this statement implausible since the narrator "cannot *know,* nor even realistically forecast, the first soldier's future." Similarly, the soldier-narrator must overhear his comrade's prayers even though they seem more likely thought than spoken. Cheatham concludes: "The first-person plural *we* [of "We went to work on the trench. . . . "] thus suggests an unrealistically double narrator, one who is both a participant in the story and at the same time an omniscient voice outside the story."[36] As the "Drafts" section below will show, these point-of-view problems resulted when Hemingway changed his mind about who should narrate the chapter.

The theme of this chapter anticipates and rebuts in advance the World War II saying, "There are no atheists in foxholes." In Hemingway's vision of war, once one is out of the foxhole or trench—out of mortal danger—this false religiosity fades. And little wonder if it arises only as a desperate expression of self-preservation. Underscoring this point, the chapter originally bore the ironic title, "Religion." What may seem self-evident to modern readers, however, would still have the power to shock readers in 1924, particularly the lowercase "jesus."[37]

What *is* genuine in this chapter is the fear, vulnerability, and aloneness a soldier experiences under artillery fire.[38] In a carefully composed sentence, Hemingway captures the terrifying danger (the bombardment "knocking the trench to pieces"), the praying soldier's pitiful efforts not to be hit ("he lay very flat"), and his fearful responses, both physiological and psychological ("sweated and prayed") Significantly, none of these responses accounts for his escape. The sentence that signifies the soldier's survival—"The shelling moved further up the line"—is flatly objective and structurally detached from his prayers. Chance—and nothing else—spares the praying soldier.[39]

The next sentence—"We went to work on the trench"—further diminishes the praying soldier's importance. Everything about this sentence isolates his experience. In place of his helplessness, "we" are doing something (rebuilding the trench); the terrifying, roaring night has become a sunny morning, "hot and muggy and cheerful and quiet." Most important, the soldier-narrator expresses no sympathy for his praying comrade in this sentence, indeed does not even refer to him except in the ambiguous "we" (which probably refers to their entire unit). Given all these facts—the desperate, self-preserving motive of the soldier's prayer, the role of chance in his survival, the narrator's cool detachment, and the contrast of the day's activities to the praying soldier's night of agony—it is hardly surprising that, once out of danger, he fails to keep his promise to Jesus and prefers to follow prostitutes instead. But the chapter's closure—"And he never told anyone"—is even more emphatically ironic, as if to nail down the shallowness of trench-borne religiosity. The narrator's detachment from the praying soldier's fear now evolves into contempt for his weak character.

Recalling the parallel images of wounding and violation in chapter 7 (Nick's sprawled legs and the twisted iron bedstead), this chapter balances alternative recourses—religion and sex—once a soldier confronts his precarious mortality. Both alternatives briefly cauterize his despair, numb his sense of vulnerability. The choice is one Hemingway would use again in *A Farewell to Arms,* when Frederic Henry reflects on why he chose to go whoring in Milan on his leave rather than visit the priest's family in Abruzzi. Drafts of chapter 8 include another anesthetic typical in Hemingway's work: drinking; the narrator (here, the praying soldier) has downed two bottles of Capri at mess before he visits the officer's whorehouse (KL 94a).

Style

The most striking feature of this chapter's style is the dramatic and structural contrast between the praying soldier's desperate monologue and the narrator's uninflected, seemingly matter-of-fact statements. Indeed, the first sentence brilliantly fuses the two voices, segueing seamlessly from narrative into monologue. The prayer's litany is repetitious—"please" appears no fewer than six times, "get me out" twice—and intermingles complex structures (the promises) and inarticulate fragments as the sentences seem to tumble into each other like shell blasts. In sharp contrast, "The shelling moved further up the line," which separates the narrator from the praying soldier, is simple and objective, followed by an equally distinctive, long run-on with three main clauses and a string of four adjectives: "We went to work on the trench and in the morning the sun came up and the day was hot and muggy and cheerful and quiet." This sentence balances the praying soldier's three terrified actions at night ("lay very flat and sweated and prayed") with three constructive and cheerful actions the next day. Finally, like chapter 7, this chapter ends with a dying fall, but the last sentence also provides a definite closure by implausibly projecting the praying soldier's behavior into the infinite future. In so doing, the sentence jerks us out of the present-time action, just as the concluding sentence in chapter 1 does, and provides a disorienting look at the soldier's future.

Sentence Structure and Sequence (★thematic center, ★★climax)		*Word Count*
monologue	1. complex-compound (f-s)	27
"	2. simple (imperative)	06
"	3. fragment	05
"	4. complex	13
"	5. compound‡ (object clause)	19
"	6. fragment	04
	★★7. simple	07
	8. compound (triple)	26
	9. simple‡ (adjective clause)	22
	★10. simple	05
	Total	134

Drafts

The evolution of this chapter shows much about Hemingway's compositional process and his techniques of objectification and autobiographical concealment. As George Cheatham has shown, Hemingway first drafted the chapter to make the praying soldier the first-person narrator, excluding the fellow soldier's voice and role altogether. In the fourth draft Hemingway rewrote the chapter in an omniscient third-person point of view, again leaving out the fellow soldier. Finally, his fifth draft recaptures the immediacy of the first three drafts but now gives the first-person narrator's role to the fellow soldier, while the praying soldier is still objectified as "he." Cheatham concludes:

> [The creation of the fellow soldier as the first-person voice] allows the narrator to maintain, grammatically, his distance from the first soldier's fear (*he,* not *I,* is afraid) and at the same time allows him to reclaim, grammatically, the cause of that fear, the experience of combat (*we,* not *they,* are in the trench). . . .
>
> Apparently, even as Hemingway obliquely confessed his fear by rewriting a personal painful experience, he at the same time denied that fear by projecting it onto a fictional other. . . . The frightened distributor of chocolates made himself over, *first,* into a frightened combat soldier, then into a dispassionately courageous combat soldier who witnessed, reported, and dissected another's fear. ("Hemingway's Process of Appropriation" 65)

This objectification appears elsewhere in *in our time.* In chapter 3, for example, the ambiguous sentence fragment "Scared sick looking at it" might originally have been the author's response to the woman *he* watched having a baby, particularly when we recall that Hemingway later imputed the experience to his fictional persona, Nick Adams: "He'd seen a woman have a baby on the road to Karagatch and tried to help her" (*Nick Adams Stories* 238). Objectification occurs again in chapter 10, as the unlucky recipient of the Dear John letter shifts from "I" to "he." What all of these transformations conceal is a first-person protagonist drawn from Hemingway's own experience who admits to fear or betrayal and humiliation. Projecting these experiences onto a third-person "he" thus expunges any hints of autobiographical shame from the narrative and permits it to assume what Cheatham calls a "dispassionate" distance from the shameful act.

One other significant development in the drafts is the gradual appearance of "the girl" and the even more belated reappearance of "Jesus." The earliest draft excludes them both:

> day my ~~a whore~~
> The next ~~night~~ leave came and that night I was drunk in the officers whorehouse in Mestre (KL 671)

In the next draft, the speaker first "didn't tell anyone that night in the officers[' mess]." Emending that, Hemingway introduces the whore:

> that night we were relieved. And
> ~~xxxx~~ the girl the next night
> I'~~xxxxxxx~~ didn't tell anyone ~~that night in the officers~~ at the Villa Rossa in at Mestre where we went after two bottles of Capri at dinner. And I've never told anybody. (KL 94a)

What didn't he tell? The ambiguous sentence leaves open the possibility that it was his abject fear and desperate prayers the soldier did not want to talk about, especially to his fellow officers. Surely, he would not try to proselytize *them!* The draft that first changes the praying soldier from "I" to "he" (KL 94a) finally gives the girl primacy but only adds "about Jesus" as an afterthought in handwriting.

These changes suggest a clear priority to the events of chapter 8: most important is the soldier-narrator's fearful prayer, appearing almost intact in all drafts; next, his efforts to forget the experience, drinking and whoring at Mestre; then his understandable reluctance to "tell" about something—either the experience or Jesus; and finally, his failure to tell "the girl" "about Jesus." The possibility that the narrator does not "tell" of his fear under fire strengthens the view that Hemingway changed narrators because he considered this thoroughly understandable fear shameful and did not wish to "tell" his readers about it in a voice they might think was his own.[40]

chapter 9 (Drevitts and Boyle)

Background and Content

The origins of this crime vignette—one of only two in the book—date to Hemingway's stint as a cub reporter on the *Kansas City Star* in 1917–18. A page-three story on 19 November 1917, which Hemingway may have written, headlined "Death Breaks Up a Gang," describes an Italian gang's robbery of a cigar store and the subsequent shooting of two gang members by two police detectives.[41] Interestingly, among the many alterations Hemingway made in his fictional version, he reduces the number of thieves to the two who were shot and changes their identity to Hungarian, retaining their Italian ethnicity only in the bigoted and false assumption of Boyle, the cop who shoots both robbers.[42] Another important difference: in the original story, the robbers were armed with revolvers and provoked the shooting by attempting "to drive their team over the detectives when ordered to stop." By omitting these facts (thus precluding the detectives' justification of self-defense), the chapter makes the robbers seem more vulnerable (two against two) and Boyle more bloodthirsty. Moreover, in "backing" their wagon out of the alley (in the chapter version), the Hungarians face away from the narrative's point of view, which implies that Boyle shot them in the back. The Italians in the actual event must have faced the detectives in attempting to run them down. As Michael Reynolds observes, "the implication [of Boyle's actions and comments] is that it was permissible to kill Italians in 1917 in Kansas City, which had a large Italian immigrant population" ("Two Hemingway Sources" 36).

Content

These changes from the newspaper story present the fictional cops as scarcely better than the criminals they kill. Boyle is bigoted, stupid, and homicidal; Drevitts is worried only about the trouble the shooting may cause them. In fact, the dialogue that occupies half the chapter simply contrasts Drevitts's nervousness with Boyle's belligerent confidence. But

Drevitts does manage to ask a crucial and logical question—"how did you know they were wops when you bumped them?"—to which Boyle can only reply with the bigot's age-old assertion: "I can tell wops a mile off." Considering how little space Hemingway devotes to the action (which he could easily have expanded to include the original robbers' attempt to run over the detectives), and considering how briefly he refers to the Hungarians, it seems clear that he wanted this contrasting study of two policemen—one brutal, the other merely weak—to be his focal point.

Style

The narrative opens with an establishing sentence and ends with a deflatingly ironic closer that does not close. Three voices are juxtaposed. The narrative voice is objective but even flatter than the image-laden descriptions in chapters 3 and 6. Indeed, the first sentence sounds like an entry in a police blotter: it lacks imagistic color, and only the colloquial "got into" (originally, "robbed") energizes the tone slightly. Contrasting this flatness, the voices of Boyle and Drevitts—invented characters—dramatize the narrative. Boyle's "ain't," Drevitts's "bumped," as well as the bullying repetition of Boyle's snarling retort to Drevitts's fear—"They're crooks ain't they? . . . They're wops ain't they? Who the hell is going to make any trouble?"—are the cops' linguistic membership cards in the tough-guy club of street crime and street punishment (drafts of the chapter were variously entitled "Crime" and "Crime and Punishment").

In the action that follows the opening sentence, two rather slight stylistic changes from the news story show Hemingway's technique of creating action through sentence structure. First, he shifts the tense of sentence three to past progressive: "The Hungarians *were backing* their wagon out of an alley" (emphasis mine). Following the summary past of "Drevitts and Boyle drove up," this shift briefly dramatizes the action before the next sentence, "Boyle shot," returns it to summary. That sentence, however, has its own color. The original news story read: "They were shot on the seat of a covered wagon" ("Two Hemingway Sources" 34). Hemingway's creation of two separate shootings in two locations and his powerful prepositions—"Boyle shot one *off* the seat of the wagon and one *out of* the wagon box" (emphasis mine)—vivify the key action by doubling it and making it dynamic. Visually and figuratively, the Hungarians are being "bumped off."[43]

Sentence Structure and Sequence (★climax)			*Word Count*
		1. simple	19
		2. simple	14
		3. simple	10
		4. simple	16
		5. complex	10
dialogue:	a	6. simple (+ speech tag)	10
"		7. simple	11
"	b	8. compound (f) (+ speech tag)	06
"		9. compound (f)	04
"		10. simple	09
"	a	11. compound-complex (+ speech tag)	20
"	b	★12. simple (+ speech tag)	10
		Total	139

Drafts

Besides the changes already noted, the drafts for this chapter show two small alterations Hemingway made to maintain the police blotter tone of the opening even as he dramatized the shooting. First, he moved the phrase "at two o'clock in the morning" to the front of the first sentence to make the opening sound less like narrative, more like a report. Second, he broke up the logical and efficient complex sentence

> Drevitts and Boyle drove up in a ford car from the Fifteenth Street police station as the Hungarians were backing the wagon out of an alley. (94a)

into a simple sequence, again trading narrative for the reportorial:

> Drevitts and Boyle drove up from the Fifteenth Street police station in a Ford. The Hungarians were backing their wagon out of an alley.

Paradoxically, the very blandness of this reportorial style intensifies Boyle's homicidal criminality by yawning at it, as a bored desk sergeant might do in writing it up, in effect confirming what Boyle assumes: "Who the hell is going to make any trouble?"

chapter 10 (the recovering soldier and Ag)

Background

This chapter can be studied in several contexts. Joined with the chapters depicting Nick's wounding and the praying soldier under shellfire (7 and 8), it rounds out the Italian war chapters, as the themes progress from soldiers' behavior under fire, to the protagonist wounded, to the protagonist recovering in a hospital and returning to the front before going home. Readers of *A Farewell to Arms* will quickly recognize this chapter as a prototype of the novel's love affair between a recovering soldier and his nurse, but with a far more cynical conclusion. And the biographically minded will recognize parallels between this love affair and Hemingway's blighted affair with Red Cross nurse Agnes von Kurowsky from July 1918 to March 1919—a romance that proved as shattering to him as his wounding and that he would rewrite yet again five years later. Since the contours of the Hemingway-von Kurowsky love affair are widely known, if not fully agreed upon,[44] my discussion of biographical origins and fictional inventions will limit itself to a few noteworthy details.

Agnes's infamous Dear John letter (actually, "Ernie, dear boy") of 7 March 1919 differs from the chapter's version in a few key respects.[45] Unlike the fictional Ag, Agnes never describes their relationship with the hurtful phrase "a boy and girl affair"; rather, she states: "I am now & always will be too old, & that's the truth, & I can't get away from the fact that you're just a boy—a kid." Ag's callow and unintentionally humorous "she expected, absolutely unexpectedly, to be married in the spring" was also Hemingway's snide alteration of "Then—& believe me when I say this is sudden for me, too—I expect to be married soon." Missing from Ag's letter are Agnes's frequent references to Hemingway as "kid,"[46] her claim that he behaved "like a spoiled child" on their trip from Padua to Milan, and her closing wish that "you'll . . . show what a man you really are [in accepting our breakup]." In fine, the Ag that Hemingway creates sounds more callow, self-centered, frivolous, and oblivious to these qualities than does the original. And Ag lacks Agnes's empathetic recognition that she was simply too old for this sometimes immature boy to seriously consider marrying him.

One source for the chapter's bitterly ironic conclusion—the young man having sex with a shop girl in a taxi and getting gonorrhea from her—appears in Hemingway's letter to Howell Jenkins, written about two months after he received Agnes's breakup letter:

> Had a very sad letter from Ag from Rome yesterday. She has fallen out with her Major. She is in a hell of a way mentally and says I should feel revenged for what she did to me. Poor damned kid. I'm sorry as hell for her. But there's nothing I can do. I loved her once and then she gypped me. And I don't blame her. But I set out to cauterize out her memory and I burnt it out with a course of booze and other women and now it's gone. (*Selected Letters* 25).

The recurring theme in Hemingway's 1920s fiction of blighted love between a wounded soldier and his nurse belies the bravado of this letter.[47] Scott Donaldson observes that Hemingway had to "get rid of it [rancor against Agnes] by writing about it" ("'A Very Short Story' as Therapy" 105), but the cure for the hurt took longer. Like Hemingway's response to his physical wounding at Fossalta, this "treatment" also required that he revisit the subject—returns that may seem more like an obsessional symptom than a cure. In part, this writing therapy had to deform a sincere Agnes into a frivolous and hurtful Ag and exorcise the latter before both could be transformed five years later into a loving, faithful, and submissive fantasy figure, Catherine Barkley.

Content and Style

The love affair between the recovering solider (referred to only as "he") and Ag progresses through seven stages: (1) the sexual affair dramatized in the present; (2) the sexual affair over the next three months encompassing his operation and recovery; (3) the couple's increasing seriousness in wanting and failing to marry before he returns to the front; (4) the letters he received at the front showing how much Ag misses him; (5) their agreement after the armistice detailing what he must do before Ag will come to the States and their argument at parting over her not being willing to come at once; (6) their separation, Ag's new love affair with an Italian major, and her Dear John letter, closely paraphrased by the narrator; and (7) the outcomes for each following the letter.

Each section conveys its theme through repeated words and phrases. The sexuality of the first two sections appears in an image that "he" finds exciting to contemplate: Ag in his bed. Thus, "Ag sat on the bed" (sentence 6); she "would not have to get up from the bed" (12); and "he thought of Ag in his bed" (14).[48] When the romance turns serious, "marriage" becomes the key word: "They wanted to get married" (17); "They felt as though they were married" (18); "they wanted everyone to know about it" (18). "Married" returns in the fifth stage, but significantly it now becomes the conditional "be married" (22, 26). And to "be married" now requires conditions ("agreed" 22, "understood" 24) before she will "come" (23, 26) and he will "come" to meet her (23). (The punning implications here seem an intentional irony: in the hospital, coming required no such conditions.) Tellingly, Ag's coming is always couched in the negative—"Ag would not come home until. . . . "; "her not being willing to come home at once"—a structural foreshadowing of the unhappy outcome, just as "so they could not lose it" is a thematic foreshadowing. Reinforcing this gloom, of course, is "quarrel" (26, 27).

The repetitions in the next stage are the most interesting because Hemingway relies on images to convey motivation. The first draft's suggestion that Ag's loneliness drove her to infidelity, slightly emended in the second draft ("It was lonely and rainy there"), now becomes fully imagistic. It is winter (32) and rainy (31, 32) and muddy (32)—the kind of weather that keeps nurses and officers indoors, where socializing becomes the chief entertainment. The key sentence (32) repeats and combines these images:

> Living in the muddy, rainy town in the winter the major of the battalion made love to Ag.

As in chapters 3 and 6, rain images despair.

Ag's Dear John letter, likewise, repeats key phrases: the devastating "boy and girl" affair (33, 34) that their romance now seems to her and how "absolutely" certain she is of everything. The conclusion parodies her hyperbole by negating it in kind: "not . . . any" (37) and "never" (38) prevail.

A quick glance at the prose paragraphs—lengthy ones for *in our time*—shows that the story is heavily narrated with no dialogue. As Robert Scholes has astutely observed, the opening, "One hot evening in Milan," the closing summary of the characters' fortunes, and even the subsequent title "A Very Short Story," combine with this story*telling* mode to parody the old-fashioned, fairy-tale format that begins "Once upon a time" and ends "They lived happily ever after" ("Decoding Papa" 114–15). As befits a fairy tale, this parody is about lovers who become separated. But it cynically reverses the "ever after" ending into "never after": "the Major did not marry her in the spring, *or any other time.* Ag *never* got an answer to her letter to Chicago about it" (emphasis mine). And for "him," the story reduces "ever-after" romantic love into a travesty of quickie sex and venereal disease. This parody of a heavily narrated, storytelling style represents still another context for chapter 10.

Within this storytelling mode, narrative time shifts several times, each marked by a corresponding shift in sentence structure. The opening paragraph dramatizes present-time action; by using simple and compound structures, sentences 1–7 slow the narrative movement to intensify individual perceptions: "There were chimney swifts in the sky. . . . Ag sat on the bed. She was cool and fresh in the hot night." The action and pace thus dramatize the romance at its most passionate stage.

Paragraphs 2 through 6, however, shift to summary exposition, interspersed with brief snippets of dramatic action or description, for instance, "[The Duomo] was dim and quiet." The sentences correspondingly change to complex sentence structure so as to compress maximal information most efficiently. This long section shatters the stereotype that Hemingway avoided complex sentences: of the twenty-nine sentences in these paragraphs, eight are complex and fifteen more contain dependent clauses or participles. At times, this compression yokes together disparate actions that might well have been separately dramatized or at least summarized in more detail:

> Living in the muddy, rainy town in the winter the major of the battalion made love to Ag, and she had never known Italians before, and finally wrote a letter to the States that theirs had been only a boy and girl affair.

The opening participle ("Living") leisurely begins an action in the indefinite present, and several intruding prepositional phrases further slow it. Since this announcement of Ag's infidelity is crucial to the narrative, both its leisurely pace and thematic importance seem to anticipate several more sentences of development. But the main clause ("the major . . . made love to Ag") yields to an entirely separate idea, Ag not knowing Italians. This statement is both punning and ambiguous: Had never known them as lovers? Had never known them at all? Had never known their romantic style and degree of sincerity? The statement begs for clarification, but once again a new action—Ag's writing the Dear John letter—is piggybacked onto the sentence and even includes that letter's most devastating sentence: "theirs had been only a boy and girl affair." The summarized action has accelerated breathlessly in this fusion. It is almost as if the narrative, having set the psychological scene of Ag's betrayal, cannot bear to recount the details of the new affair and, after an explanatory swipe at Ag's naiveté, jumps ahead to the crucial fact from "his" perspective: the Dear John letter and its most destructive claim. Underscoring the sentence's climactic import is its length: at forty-three words it is the longest by far of the chapter's many long sentences.

In glaring contrast to this section's reliance on complex structures, one fragment stands out: "Only get a job and be married." Its difference heightens its thematic importance, for this is the most extreme expression of "his" reformed, quasi-puritanical seriousness in fulfilling Ag's expectations.

In Ag's breakup letter, Hemingway again shifts the style, not simply to summarize its contents, or to capture Ag's voice objectively, but to satirize her savagely. Following the startling compressions of sentence 32 ("Living in the muddy. . . . ") and its coup de main of the "boy and girl affair," the next sentence ("She was sorry. . . . ") blathers into a run-on with three main clauses as well as a clumsy compound predicate in the middle:

> She was sorry, and she knew he would probably not be able to understand, but might some day forgive her, and be grateful to her, and she expected, absolutely unexpectedly, to be married in the spring.

The ludicrous "expected absolutely unexpectedly" presents Ag as an airhead, an impression reinforced by the repetitions and hyperbolic prose throughout: "she believed in him absolutely"; "She *knew* it was for the best" (emphasis mine). Her sentence—"She loved him as always, but she realized now it was only a boy and girl love"—is both nonsensical (How can she love him "as always" if she's now in love with the major?) and thoughtlessly cruel in repeating the "boy and girl affair." Finally, by restating the letter's contents in third person, the entire passage robs Ag of whatever dignity her own voice might have conferred. Scholes is exactly right in concluding that this pseudo-objective retelling of the crucial letter is really out to get its author ("Decoding Papa" 118).

The most dramatic shift of style occurs in the "unhappily ever after" denouement. The sentences telling the outcome of Ag's and the Major's love affair now assume a kind of deadpan factuality of simple statements. But as Scholes and others have observed, the "never after" extensions into infinity, (echoing "And he never told anyone" of chapter 8) acquire a vengeful glee in underscoring Ag's failure ("Decoding Papa" 120). In their pseudo-objective finality, the simple structures *reinforce* her failures, linger over them by devoting entire sentences to each. By contrast, "his" fate—that of the chapter's real protagonist—is dramatized into a complex (and unintentionally ambiguous) sentence.[49] If his outcome is equally dismal and even more bitterly antiromantic, at least he has actively participated in achieving it.

Paragraph	*Sentence Structure and Sequence* (*thematic center, **climax)	*Word count*
1.	1. compound	23
	2. simple	07
	3. compound	11
	4. compound predicate	10
	5. simple	10
	6. simple	05
	7. simple	09
2.	8. simple	08
	9. simple‡ (infinitive clause)	06
	10. complex-compound	21
	11. complex	23
	12. complex	22
	13. compound	12
	14. simple	04
	15. complex	14
3.	16. complex-compound predicate	14
	17. compound‡ (participle)	14
	18. triple compound	21
	*19. compound‡ (2 object clauses, 2 infinitive clauses)	25
4.	20. simple‡ (object clause)	13
	21. compound-compound predicate	18
[Ag's style]	22. simple‡ (multiple adverbial clauses)	30
5.	23. simple‡ (object clauses)	18
	24. complex	20
	25. compound‡ (object clause)	21
	**26. fragment	08
	27. simple‡ (object clause)	21
	28. complex-compound predicate	23
	29. simple‡ (participle)	09
6.	30. simple	09
	31. complex	11

	32. compound‡ (adverbial clause)	17
[Ag's style]	★33. compound‡ (participle, object clause)	43
"	34. triple compound‡ (compound object clause, infinitive clause)	36
"	35. compound‡ (object clause)	17
"	36. compound predicate‡ (object clause)	13
"	37. simple‡ (object clause)	07
7.	38. simple	13
	39. simple	12
	40. simple‡ (participle)	21
	Total	639

Drafts

As Scholes and others have demonstrated, Hemingway objectified this chapter, just as he did chapter 8, by changing the first-person narrator of the original draft to the unnamed third-person "he." In so doing, the author attempts to conceal the story's autobiographical origins and its narrative bias for "him" and against Ag in what purports to be an objectively told story.[50]

The drafts of chapter 10 (the first candidly labeled "Personal," the second sardonically entitled "Love") show that the chapter evolved in Hemingway's imagination from a rather wistful, first-person recollection of the loss of true love to an increasingly bitter third-person narrative that intensifies Ag's sins, while presenting the young man as being ever more sinned against. The short first version (KL 633), a two-page handwritten draft, presents the couple in a mutually loving relationship, writing letters to each other from different parts of the hospital when they are not in bed together, with the narrator concluding "We loved each other very much." As in the final version, the lovers want to marry in Italy but cannot meet the state's bureaucratic requirements; thus, "After the armistice I went home to get a job so we could get married." Ag's infidelity is implied so vaguely that the reference to her *not* marrying the major and to the Dear John letter comes with the same shocking suddenness that its real-life counterpart must have had for Hemingway:

> It was lonely there and there was a battalion of Arditi quartered in the town.
> ~~She didn't marry the Major so she wrote me~~ [. . .] ~~after a while~~
> When the letter came saying ours had been only a kid affair I got awfully drunk.

Similarly, Ag's failure to marry the major appears simply as naive telling:

> The major never married her
> ~~didn't marry her after all.~~ (KL 633)

Instead of malice toward Ag's infidelity, the conclusion emphasizes the narrator's hurting responses: he gets "awfully drunk" and then gets "a dose of clap from a girl in Chicago riding in a yellow taxi."

The second draft (KL 94a) distances the narrative from the author by using third person and darkens the romance considerably by omitting the lovers' exchange of letters in the hospital, adding their quarrel on the train (without giving its cause), and developing Ag's affair with the major. The narrator both asserts Ag's naiveté—"she had never known Italians before"—and has her acknowledge it, while snubbing her in return:

> She never got an answer to her second letter to Chicago saying it had all been a mistake about the major.

As Paul Smith points out, the much more fully developed published version—nearly twice as long—suggests a lost third draft (26). The additions and deletions here continue to expunge the romantic treatment of the affair in earlier drafts: gone is the sentimental "They loved each other very much." And the romance becomes increasingly imbalanced: paragraph 5, for example, develops the conditions that "he" must fulfill before Ag will consent to come to the States and marry him. Scholes and other critics have noted the one-sidedness of these demands—he must get a job, stop drinking—and the absurdity in his not even "wanting" to see his friends. Thus, she continues her single life, while he virtually relinquishes his in wanting "Only to get a job and be married." The published version also develops Ag's devastating Dear John letter, and it lingers deliciously over her failure to marry the major. Yet, in its carefully nuanced imagery of winter in Torre di Mosto, it also creates a more empathetic context for Ag's infidelity. All of these additions develop her characterization and intensify the bitterness of the antiromantic conclusion.

chapter 11 (the revolutionist)

Background

This portrait of a revolutionary classifies chapter 11 as political, but it differs significantly from the other political chapters: 3, 6, and 18. While chapters 6 and 18 dramatize the mortal risks of practical politics once a revolution has occurred—mass executions, house arrest—this one studies the psychology of a very young true believer, one who would create such a revolution. And while the other three chapters evolve from real events in 1922 resulting from the Greco-Turkish War, this fiction is built on and subtly alludes to a broader political oscillation of revolution and reaction in Hungary and Italy from 1919 to 1922.

Both Hungary and Italy experienced revolutions in the political vacuum created by the armistice of World War I. A Bolshevik commune briefly established itself in Budapest in the spring and summer of 1919, only to be brutally overthrown by the "White Terror," a far-right reaction led by the proto-fascist, Milan Horthy. A Magyar, the revolutionist in chapter 11 "had suffered very much under the whites," who "had done some very bad things to him." His torture also helps explain why the revolutionist is on the move and now in nearby Italy. And, in an example of Hemingway's art of omission, it explains why this lover of Renaissance art "did not like Mantegna," since Mantegna's *Crucifixion* in Milan depicts Christ's death with a graphic realism unmatched by any other Italian Renaissance painter—and unredeemed by the promise of resurrection.[51] Frederic Henry would later coach Catherine Barkley on Mantegna's "bitter nail holes" so shockingly evident in Christ's foregrounded feet. For the Hungarian revolutionary, the painting is a reminder not only of how he was tortured for his own faith, but how his martyrdom might ultimately prove futile.

Italy, too, wavered between extremes in 1919. Its soon-to-be fascist dictator, Benito Mussolini, began his political career as a socialist, writing for the socialist newspaper, *Avanti*. It is noteworthy that the revolutionist wraps his pictures of Renaissance art in a copy of this newspaper—a symbolic anticipation of just how "badly" the Leftist movement would go in the next years.[52] For readers of 1924, the revolutionary's hopes of 1919 look all the more quixotic after Mussolini's fascist government had established itself in 1922.[53]

Although chapter 11 is relatively unimportant in the Hemingway oeuvre, the story bears several interesting linkages to other chapters of *in our time* and to subsequent novels. Paul Smith feels that it resembles chapter 10 in being "a narrative of disillusionment" (31), although it is doubtful whether that disillusionment applies to the revolutionist himself. Moreover, the two chapters differ markedly in their tone: this one understates what chapter 10 shouts in bitter irony. Both the narrator's tone and point of view resemble chapter 8, in which the first-person narrator also describes a "comrade" with cool detachment. Jake Barnes would later describe Robert Cohn in *The Sun Also Rises* as "a nice boy" and "very shy," and like the revolutionist's political idealism, Cohn's romantic idealism did not at all suit his time and place. *A Farewell to Arms* returns to the motifs of being on the run, going underground, and viewing Switzerland as a haven. Like the revolutionist, Frederic Henry is aided by a loose underground working in the Italian railway stations, but Henry's political luck is better in Switzerland: his arrest is temporary, whereas the revolutionist of chapter 11 lands in a Swiss jail. Finally, the revolutionist's naive idealism anticipates similar sentiments expressed by a young Cuban revolutionary to his prisoner, Harry Morgan, in *To Have and Have Not.* Once again, the narrator, Morgan, is deeply skeptical.

Content and Style

The futility of revolutionary idealism in the postwar world is an unmistakable theme in this chapter, but critics disagree somewhat as to whether the protagonist is simply naive or someone whose faith in the revolution has become "precarious" and maintained only through a kind of psycho-social withdrawal symbolized by his eager anticipation of walking alone over the Saint Bernard Pass into Switzerland. In fact, these two views can be easily merged in Eric Hoffer's characterization of the true believer—one whose psychological need to cling to the true faith will withstand any number of reality shocks.[54] The revolutionist's fondness for the early Renaissance masters—Giotto, Masaccio, Piero della Francesca—hints at his identification with their themes of martyrdom and resurrection; ironically, the revolution he works for would, if successful, proscribe these images.

The narrator tells us that the revolutionist "believed altogether in the world revolution" despite his past experience.[55] Confronted with the narrator's bleak assessment of Italy's ripeness for revolution, the revolutionist again resorts to denial and theory: "But it will go better, he said. You have everything here. It is the one country that everyone is sure of. It is the starting point of everything." Hemingway uses several stylistic techniques to undermine this fanatical optimism. His narrator, like the narrator in chapter 8, is only ostensibly a "comrade"; in fact, his skeptical detachment counterpoints the protagonist's mentality. He answers the revolutionist's question bluntly and negatively, and he does not respond to the revolutionist's hyperbolic optimism ("it will go better," and so on). Also familiar is the ironic fall of the last sentence following the revolutionist's repeated statements about his eagerness to walk into Switzerland; similarly deflating denouements appear in chapters 5, 10, 13, and 18.

Hemingway's most subversive device, however, is the chapter's insistent hyperbole. Nowhere in *in our time* do we find more *verys* (eight in thirty sentences). Nearly all describe the revolutionist. He is "very shy" (repeated three times), "very nice," suffered "very much," thanks the narrator "very much," and was "very eager" to walk over the pass. The narrator's contrary assessment of Italy's political situation mocks this absolutism: the movement is going "very badly." Other phrases are also extreme:

> aid him in *any* way
> He was . . . *quite* young
> He had *no* money
> The people were *all* kind
> he believed *altogether* in world revolution
> You have *everything* here.
> It is the one country that *everyone* is sure of.
> It will be the starting point of *everything.*

By contrast, when the narrator does not describe, quote, or answer the revolutionist—that is, when he appears to speak in his own voice about his own interests—that voice becomes moderate and rather similar to Jake Barnes's: "We had a good trip together. It was early September and the country was pleasant."

As with Ag's hyperbole in chapter 10, these extremities, repeated with Steinian "insistence," undermine the character. But where hyperbole makes Ag appear shallow, it makes the revolutionist seem unworldly and fanatical, unable to see the world in grays or to live with uncertainties. Significantly, the most overstated passage is the revolutionist's declaration of faith—"But it will go better . . . You have everything here. It is the one country that everyone is sure of. It is the starting point of everything"—in which the first sentence is melioristic, the other three hyperbolic. The narrative mimics not only the revolutionist's absolutism but also his speech patterns in a paragraph recounting his Italian experiences. Note how sentences 9 and 10 invert subject and object to capture the revolutionist's syntax: "Giotto . . . he bought reproductions of. . . . " and "Mantegna he did not like." Finally, Hemingway's original title for this chapter, "Youth," completes this character study of naive idealism, of the true-believing martyr destined to sustain innumerable hardships as he forces his two-dimensional ideology onto a three-dimensional world that has little use for either idealism or naiveté.

Paragraph	*Sentence Structure and Sequence* (★thematic center, ★★climax)	*Word Count*
1.	1. simple‡ (multiple participles & clauses)	50
	2. simple	07
	3. compound	19
	4. compound	15
2.	5. simple	05
monologue	6. simple (+ speech tag)	07
"	7. simple	05
reported	8. compound predicate (3)	12
monologue	9. compound predicate‡ (adverbial clause)	19
	10. simple	05
3.	11. compound‡ (adverbial clause)	24
	12. simple	06
	13. compound	09
	14. simple	11
	15. simple	09
	16. simple	06
	★★17. simple	11
4. dialogue a	18. simple (+ speech tag)	10
" b	19. fragment (+ speech tag)	04
" a	20. simple (+ speech tag)	07
"	21. simple	04
"	22. simple‡ (noun clause)	10
"	★★23. simple	08
	★ [climax via omission]	
5.	24. complex	25
	25. simple	09
monologue	26. simple (+ speech tag)	10
	27. simple‡ (object clause)	15
	28. compound‡ (object clause)	17
	29. simple‡ (adverbial-infinitive clause)	14
	30. complex (elliptical)	14
	Total	367

chapter 12 (the gored horse)

Background

The five bullfight chapters (12–16) were all written after Hemingway had seen several bullfights in Spain and, indeed, had become a passionate devotee of them on his two trips there in the summer of 1923. Originally titled as a group, "Toros y Toreros," these chapters presume an understanding and intimacy that chapter 2 lacks.

In *Death in the Afternoon,* Hemingway described the bullfight as a highly structured tragedy that can be performed more or less well, but always results in the death of the bull (16). The more skillfully the bullfighter performs, the closer he works to the bull's horns, that is, to mortal danger. This blending of the greatest possible risk with the highest level of control and skill to master that danger produces the aesthetic frisson of a great bullfight. For a writer intent on mastering *his* art—and exposing his writing to maximal risk through experiment in order to achieve a style of his own—the bullfight was both an exemplar of professionalism and a rich subject, merging complex action, skill, and character in life-and-death situations.

Content

In some ways, chapter 12 is the most impressive and experimental chapter of this book. Although its reportorial style links it to chapters 3 (the civilian retreat) and 6 (the cabinet ministers' execution), and to the openings of 9 (Drevitts and Boyle) and 17 (Sam Cardinella's execution), its narrative action seems more radically "present" and fragmentary than the others. More than any other chapter, it begins and ends in medias res, lacking both the establishing openings of 6, 9, and 17, the imagistic framing of 3 (the civilian retreat), and even a "dying fall" closure. Its subject, the disemboweling of a picador's horse, is the goriest in the book, and the objective point of view forces us to look directly at it, refuses to cushion the blow either by softening the descriptors in figurative language or by rationalizing its necessity to the bullfight. The chapter simply narrates the horse's situation—what it does, what is done to it, how it looks—just after it has been gored and has fallen.[56] En route to Spain, Robert McAlmon tell us, he and Hemingway encountered a similarly repellent sight, a dead dog on a flatcar; Hemingway's response was to study the dog carefully and make notes on the condition of its corpse, urging the sickened McAlmon to adopt a "detached and scientific attitude" toward it.[57] In this chapter, Hemingway does precisely that for what is arguably the bullfight's most repellent event.

The way that this narrative fuses vivid verbs and adverbs—"whack whacked," "swung backward and forward," "cantered jerkily" "nervously wobbly"—with ambiguous contexts and uncertain outcomes is especially effective in creating tension. We don't know who "They" are, at first, nor why they are "whacking" the horse on its legs. Nor does our first reading tell us why the horse had fallen earlier. Although "picador" of sentence 2 explains the context, the next sentence shocks the unprepared reader: "The horse's entrails hung down in a blue bunch and swung backward and forward as he began to canter, the *monos* whacking him on the back of his legs with the rods." The lucid actions that follow are all framed in uncertainty: the horse that "cantered jerkily," "stopped stiff," and was "nervously wobbly" teeters on the verge of final collapse. Is his cantering pathetic or grotesquely comic?[58] The bull looms, may charge again at any moment, yet "could not make up his mind to charge." (What happened to its blood lust? Is it a bad bull?) Without resolving these uncertainties into closure, the piece simply stops.[59]

Style

The sentences build to the chapter's first shock in sentence 3—"The horse's entrails. . . . "—a sentence that is twice as long as any other and the only one with a dependent clause and participle. From this apex, the sentences taper off, first to simple and compound structures, then to simple only. Thus, as we come to realize what is actually occurring with sentence 3, the simple sentences (7–9) slow the sequence into separate actions that intensify our perception: "Blood pumped regularly from between the horse's front legs. He was nervously wobbly. The bull could not make up his mind to charge." Symmetrically, the gruesome echo of sentence 3 (entrails hanging, blood pumping) comes three from the end, while the unstated climax—the *anticipation* of collapse in sentence 8 ("He was nervously wobbly")—stands out as the shortest, a scant four words.

Sentence Structure and Sequence (★thematic center, ★★*unstated climax)*	*Word Count*
1. compound	14
2. compound predicate (3)	14
★3. compound predicate‡ (adverbial clause, participle)	32
4. simple	06
5. compound, compound predicate	15
6. compound predicate (3)	15
7. simple	09
★★8. simple	04
9. simple‡ (infinitive clause)	10
Total	119

Drafts

One draft of this chapter reveals how Hemingway excised all but the present moment of action. Originally, he included both the explanatory past and the intended future:

> Blood pumped regularly from the horses
> T as he lay on the sand with his
> forelegs ~~where~~ the bull had gored him after he was lifted over and
> legs up
> ripped by the charge. He was bleeding so regularly they were worried and were trying to get him out so the bull would charge him again before he keeled over. He cantered jerkily. (KL 94a)

A later draft deletes this explanation of the goring. In place of the *monos'* intention ("trying to get him out so the bull would charge him"), the final version presents unexplained action: "one of the *monos* held his bridle and walked him forward."

chapter 13 (the bad bullfighter)

Background

This portrait of a failed bullfighter is usually contrasted to the next chapter's depiction of Villalta's consummate artistry. But this chapter's real complement is chapter 2, as the two share nearly identical motifs and style in depicting success and failure in the bullring. That chapter ended with "the kid" puking after killing five bulls "while the crowd hollered and threw things down into the bull ring." This one begins: "The crowd shouted all the time and threw pieces of bread down into the ring." Both chapters are more about the crowd's responses (strikingly similar up to a point) to good and bad performances as seen from the stands. This chapter adds a first-person epilogue that anticipates chapter 15.

In *Death in the Afternoon,* Hemingway refers to a cowardly bullfighter, Domingo Hernandorena, a "short, thick-ankled, graceless Basque," in language similar to that of chapter 15. Compare:

> That night at the café I heard no word of sympathy for him. He was ignorant, he was torpid, and he was out of training. Why did he insist on being a bullfighter? (19)

and:

> Afterwards I saw him at the café. He was very short with a brown face and quite drunk and he said after all it has happened before like that. I am not really a good bullfighter. (chapter 13)

Content and Drafts

The parallels and contrasts between chapters 13 and 2 are numerous. In the dramatized bullfights in each, the kill is slow and labored: the "bad sticking"[60] here recalls "the kid"'s five attempts to "get the sword in." In the first draft, Hemingway was far more explicit about the bad bullfighter's performance:

> He was simply awful with the cape and he wouldn't fight
> the bull. He kept dodging back of the little wooden funk boxes along
> the barrera and the crowd got angrier and angrier. Finally the bull
> bled so much from the bad sticking and folded
> was too tired and ~~had been struck so many times with the sword and~~
> his knees and lay down
> ~~lay down and.~~ . . .

The published version virtually erases the torero's presence: sentences 1 and 3 describe the crowd's angry responses; sentence 2, the bull's fatigue and the cuadrilla's coup de grâce. The hapless bullfighter appears only halfway through the chapter, as if the narrative punishes him for incompetence by snubbing him. In his stead the crowd "performs." And while the *kid*'s life-and-death struggle in chapter 2 briefly succeeds in silencing *his* crowd, this crowd not only upstages the bullfighter, but literally fills the stage, symbolically emasculating and cashiering him. Narrated by an anonymous, detached observer in the stands, the scene becomes pure farce: "two men grabbed him and held him and some one cut off his pigtail and was waving it and a kid grabbed it and ran away with it."

Suddenly—and atypically—the scene, action, narrative voice, and tone change with the briefest of transitions: "Afterwards." The objective voice becomes first person (contrast the involved narrator of chapter 2 who never shifts into "I"); the crowd and tumult of the bullring vanish like a bad dream, giving way to a café, where it is quiet enough for the principals to converse; and, unlike the kid in chapter 2, the bullfighter shifts from performer viewed externally to a character with hints of a personality. This mini-encounter between the unidentified narrator and the bad bullfighter anticipates a similar meeting in chapter 15. In both chapters, the first-person narrator encounters a drunken bullfighter. In fact, this bullfighter's "brown face" may identify him as Luis, the "Mexican savage" of the later chapter. Similarly, the narrator of chapter 13, who knows the bad bullfighter well enough to converse with him in the café, may be the bullfighter-narrator of chapter 15, who tries to retrieve the drunken Luis from the public square. But as in chapters 8 and 11, the first-person narrator is peripheral to the action, here not even providing the ironic undercutting that he does in these other chapters. His function here is merely to provide a close-up look at this failed bullfighter.

Equally important, the chapter's mode changes from action—incompetent performance and retribution—to attitude: resignation and cynical acceptance. Numbed by drink, the bullfighter is detached enough to acknowledge that today's performance was no fluke, resigned enough to accept his incompetence. Lacking remorse, his candor ("I am not really a good bull fighter") seems almost insouciant.

Style

Although the first-person voice in chapter 13 is more conventional than its colloquial counterpart in chapter 2, the sentence structure in the two chapters is nearly identical in fusing actions into long compound sentences joined by *and*s. The first three sentences steadily build these fusions: sentence 1 begins moderately with a compound predicate. The next compound sentence fuses three actions in its first half ("was tired," "folded," "lay down") and two in its second half ("leaned over," "killed"). The climactic sentence 3 stands out as a long run-on (though no match for the seventy-four-word monster in chapter 2[61]), symmetrically alternating four compounded actions with three compound predicates:

> The crowd came over the barrera and around the torero **<u>and</u>** two men grabbed him **and** held him **<u>and</u>** someone cut off his pigtail **and** was waving it **<u>and</u>** a kid grabbed it **and** ran away with it. (emphasis mine)

By contrast, the concluding sentence that summarizes the theme of incompetence is short and simple—another instance of highlighting a theme by sharply varying sentence length or structure.

Sentence Structure and Sequence (*thematic center, **climax)		*Word count*
	1. compound predicate‡ (participle)	26
	2. compound-compound predicates	34
	**3. run-on: compounds (4)-compound predicates	39
	4. simple	07
monologue	5. compound (f-s)	22
"	*6. simple	08
	Total	136

chapter 14 (Villalta)

Background

In the first of two dispatches on bullfighting that Hemingway wrote for the *Toronto Star* (20 Oct. 1923), a knowledgeable viewer describes the torero Nicanor Villalta as "the great one." Hemingway continues: "I had noticed Villalta. He was straight as a lance and walked like a young wolf" (*Dateline: Toronto* 342). This perception had stayed with Hemingway once he had seen Villalta perform in the summer of 1923. Drafting chapter 14, he began and immediately crossed out: "~~There was one great killer and that was~~ Villalta" [KL 94a].[62] Chapter 14 twice refers to Villalta's stance: "when the bull charged he swung back firmly like an oak when the wind hits it" and "Villalta standing straight."[63] Villalta is clearly "the great one" of *in our time,* the supremely skillful, commanding bullfighter, whose mastery offsets the bad bullfighting of chapter 13 and whose success opposes Maera's goring and death in chapter 16. Among chapters that have systematically deflated clichés of the hero, the narrative accords him heroic status in the one realm where heroism was still meaningful to Hemingway.

Content

Hemingway's intent is transparent in this chapter: to capture a great bullfighter in action. The reader's gaze is not deflected to the crowd's behavior or to contretemps outside the bullring. It stays squarely on Villalta, perceiving in minute detail what he does and how he does it. In fact, the opening sentence stresses how close-up our perspective is: "If it happened right down close in front of you, you could see Villalta snarl at the bull." This daring descent into informal second person has misled one critic into assuming that the entire chapter is narrated in second person.[64] It isn't. The narrative quickly shifts to third person, focusing on "he" and tempering its admiration with factual precision akin to the dispassionate voice of chapters 3, 6, and 12. "You" (that is, the reader) is understood as having this privileged, close-up perspective; thus, the narrator can relay actions—Villalta's snarl, his curse, his calling "Toro!"—that the audience further back would miss. We are insiders, and the narrator gives us an insider's view and appreciation of the action, of knowing which actions to focus on and how to perceive them.[65]

Style and Action

Many chapters of *in our time* present action, but in no other chapter is action more complex, spatial, and simultaneous, hence more difficult to render into linear prose. In constructing the climactic confrontations between two supreme specimens of their kind—the masterful bullfighter and the brave bull—Hemingway brings together several techniques he has experimented with to get "the sequence of motion and fact which made the emotion."

In previous chapters, sentence structure conveys the pace of actions and corresponding states of mind in the narrator or protagonist: simple sentences slow and isolate events; compounds tend to run actions together into accelerating, breathless sequences. Yet the actions themselves remain essentially linear and chronological, for example the long second sentence of chapter 2. Here, however, the narrative must encompass separate actions occurring simultaneously (or in close succession) and coming together in space: Villalta's stance, his handling of the cape, his sword-work, his calling to the bull, his gesture to the crowd, the bull's looking, charging, bleeding, caving, the crowd's roaring. Not only does Hemingway vary his sentence structures to suggest the simultaneity of these actions, he manipulates the structures themselves to alter the time sequence and subvert linearity, jumping forward to anticipate actions, freezing the action into a momentary tableau, then overlapping it to summarize.

Consider the second paragraph (sentences 3–8):

> [3] When he started to kill it was all in the same rush. [4] The bull looking at him straight in front, hating. [5] He drew out the sword from the folds of the muleta and sighted with the same movement and called to the bull, Toro! Toro! and the bull charged and Villalta charged and just for a moment they became one. [6] Villalta became one with the bull and then it was over. [7] Villalta standing straight and the red hilt of the sword sticking out dully between the bull's

shoulders. [8] Villalta, his hand up at the crowd and the bull roaring blood, looking straight at Villalta and his legs caving.

The opening complex sentence signals the beginning of the new action ("*started* to kill") but immediately jumps forward into summary—"it was all in the same rush"—that spans all of Villalta's subsequent actions until the kill is over (sentence 6). Sentence 4—a fragment—pulls back into the radically present time of participials: "the bull *looking* at him straight in front, *hating*."[66] Here, as in the first paragraph, Hemingway sacrifices conventional grammar ("The bull *looked* at him") for the ongoing participial time that continues the bull's actions into the next sentence. Sentence 5, depicting the multiple and simultaneous actions of the kill, shifts into the run-on mode of chapters 2 and 13, fusing four complete actions into a compound structure linked by *and*s, the first carrying a triple predicate:

1) He drew out the sword from the folds of the muleta
and sighted with the same movement
and called to the bull, Toro! Toro!
2) and the bull charged
3) and Villalta charged
4) and just for a moment they became one.

Six actions become one, unimpeded by separating commas. The climactic sentence 6, sharply contrasting in its brevity and single compound structure, moves both backward and forward in time. Repeating "became one with the bull" reinforces and freezes the key image of the preceding sentence (and of the chapter), providing closure. But the narrative suddenly jumps ahead (as sentence 3 did) into flat summary—"and then it was over"—a statement that presumes foreknowledge to *know* that "it" was over and is thus retrospective. This statement also reinterprets the preceding actions, telling us that the climactic moment of their becoming one is also the end of the kill.[67] But not the end of the bullfight. The next two sentences boldly return to participles, again waiving conventional grammar for a tableau effect that freezes the simultaneous, linked gestures of bullfighter, bull, and crowd:

Villalta *standing* straight
and the red hilt of the sword *sticking* out dully between the bull's shoulders.

Villalta, his hand up at the crowd
and the bull *roaring* blood,
looking straight at Villalta,
and his legs *caving*

Only the last participle, "caving," conveys a genuinely progressive action: the bull is on his way down.[68]

Repetitions and transformations of key phrases establish their importance almost subliminally, like sound repetitions in poetry. Villalta "swung back" from two charges, and each time, he does so "firmly." Similarly, the narrative twice traces the gracefully curving arc of Villalta's muleta: "the muleta trailing and the sword following the curve behind. . . . the muleta curving." Continuing these repeated participles, the bull is "looking" at Villalta "straight in front" before the torero starts his kill and "looking straight" at him after he plunges in the sword. The direct eye contact heightens the intensity of their confrontation: the bull never stops "hating" and wanting to kill Villalta, but after Villalta strikes, "hating" becomes "roaring [blood]" and "caving." In separate statements, both opponents "charge" each other, and "just for a moment they became one." This climactic fusion receives the chapter's most emphatic echo to convey a mystic union of man and beast, killer and killed, life/sex and death.

Chapter 14 displays Hemingway at his experimental best. Like a bullfighter whose capework anticipates and controls the bull's shifting charges, he gauges and varies his sentences to manipulate time in the sequence of separate and simultaneous actions: here accelerating them, there freezing them, jumping forward and backward, overlapping and repeating, breaking grammatical conventions, and, contrary to later stereotypes of his writing, employing a range of structures *except* simple sentences.

Sentence Structure and Sequence (*thematic center, **climax)	*Word Count*
1. complex-compound (both halves)	52
2. compound predicate (3) (absolute + participles)	28
3. complex	12
4. fragment‡ (2 participles)	09
5. run-on: (4 compounds+compound predicate)	39
**6. compound	11
7. fragment‡ (2 participles)	17
8. fragment‡ (absolute + 3 participles)	20
Total	188

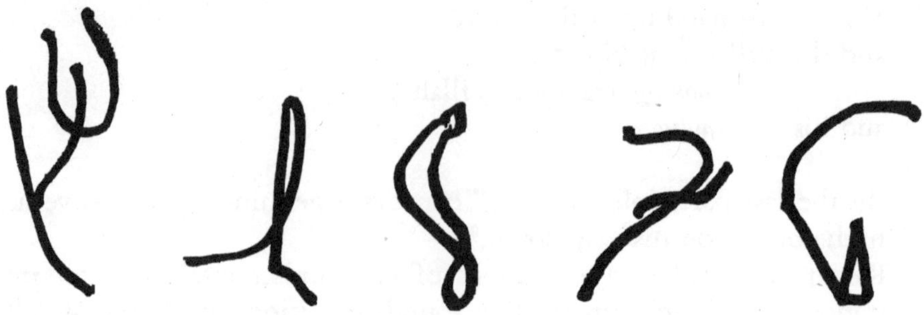

(a) (b) (c) (d) (e)

Drafts

The drafts for chapter 14 contain one element nowhere else evident in the *in our time* papers: Hemingway's diagrams of actions he describes verbally. At the bottom of one sheet (KL 94a) are five curving line drawings that I believe represent Villalta's various stances (see above).

Note particularly how (b) images his "standing straight" with the curving line of one leg (or the muleta) following, while (e) shows him curving far forward, as when he goes in over the horns for the kill. The draft's diction clarifies this motion: "He *folded over* and became one with the bull" (emphasis mine). Drawing (d) can be read variously: it may show Villalta as he "swung back firmly like an oak when the wind hits it, his legs tight together," or it may depict a stance of triumph: "Villalta, his hand up at the crowd. . . . " Whatever their artistic limitations, these drawings reveal how seriously Hemingway approached the problem of capturing Villalta's moves and stances.

chapter 15 (the drunken bullfighter)

Background

Like chapters 2 and 13, and 13 and 14, chapters 15 and 16 form a pair within the bullfight sequence. Where 13 and 14 contrast incompetence with skill and courage, this pair opposes fear and courage, escapism and fatalism, vitality and death. The two chapters are also causally connected as Luis's irresponsibility in getting drunk and incapacitated endangers the other two bullfighters, who must kill Luis's bulls. Maera clearly recognizes this danger at the conclusion of 15, and chapter 16 dramatizes the consequences in Maera's death.

Content

Chapter 15 abandons detached description for an imaginary mini-drama in which the first-person narrator is now a bullfighter—another fantasy projection of Hemingway, the bullfight enthusiast. But in positioning his narrator with the sober Maera as he tries to rein in the drunken Luis, Hemingway constructs a rather two-dimensional conflict of responsible and irresponsible bullfighters. Michael Reynolds found this invented scenario as convincing as the Villalta chapter (*The Paris Years* 139), but its dramatic contrasts seem rather obvious and wooden. The narrator and Maera (the responsible bullfighters) fatalistically accept that they will face the mortal consequences of Luis's drunkenness:

> Yes, Maera said, and who will kill his bulls after he gets a *cogida?*
> We, I suppose, I said.
> Yes, we, said Maera. We kill the savages' bulls, and the drunkards' bulls, and the *riau-riau* dancers' bulls. Yes. We kill them. We kill them all right. Yes. Yes. Yes.

Even Hemingway's usually taut dialogue goes flabby in the narrator's speech to Luis: "I said, Don't be a damn fool, Luis. Come on back to the hotel."

If anything rescues this chapter it is the understated characterization of a bullfighter whose fear of death expresses itself in his desperate clinging to an image of protean vitality, the *riau-riau* dance:

> When they stopped the music for the crouch he hunched down in the street with them all and when they started it again he jumped up and went dancing down the street with them. He was drunk all right. . . .
>
> Then the music started up again and he jumped up and twisted away from me and started dancing. I grabbed his arm and he pulled loose and said, Oh leave me alone. You're not my father.[69]

Even the approach of the *riau-riau* dancers exudes vitality as Hemingway employs his "sensations first" technique to achieve the verisimilitude of the narrator's perceptions: "I heard the drums coming down the street and then the fifes and the pipes and then they came around the corner, all dancing. The street full of them."[70] But between Luis's desperate grab at life and Maera's despairing fatalism, the narrator's characterization pales.

Style

This chapter sharply contrasts a variety of sentence structures. It begins in the manner of chapters 2 and 13 with present-time actions (via participles) linked by *and*s:

> I heard the drums com*ing* down the street *and then* the fifes and the pipes *and then* they came around the corner, all danc*ing.* (emphasis mine)

This pattern continues in sentences 3 and 4:

> Maera saw him *and then* I saw him. *When* they stopped the music for the crouch he hunched down *and when* they started it again he jumped up and *went* danc*ing* down the street with them. (emphasis mine)

But interspersed with these loose coordinate structures are a fragment and a short simple sentence: "The street full of them. . . . He was drunk all right." This pattern continues in the remaining narrative paragraphs (2 and 4), and in each case, the contrasting simple sentence is the thematic crux of that paragraph: Maera was drunk; he had bulls that afternoon; and he rejects the narrator's authority ("You're not my father"). This thematic juxtaposition of relatively long and short sentences also highlights the closing dialogue, the narrative winnowing finally into one-word fragments expressing Maera's despair and resignation:

> Yes, Maera said, and who will kill his bulls after he gets a *cogida?*
> We, I suppose, I said.
> Yes, we, said Maera. We kill the savages' bulls, and the drunkards' bulls, and the *riau-riau* dancers' bulls. Yes. We kill them. We kill them all right. Yes. Yes. Yes.

Sentence Structure and Sequence (*thematic center, **climax)	*Word Count*
1. compound	24
2. fragment	05
3. compound	08
4. complex-compound (for both halves)	34

		*5. simple	05
dialogue	a	6. compound (f-s)	10
"	a	7. compound predicate‡ (adverb clause)-compound (f-s)	29
"	a	*8. simple	08
		9. compound (f)	15
dialogue	a	10. simple (imperative) (+ speech tag)	08
"		11. imperative simple	06
		12. compound-compound predicate	18
narr/dia.	b	13. compound (f-s)	14
dialogue	b	*14. simple	04
		15. compound‡ (participle, infinitive, object clause)	22
		16. complex-compound predicate	11
dialogue	a	17. simple (+ speech tag)	11
dialogue	c	*18. complex (+ speech tag)	14
dialogue	a	*19. simple (elliptical + speech tag)	05
dialogue	c	20. fragment (+ speech tag)	04
"		**21. simple	15
"		22. fragment	01
"		23. simple	03
"		24. simple	05
"		25. fragment	01
"		26. fragment	01
"		27. fragment	01
		Total	282

chapter 16 (Maera's death)

Background

Like Nicanor Villalta, Manuel Garcia Maera was a bullfighter whom Hemingway saw, admired, and immortalized in 1923. First, however, Hemingway had to kill him off—an invention that no doubt would have disturbed the real Maera (had he read this chapter) since he was only superficially injured in the Pamplona bullfights of 1923. The author describes this injury in his *Toronto Star* dispatch of 27 October:

> The sword shot out of his hand and the bull caught him. He went up in the air on the horns of the bull and then came down. Young Algabeno flopped his cape in the bull's face. The bull charged him

> and Maera staggered to his feet. But his wrist was sprained. (*Dateline: Toronto* 352–53)

Hemingway showed his first version of Maera's death to Pound, who must not have liked it. On 6 August, Hemingway wrote him: "Have redone the death of Maera altogether different. . . . The new death is good" (*Selected Letters* 91).

Content

Although Hemingway initially planned to continue the first-person perspective of chapter 15, making the narrator a fellow bullfighter, his final version of this chapter tries an interesting experiment with point of view. Previous third-person perspectives in the bullfight chapters observed the action from the stands. Here, the narrative perspective stays very close to Maera's consciousness, as he is gored repeatedly, carried off to the infirmary, and dies there. Except for a few explanatory sentences that digress from this point of view, the reader feels what Maera feels, sees and hears only what falls within his perceptual range, and infers what he would have inferred. It is this imaginative rigor in restricting and focusing the point of view that makes the experiment so effective.[71]

Significantly, the chapter begins in medias res *after* Maera has been gored and knocked to the ground. In fact, the opening sentence is deceptively tranquil: "head on his arms, his face in the sand," Maera might be relaxing on a beach. But the impression quickly vanishes with "sticky from the bleeding." Since Maera lies face down, he does not see the bull coming; he feels it. More precisely, he anticipates and feels the point of maximal danger and pain, the bull's horn: "Each time he felt the horn coming. Sometimes the bull only bumped him with his head. Once the horn went all the way through him and he felt it go into the sand."[72] As discussed in Chapter Four, the sentence describing how the bull is pulled away may represent Maera's experienced assumption rather than a point-of-view digression. Certainly, he can hear the swearing and sense that "the bull was gone." Rather than summarize Maera's removal (for instance, "Several men carried him to the infirmary"), the next long sentence presents the route of the men carrying Maera in a linear series of phrases: "toward the barriers[,] through the gate[,] out the passage way[,] around under the grand stand[,] to the infirmary." The effect is cinematic: as if watching jerky film shot from a handheld camera, the reader accompanies the stretcher on its cumbersome route. Once inside the infirmary, however, the point of view does shift for ironic effect:

> They laid Maera down on a cot and one of the men went out for the doctor. The others stood around. The doctor came running from the corral where he had been sewing up picador horses. He had to stop and wash his hands.[73]

Except perhaps for the concluding sentence, we now stay strictly within Maera's consciousness. We hear a "great shouting" from the "grandstand overhead" but we don't know what causes it, only that the bullfight continues without Maera. We never know what Maera wants to say because he "found he could not talk." He dies a lonely, painful, unromantic death, unable to communicate, attended by a horse doctor and several gawkers.[74]

Style

The sentence sequence aligns itself with point of view by relying predominantly on simple sentences, particularly when the narrative conveys the waning moments of Maera's consciousness. Separate statements convey his discrete sensations and perceptions. "Then," ordinarily a clumsy transition, reinforces this separateness in Maera's last, distorted sensations, as do the parallel, simplistic repetitions:

> Maera felt everything getting larger and larger and then smaller and smaller. Then it got larger and larger and larger and then smaller and smaller. Then everything commenced to run faster and faster as when they speed up a cinematograph film. Then he was dead.[75]

Sentence Structure and Sequence (*thematic center, **climax)	*Word Count*
1. simple	13
2. simple	08
3. simple‡ (participle)	07
4. simple	09
5. compound‡ (object clause)	17
6. simple	07
7. compound predicate	12
8. simple	05
9. compound predicate (with six prepositional phrases)	29
10. compound	17
*11. simple	04
12. simple‡ (adverbial clause)	15

13. compound predicate	08
*14. simple	11
15. compound predicate‡ (object clause)	11
16. simple	12
17. simple	13
18. complex (adverbial clause)	16
**19. simple	04
Total	218

Drafts

Hemingway was not exaggerating when he told Pound that his revised death of Maera was "altogether different." No other chapter in *in our time* underwent such drastic revision. Originally, the death scene in the infirmary occupied the whole chapter (KL 564, 564a, 94a). The onlookers are gone; in their place, the narrator ("Martin," in one version), a fellow bullfighter, visits Maera on his deathbed and sees "the sheet pulled up to his chin. There was a big hump under the sheet where he was bandaged" (KL 564a ts.). The scene is detailed: "The Doctor sat on a chair in the corner. It was very hot and dim in the room and the shutters were closed" (KL 564 ms.). Maera recalls to the narrator the goring that Hemingway would dramatize in the revision:

> ~~When I slipped I lay quiet and he~~
> he knocked me over I was off balance and I lay quiet
> twice
> and he hit me ~~four times~~ with his head and I knew I was all right and then he
> got me with the horn and rolled me over and I kept waiting for Luis to do the
> quite and waiting for the quite to take him away and one after another he got
> in my belly
> me three times ~~in the intestines~~ with the horn. Each time it was an hour between. (KL 564 ms.)

The last subjective exaggeration—"an hour between" each goring—is notably missing from the final version, left for us to imagine as "Each time he felt the horn coming."

The doctor quickly breaks up the meeting, telling the narrator (ordering him in one version) to leave and reassuring Maera that he won't die. In the scene's closing (as well as in Maera's greeting to the narrator), Maera affirms repeatedly that "I'm going to die" and that "it hurts so." His final words to the narrator are "Tell Luis I'm going to die," an ironic closer since Luis, we know from the preceding chapter, has indirectly caused Maera's condition by being too drunk to kill his own bulls.

Though Pound's specific advice to Hemingway is unknown, given Pound's aesthetics of the image ("that which presents" rather than describes), he may well have suggested dramatizing the goring rather than having it recounted. If so, it was good advice. Hemingway's final version is far more dynamic, and its narrative perspective—approaching, but not quite achieving, pure stream-of-consciousness—is more imaginative and experimental than the deathbed scene he rejected. That draft was not completely wasted, however, for Hemingway recycled Maera's pain and recognition that he is dying, as well as the doctor's false assurances, in Catherine Barkley's death scene in *A Farewell to Arms.*

chapter 17 (Sam Cardinella's execution)

Background

In the same letter to Pound that speaks of rewriting Maera's death (c. 6 August 1923), Hemingway closes with "I will commence the hanging." Pound must have already seen a plan (or at least heard Hemingway describe the intended chapter) to understand that cryptic reference. Sam Cardinella was a Chicago gangster hanged for murder in the Cook County jail on 15 April 1921.[76] The execution, which received much press and public attention, impressed Hemingway, who was living in Chicago at the time. He mentions it in at least two separate letters. To his father he writes on the same day:

> They hanged Cardinella[77] and Cosmano and some other Wop killer today. Lopez, who was to hang, was reprieved. Cardinella is a good man to swing I guess. Passed the County Jail in the morning and there was a big crowd standing outside waiting for the event. (*Selected Letters* 46)

About four months later, he describes what for him were key facts about the hanging in a letter to Bill Smith.[78] By now, it was not just justice meted out that interested the young writer, but the way Sam Cardinella responded to the imminence of his own hanging: first, complete denial until the last minute; then, violent, futile resistance, forcing guards to carry him to the scaffold and tie him to a chair for the hanging. But as the sensational *Chicago Tribune* account of the execution indicates, Hemingway was already embroidering the events, inventing Cardinella's denial to contrast with his resistance:

> For hours before the death march, Cardinella paced his cell, wringing his hands, moaning and slobbering. . . . When the death march time arrived, he fought his guards like a maniac until he was exhausted. Finally he was carried to the scaffold in a chair, unable to stand erect, and, gibbering insanely in Italian, half insensible from fear, still cringing in the chair, he was executed. (qtd. in Reynolds, *The Young Hemingway* 216)

Earlier, in January 1921, Hemingway had written a poem depicting the execution of another member of the Cardinella gang along with a black man. The poem sharply contrasts the white man's complete breakdown on the scaffold—he "had to be held up . . . he drooled from his mouth and slobber ran down his chin"—with the black man "standing straight and dignified like the doorman at the Blackstone." Details that he would later recycle in chapter 17 are also present in the poem: "the high corridor of the county jail," the priest ministering to the white prisoner, and a sardonic conclusion, as the narrator associates the black man with a black star of the *Ziegfield Follies* (Reynolds, *The Young Hemingway* 215):

> It gave me a bad moment,
> I felt sick at my stomach
> I was afraid they were hanging Bert Williams.
> ("To Will Davies," *88 Poems* 21)

From these sources, several elements emerge as keys to Hemingway's fascination with these executions: first and most important, how the prisoners conducted themselves as they faced death. The setting and details also matter: for example, the poem parallels the hanging judge's "black cap" with the "black bag" to go over the prisoner's head. Finally, satiric or darkly comic qualities undermine the solemnity of the execution. The black man's courage is demeaned by the comparison to a doorman's dignity and to a vaudeville performer, and the speaker's "bad moment" is obviously ironic.

Content

In its content and style, chapter 17 recalls the execution of the Greek cabinet ministers in chapter 6.[79] Although the behavior of the prisoners is a study in opposites—the ministers' quiet dignity versus Sam's abject fear—both executions are messy. Both chapters begin with a factual establishing sentence, starting with the impersonal, unidentified "They" who "shot" (6) or "hanged" (17) their prisoners and then locating the precise time and place. This quasi-journalistic style predominates in both chapters, though each modifies it with fictional devices: chapter 6 with symbolic imagery, chapter 17 with dialogue and satirical irony.

The tone of the opening paragraph is somber as it sketches the scene—the "high and narrow" corridor foreshadowing the verticality of the gallows and the drop—and studies the other prisoners' responses to a hanging that they are forced to witness ("The men had been brought in for the hanging"). Although the published version does not clarify how soon the prisoners on death row are to be executed (in the historical event, several were executed the same day), their responses are variations on the theme of fear:

> Three of the men to be hanged were negroes. They were very frightened. One of the white men sat on his cot with head in his hands. The other lay flat on his cot with a blanket wrapped around his head.

Events quickly become strange and ludicrous, however. Hagemann notes the odd, Kafkaesque image of the procession coming out "onto the gallows through a door in the wall" ("Only Let the Story End" 55). Momentarily, it seems almost regal, the monarch carried by his subjects with two priests dignifying the procession. But the dismissive sentence that follows—"He had been like that since about four o'clock in the morning"—suggests (with uncharacteristic vagueness) that Sam cannot be made to walk to his death, hence must be carried. This loss of control pervades the next paragraph, which comically juxtaposes the priest exhorting Sam to "Be a man, my son" with Sam losing "control of his sphincter muscle."[80] Like the chapter that forces us to watch the gored horse, this one forces us to smell, so to speak, in its revolutionary frankness. The mess may disgust the guards, but their abruptly dropping him is slapstick. In dialogue and dress (the derby hat) that anticipate Al and Max in "The Killers," the guards place Sam on his throne.

The focus of the concluding paragraph is especially subtle in the way it directs our attention away from Sam and positions us with his attendants. The long opening sentence focuses on the group "all" stepping back onto the scaffolding behind the drop, where it is safe. Attention to the construction of the drop further deflects our attention from Sam, who finally and briefly appears "sitting there strapped tight." Immediately, the sentence shifts to his final attendant, the younger of the two priests, who kneels beside Sam perhaps because he is more devoted to his calling than his older colleague—or has less seniority. Hemingway saves his best joke for last: the younger priest "skipped back onto the scaffolding just before the drop fell." If his kneeling prayers prepare Sam for the next world, the priest still wants to live in this one, as his anxious, self-preserving skip indicates.[81] Meanwhile, Sam has disappeared from the narrative, just as he disappears from the scaffolding: it is "the drop" that falls, not Sam. Our attention is with the survivors who have saved their own skins.

Style

As noted above, this chapter skillfully blends tension and humor—both slapstick and satiric—to achieve an effect more unsettling than either could achieve alone. Anticipation and foreshadowing continuously build tension, while botched rituals and ironic reversals momentarily—but only momentarily—relieve it. The "high and narrow" corridor anticipates the verticality of the gallows and the drop, just as the blanket "wrapped around" the head of one prisoner foreshadows the noose soon to be wrapped around his neck. "Hanged" and "to be hanged" resound in the first paragraph like a tolling bell. The drop "swung" as Sam will swing. The priest "skipped" as Sam will skip and kick in air. Ironies abound. The prisoners are forced to witness their own fate, but several keep from looking. Sam is quivering jelly treated like royalty. The priest's exhortation to "Be a man, my son" turns hypocritical in his own scurrying for safety. The cap, which, like the blindfold, is intended to spare the prisoner the agony of witnessing his final moment, terrifies Sam into messing his pants. Note how Hemingway lets us envision what Sam sees: "When they came toward him with the cap to go over his head . . . "[82] Finally, the closing refuses to close, refuses to release the chapter's building tension. Like the other execution chapter, this one deflects the execution itself into a dependent clause—"just before the drop fell" (cf. "When they fired the first volley . . . ")—leaving our final gaze on a comic action "just before."

As with other chapters in the journalistic mode, simple sentences (or simple sentences with a brief embedded clause) prevail. Of the twenty-two sentences, fourteen are simple and four others have short modifying clauses. The long, complex penultimate sentence (forty-four words) sets us up for the comic anticlimax (the priest skipping) of eleven words.

Sentence Structure and Sequence (*thematic center, **anticlimax)		*Word Count*
	1. simple (establishing sentence)	17
	2. simple	13
	3. simple	05
	4. simple	09
	5. simple‡ (adjectival infinitive clause)	12
	6. simple‡ (adjectival infinitive clause)	09
	7. simple	04
	8. simple	15
	9. simple‡ (adverbial past participle)	14
	10. simple	12
	11. simple	10
	*12. simple	05
	13. simple	12
	14. complex-compound	20
monologue a	*15. simple (imperative + speech tag)	08
	*16. complex	21
	17. simple‡ (adjectival clause)	10
	18. simple	04
dialogue b	19. simple (elliptical + speech tag)	10
dialogue c	20. simple (imperative + speech tag)	10
	**21. complex	44
	**22. complex	11
	Total	275

Drafts

The way that Hemingway worked over the last two sentences in the draft (KL 94a) and published versions of this chapter epitomizes his struggle with the aesthetic question "How much is enough?" Originally, the penultimate sentence ended plainly and showed Sam's aloneness as it focused on other matters:

> When they all stepped back on the scaffolding back of the drop, which was very heavy, built of oak and steel and swung on ball bearings, Sam Cardinella was left sitting there in a chair xxxxxxx. (KL 94a)

With each revision, Hemingway adds details emphasizing Sam's forlorn, pinioned helplessness in his last moments. This same draft inserts a vivid participle:

> strapped
> . . . Sam Cardinella was left sitting there / in a chair xxxxxxx.

Chapter 17 drops the redundant "in a chair" but underscores his bondage:

> Sam Cardinella was left sitting there strapped tight.

But Hemingway still wasn't finished. He adds another grim detail to the 1925 *In Our Time,* showing us, in effect, how "prepared" Sam now is (and forcing us to see—feel—the crucial element):

> Sam Cardinella was left sitting there strapped tight with the rope around his neck . . .

As Sam becomes increasingly bound and helpless, the priest by his side acquires more prominence. Initially, his skipping lacked a logical connection to Sam:

> strapped
> . . . Sam Cardinella was left sitting there / in a chair xxxxxxx. The younger of the two priests skipped back onto the scaffolding just before the drop fell. (KL 94a)

Chapter 17 adds the essential linkage:

> Sam Cardinella was left sitting there strapped tight, the younger of the two priests kneeling beside his chair. The priest skipped back. . . .

Still not satisfied, Hemingway gives the priest a gesture in the 1925 *In Our Time:*

> Sam Cardinella was left sitting there strapped tight, the younger of the two priests kneeling beside his chair holding up a little crucifix. The priest skipped back. . . . (*Chapter* XV)[83]

Hemingway's intent is unmistakable in these changes. Each revision, in increasing Sam's helplessness, makes him more remote, less visibly human, than the initial image of his "sitting there." Conversely, the revisions give the younger priest more professional (and stereotypical) stage business—kneeling, holding up a "little" crucifix—thus making his final skip to safety more comic. Like the cops in chapter 9, authority figures are scarcely more sympathetic than the criminals they help execute. But the irony of chapter 17 has become rather heavy-handed satire as *Chapter XV.*

chapter 18 (the king in the garden)

Background

The closing chapter of *in our time* also closes out the book's glimpses of the aftermath of the Greco-Turkish War with this study of a powerless king. George II was installed and then placed under house arrest by the revolutionary committee after his father, King Constantine, fled to England. Although Hemingway no doubt read news stories about the hapless king,[84] it was the movie-news cameraman, Shorty Wornall, who provided him the material for this chapter as Hemingway was writing the later chapters in summer 1923. He writes Pound around 6 August: "My pal Shorty, movie operator with me in Thrace, just brings the dope on the King. Edifying" (*Selected Letters* 92).

Hemingway lost no time converting into fiction Wornall's account of his garden chat with the royal couple, and, as with the narrative about the Greek refugees, he "double-dipped," including Wornall's account in a *Toronto Star* dispatch.[85] The two texts are quite similar. In both, the queen is "clipping a rosebush." The uncanny introductions are virtually identical: " 'This is the queen,' said George. 'How do you do?' she said" (*Dateline* 295). As in the chapter, they all have "whiskey and soda at a table under a big tree"; "the king was glad to have somebody to talk to"; and "Like all the Greeks, he wants to get over to the States."

Content and Style

Unlike his *Star* dispatch, however, Hemingway's chapter subtly blends two qualities that began *in our time:* a sense of unreality and muted menace. The nursery rhyme opening, the garden setting, and the royal couple's offhand introductions and mundane actions (reminiscent of Czarist nobility driving taxis in Paris) all contribute to the scene's strangeness. Beginning in the middle, the narrative heightens this unreality by omitting identifiers (*which* king?) and explanatory context (why "glad"? Who is the narrator?)

Not until the king starts his monologue does this dislocated fairy tale gradually yield to the contemporary realism of power politics. The king reveals they are under house arrest by a "revolutionary committee," which explains both the gardening and why he is glad to see someone new. For a political prisoner, though, he is strangely sympathetic to his captors, who have executed his father's cabinet ministers:

> Plastiras is a very good man I believe, he said, but frightfully difficult. I think he did right though shooting those chaps. If Kerensky had shot a few men things might have been altogether different.[86]

Suddenly, however, the reality principle rips through the affability of this garden chat: "Of course the great thing in this sort of an affair is not to be shot oneself!" Though delivered with the same directness and good humor as the introductions, the statement betrays the tension lurking in the garden and thus undermines the hyperbolic "It was very jolly."

Closing out this satire of anachronistic royalty is a flippant anticlimax that reduces this already reduced "king" to being just another Greek, and an unpatriotic one at that: "Like all Greeks he wanted to go to America."[87] A book of "unwritten stories" that begins with the anti-heroic, flat statement "Everybody was drunk" thus ends with an anti-romantic fable of royalty who have become gardeners.

Sentence Structure and Sequence (*thematic center, **anticlimax)		*Word count*
	1. simple	07
	2. simple	07
	3. simple	05
monologue a	4. simple (+ speech tag)	06
	5. simple	06
monologue b	6. simple (+ speech tag)	07
	7. compound	17
monologue a	8. simple (+ speech tag)	07
" (reported)	9. simple (+ speech tag)	16
"	10. simple‡ (object clause + speech tag)	13
"	11. simple‡ (participle)	09
"	12. complex	13
"	*13. simple	17
	14. simple	04
	15. simple	06
	**16. simple	09
	Total	149

Drafts

The draft for chapter 18 shows how carefully Hemingway constructed the mysterious opening of a king and queen "working in the garden" and "very glad to see" the narrator (who, like his first-person counterpart in chapter 13, is virtually a cipher). The initial version of the opening gives the game away immediately:

> ~~The king was shut up in the garden. The revolutionary committee xx would not let him go outside at all. He was glad to see me.~~ (KL 94a)

The revised version immediately below the cross out is better but still explains too early:

> The king was working in the garden. The revolutionary committee would not allow him to go outside the palace grounds. He seemed very glad to see me. (KL 94a)

This version marks for relocation the explanatory second sentence, leaving the text as it appears in chapter 18, a modern, uneasy fairy tale with rifles concealed just behind the rosebushes.[88]

Epilogue

After *in our time*

I. From Chapters to Stories

In retrospect, *in our time* was Hemingway's most experimental book. The short stories that poured out of him in 1924 and the novels he began writing soon after were established genres, and Hemingway respected their generic conventions, even as his subjects and style breathed new life into these forms. As his critical and popular success in these genres soared, the terse "unwritten stories" of 1923 were quickly left behind. Integrated into the 1925 *In Our Time,* the genre was then abandoned by its author and undervalued by his critics.

This reversion to familiar genres offers several insights into the development of Hemingway's career and style, both of which were still clarifying in 1923–24. Certainly, he had no intention of remaining a radical modernist, à la Stein, publishing only in avant-garde presses and paying for the privilege (as Stein mostly did). His desire for popular success was too great: "I want, like hell, to get published," he had confessed to Edward O'Brien in May 1923 (*Selected Letters* 82). If he had rejected his earlier, unsuccessful path to that success in the slick, *Saturday Evening Post* type of story—and writing *in our time* obliterated *that* genre for him once and for all—he had not abandoned the goal. Thus, when Edward O'Brien wrote him in November 1923 that he had chosen "My Old Man" for *Best Short Stories of 1923* and even wanted to dedicate the volume to Hemingway, the young writer was ecstatic:

> Your letter couldn't have had any greater effect if it had been to inform me that I'd just been given 1 million dollars, the V.C., a renewable annual pass entitling self and family to the royal suite on the Mauretania—with the promise that I would only have to make one more crossing, and the news that I had been elected to

> the Academie to replace Analole France. (c. 20 Nov. 1923, *Selected Letters* 103)

Even better, O'Brien "wants to know if I've got enough stories for a Boni and Liveright book," Hemingway eagerly announced to Sylvia Beach and added, "I'll get on your shelves yet" (6 Nov. 1923). That Hemingway wrote the same news to Edmund Wilson and Jim Gamble (*Selected Letters* 98, 105, 107) shows how enticed he was by the prospect of being published by a recognized commercial press. As Leonard Leff points out, "Liveright was publishing moneymakers [at the time] . . . the sorts of books that earned authors huge returns and Hollywood offers."[1] Hemingway expressed his ambitions to O'Brien seven months later:

> What I would like to do would be bring out a good fat book in N.Y. with some good publisher who would tout it and have In Our Time [sic] in it and the other stories, and about 15 or 20 others. How many would it take? (*Selected Letters* 117)

Tellingly, he had asked O'Brien the same question in response to O'Brien's original inquiry: "How many stories would I need for a Boni Liveright book?" (*Selected Letters 104*). "Stories," not chapters. As soon as he returned to Paris from Toronto in January 1924, he started producing them at an astonishing rate—eight in five months and twelve by March 1925 (Smith, *Reader's Guide* xvi). By contrast, he had written only one short story, "Out of Season," while composing *in our time,* two others in 1921–22, and none at all in the four months he spent in Toronto writing full-time for the *Star.* As O'Brien had predicted, Boni & Liveright published a book of these stories (interspersed with the 1923 chapters) in 1925, launching Hemingway's public career.

O'Brien's influence here continues a pattern that undermines the self-image Hemingway retrospectively invented in *A Moveable Feast* of a single-minded young writer who relentlessly pursued his aim—to make himself into a serious artist—from the moment his boat docked at Cherbourg. As Chapter Two shows, a collaboration of factors turned Hemingway to the modernist experimentation of *in our time:* the influence and advice of his avant-garde mentors, Pound and Stein particularly; the loss of nearly all the early manuscripts he had with him in Paris, making it easier to follow Stein's advice to "begin again" in a new form; the milieu of Parisian modernism; and, most important by far, two commissions—guarantees of publication—that both sought "contemporary English prose." But the experiments of *in our time* were not even in print when O'Brien's award and query about more stories appeared, returning Hemingway's interest to the short story and to finding a commercial publisher.[2]

If this scenario makes Hemingway seem rather wayward and passively opportunistic in determining and pursuing his professional goals, two mitigating factors should be considered. First, among the multiple careers that beckoned when he arrived in Paris—journalist, poet, satirist, fiction writer, avant-gardist—he had already ruled out two major vocations, journalist and poet, by the end of 1923. Gertrude Stein had advised him early on to give up journalism if he wanted to become a serious writer, but now the wisdom of this advice was unmistakable: the traveling assignments had become increasingly onerous, increasingly costly to his creative momentum. No sooner had he returned to Paris in March 1923 bearing the six "In Our Time" pieces for the *Little Review,* then he had to travel to Germany to do a series of features. The straight journalism he worked at in Toronto during the fall of 1923 was tedious and all-consuming: "It is impossible for me to do any writing of my own," he complained to Sylvia Beach. "The paper wants all day and all night. Much longer and I would never be able to write anymore" (*Selected Letters* 97). Thus, he decided once and for all to cut the cord and return to Paris and creative writing—full-time—as soon as possible.

Hemingway's feelings about his poetry were more ambiguous. *Three Stories & Ten Poems* (published August 1923) did not arouse much interest in his poems. Edmund Wilson's review of this book and *in our time,* so laudatory of the prose, flatly dismissed the poetry: "Mr. Hemingway's poems are not particularly important" ("Dry Points" 119). His two mentors were ambivalent. Pound had placed Hemingway's poems in *Poetry* and the *Little Review,* and in early 1924 had mildly praised the poetry to Ford Madox Ford: "He writes very good verse." But Pound was far more enthusiastic about Hemingway's prose: "he's the finest prose stylist in the world" (Baker, *A Life Story* 123). After 1923, Pound did not continue promoting Hemingway's poetry. By contrast, Stein, in her review of *Three Stories,* seemed to prefer the poetry: "I should say that Hemingway should stick to poetry and intelligence and eschew the hotter emotions and the more turgid vision [of the stories]" (qtd. in Reynolds, *The Paris Years* 153). But tautology renders her praise meaningless: "as he sticks to poetry and intelligence it is both poetry and intelligent." In 1924, Hemingway gained a new outlet for his poems, the German quarterly *Der Querschnitt,* where he published five of them. On that basis, Carlos Baker argues that Hemingway "had not yet decided to abandon poetry" in 1924 (*The Writer as Artist* 28). But Hemingway himself, responding to Eugene Jolas's criticism of "The Soul of Spain" and "The Earnest Liberal's Lament" in *Der Querschnitt,* admitted that the poems "were not intended to be serious" and implied in *A Moveable Feast* (71) that he published in *Der Querschnitt* for the money.[3] Tellingly, when he announced to Gertrude Stein in late 1923 that he was quitting journalism, he described his new ambition only in terms of fiction: "I have some good stories to write." (*Selected Letters* 102).

Another, more important factor mitigates against the image of literary opportunism. In deciding to abandon the modernist miniature and write short stories, Hemingway did not repudiate the modernist techniques he developed in those miniatures. The experiments he tried out in *in our time* shaped the fiction he produced in 1924. He adapted as much as adopted, sanding the edges of raw experiment into a consistent and unified style.

II. The Fate of Experiments

Not everything in *in our time* was used, of course, and in returning to more traditional genres, Hemingway shelved some of the chapters' bolder experiments with sentence structure and narrative perspective. The elided particles (for instance, "and each swing the crowd roaring") yielded to conventional phrasing ("and *at* each swing") as early as the 1925 *In Our Time.* Abrasive fragments—"The street full of them"—likewise grew into complete sentences. Point of view and narrative voice no longer seemed to jump abruptly from speaker to speaker, as in chapter 8 (the praying soldier), where "He" becomes "We," then returns to "He." The stories and novels of the 1920s maintain a consistent narrative perspective, typically the protagonist's, conveyed in first or third person. In this respect, *in our time*'s least typical narrative style, which stays closely focused on Nick in chapter 7, is the most predictive of Hemingway's future writing. More than a decade would elapse before Hemingway experimented again with multiple narrators in *To Have and Have Not,* and, unlike the ambiguous narrative voices of *in our time,* that novel's narrators are clearly identified.

Those murky, half-hidden narrators, so typical of *in our time,* illustrate how Hemingway adapted his experiments to conventional genres. *The Sun Also Rises,* for example, reveals immediately that a character narrates the novel in first person: "Robert Cohn was once middleweight boxing champion at Princeton. Do not think that I am very much impressed by that as a boxing title, but it meant a lot to Cohn." But the novel does not identify the speaker by name for several pages or give his occupation until Chapter 2. The beginning of *A Farewell to Arms* is even more ambiguous: "In the late summer of that year we lived in a house in a village that looked across the river and the plain to the mountains." What year is "that year"? Which village? What river? Which mountains? And who are "we"? The chapter never tells us. The curiously generic quality of these nouns makes them seem emblematic, which has led one critic to identify river, plain, and mountain as the novel's central symbols and critics generally to consider the first chapter an imagistic microcosm of the entire novel (Baker, "The Mountain and the Plain" 47–60). Once again, however, this calculated ambiguity clarifies into a particular setting and identifiable narrator by Chapter II. The experiments with ambiguous narrative voices and contexts taught Hemingway how to create immediacy by beginning in medias res yet cloud the context to focus the reader's attention on the narrator's tone, on journalistic details ("at six o'clock in the morning in the corridor of the county jail"), on the quality of the action ("They whack-whacked the white horse on the legs and he knee-ed himself up"), or on suggestive images ("against the wall of a hospital"). But where *in our time* often maintains that ambiguity throughout a chapter—for example, the unidentified first-person narrators in chapters 2 ("the kid" kills five bulls) and 13 (the bad bullfighter)—the stories and novels clarify it relatively soon.

Controlling narrative distance in these brief chapters concerned Hemingway as much as characterizing the narrative voice. The positioning of this voice was therefore crucial to the kinesthetic, psychological, and expressive effect of each scene: If the narrator is an observer, as in many of the bullfight chapters, how close to the action is he? How knowledgeable (in delineating the bullfighter's technique) or impressionistic (in reporting the crowd's hijinks)? If a participant, what could he reasonably know or see from the middle of an action? The officer in chapter 4 never tells us *why* the Germans came over the wall so ill-advisedly. Presumably, he does not know. The kitchen corporal in chapter 1 *reports* the bizarre and drunken antics of his battery, but he has no way of knowing at the time where these events are taking him. And as the perspective in chapter 3 narrows from a distant view to the plodding Greek civilians, the procession really seems to have "No end and no beginning" for the narrator.

The risks Hemingway took working within these distances did not always succeed, as when the point of view in chapter 16 briefly shifts from Maera's consciousness to an external view of the hurrying doctor. But the stories that followed *in our time* show how much he learned from these exercises in controlling narrative perspective and distance. In the famous opening of "The Killers," we see the sudden appearance of Al and Max from inside the lunchroom, where Nick Adams sees it sitting at the counter: "The door of Henry's Lunch-Room opened and two men came in." They might have come from anywhere or nowhere—the story never tells us. They are simply—and suddenly—*there* from Nick's vantage point. Likewise, when they leave, "The two of them went out the door. George watched them, through the window, pass under the arc-light and cross the street." Poof! They're gone.

Just as the *in our time* chapters establish the narrator's perceptual distance, so they explore varieties of tone to establish the narrator's expressive distance from other characters or from the action. In particular, Hemingway tried out undercutting tones through irony, satire, and parody. To be sure, some of these methods badly needed adjustment, notably the malicious irony of chapter 10 (the recovering soldier and Ag). More subtly, the narrators of chapters 8, 11, 13, 15, and 18 put skeptical distance between themselves and the characters they describe—the praying soldier, the blinkered revolutionist, the incompetent and irresponsible bullfighters, the ineffectual king—by presenting their self-incriminating statements without comment or by changing the subject. Positioning a narrator apart from or between significant characters or ideologies became one of Hemingway's most effective devices to achieve irony, sometimes through direct comment, but often by merely juxtaposing these contrasting stances and having them, in effect, cancel each other out, as did the drunken lieutenant's antics and the nervous adjutant's fears in chapter 1. In the opening lines from *The Sun Also Rises* quoted above, Jake Barnes undercuts Robert Cohn's achievement as soon as he cites it. As much an observer of the other characters as a participant in the action, Jake is perfectly situated to narrate and subvert simultaneously. Ironic "canceling," admirably concise and understated, lent itself especially to short stories such as "In Another Country," which positions the narrator squarely between the optimistic doctor and his machines, the patriotic Arditi soldiers, and the disillusioned major.

Hemingway continued to write in the subversive genres of satire and parody, though they gradually faded in importance after *The Torrents of Spring* (1926). A direct descendent of the fairy tale parody of chapter 10 is "Mr. and Mrs. Elliot"—Hemingway's version of *Hugh Selwyn Mauberley*—which satirizes Victorian sexuality and aesthetics and parodies the fairy tale in its closing: "and they were all quite happy." More relentlessly satirical than chapter 10, it shares that chapter's style of heavily narrated storytelling with little action or dialogue. Like chapter 10, it also relies on complex sentences to compress the historical past of this couple—only here, even the subordinating conjunctions seem to smirk as Hemingway satirizes the style itself in its Victorian (Jamesian?) turgidity:

> She had seemed much younger, in fact she had seemed not to have any age at all, *when* Elliot had married her *after* several weeks of making love to her *after* knowing her for a long time in her tea shop *before* he had kissed her one evening. (*In Our Time* 85, emphasis mine)

From chapter 11, which depicted the revolutionist, "Mr. and Mrs. Elliot" borrows another undercutting device, the inflated intensives *very* and *quite,* which the story joins to repeated key words—*tried* and *sick*—in the opening paragraph to establish the Elliots' view of married sex (solely for procreation and sickening drudgery in practice) and the narrator's mocking contempt for them:

> Mr. and Mrs. Elliot tried very hard to have a baby. They tried as often as Mrs. Elliot could stand it. They tried in Boston after they were married and they tried coming over on the boat. They did not try very often on the boat because Mrs. Elliot was quite sick. She was sick and when she was sick she was sick as Southern women are sick. That is women from the Southern part of the United States. Like all Southern women, Mrs. Elliot disintegrated very quickly under sea sickness. (*In Our Time* 85)[4]

As these passages suggest, Hemingway typically blended varieties of narrative mode, voice, and sentence rhythm—elements he intensively explored in *in our time*—to capture the right distance, tone, and "sequence of motion and fact." In Jake Barnes's contemptuous description of the homosexuals accompanying Brett Ashley to the *bal musette,* for example, note how the passage fuses precise description (for example, "newly washed"), repetition of key images and sounds ("white hands," "wavy hair"), recreation of their voices, and finally repetition of a key, contrasting sentence ("With them was Brett") to express Jake's disgust at seeing his former love in this company:

> A crowd of young men, some in jerseys and some in their shirt-sleeves, got out. I could see their hands and newly washed, wavy hair in the light from the door. The policeman standing by the door looked at me and smiled. They came in. As they went in, under the light, I saw white hands, wavy hair, white faces, grimacing, gesturing, talking. With them was Brett. She looked very lovely and she was very much with them.
>
> One of them saw Georgette and said: "I do declare. There is an actual harlot. I'm going to dance with her, Lett. You watch me."
>
> The tall dark one, called Lett, said: "Don't you be rash."
>
> The wavy blond one answered: "Don't you worry, dear." And with them was Brett. (*The Sun Also Rises* 20)

These techniques—imagistic repetition and contrasting sentence structure to highlight a key fact—come straight from the chapters. Their purposes have not changed: to recreate action, suggest theme, evoke psychological and emotive states. But here they achieve a fluidity far beyond the journeyman's explorations of *in our time.* What Hemingway taught himself about writing sentences in that book matured into a style that could employ virtually any combination of sentence structures to suggest multiple types of meaning. In the passage quoted above, note how the simple sentences shorten to an important fact ("They came in"), then expand in a complex sentence, then contract to a terse sentence to express the key fact ("With them was Brett"). The culminating compound ("She looked very lovely and she was very much with them") promises at first to relax the structural tension but instead builds on it by repeating the critical phrase "very much with them." By contrast, the abrupt, simple sentences that begin "The Battler"—"Nick stood up. He was all right"—do more than start the story as if the narrative itself were abruptly thrown off a train. They convey Nick's psychic shock and instinctive rebound in recognizing what has just happened to him and reassuring himself that he is still "all right." Remarkably, both the action and diction thematically foreshadow the central theme of outsiders getting physically busted and not being "all right."

Compound sentences—the rhythm in which Hemingway most naturally composed—appear everywhere in his mature prose. Even the self-conscious run-ons of chapters 2 ("the kid" kills five bulls) and 13 (the bad bullfighter) have a place. In the celebrated opening paragraph of *A Farewell to Arms,* these compounds acquire biblical solemnity as they combine with participles to effect the rolling cadence of endlessly moving troops, colored in repeated images of early death:

> Troops went by the house and down the road and the dust they raised powdered the leaves of the trees. The trunks of the trees too were dusty and the leaves fell early that year and we saw the troops marching along the road and the dust rising and leaves, stirred by the breeze, falling and the soldiers marching and afterward the road bare and white except for the leaves. (3)

The appendix shows how chary Hemingway was of complex structures: their explanatory potential runs counter to his evolving techniques of understatement and omission. Yet composing the chapters also taught him the value of complex sentences, not just to convey information efficiently, but to arrange related actions into a hierarchy in which the lesser images or actions both subserve and build to the key image. In "Indian Camp," when Dr. Adams discovers that the Indian father has slit his throat, the doctor orders his own young son removed from the shanty: "There was no need of that. Nick, standing in the door of the kitchen, had a good view of the upper bunk when his father, the lamp in one hand, tipped the Indian's head back" (18). As Nick's positioning compels him to witness this grisly scene, so the precise arrangement of clauses and phrases does not release the crucial action—"tipped the Indian's head back"—until the end. The sentence closes with a click, forcing the reader to visualize what Nick sees. A more dramatically complex sentence in "Cross-Country Snow" self-reflexively points to the author's obsession with capturing exactly "the sequence of motion and fact which creates the emotion":

> George was coming down in telemark position, kneeling: one leg forward and bent, the other trailing; his sticks hanging like some insect's thin legs, kicking up puffs of snow as they touched the surface and finally the whole kneeling, trailing figure coming around in a beautiful right curve, crouching, the legs shot forward and back, the body leaning out against the swing, the sticks accenting the curve like points of light, all in a wild cloud of snow. (*Complete Short Stories* 108)

The Steinian participles (*coming, trailing, hanging, kicking, kneeling, trailing, coming, crouching, leaning, accenting*) create simultaneous and parallel actions, just as they do in the Villalta chapter: "the muleta trailing and the sword following the curve behind."

Where the chapters experiment with making one sentence structure dominant while a contrasting structure often conveys the central theme or climax, the later fiction typically blends these structures to achieve a particular rhythm and thematic impact. In this passage from "In Another Country," note how the lengthening complex and compound sentences accompany, and in a sense enable, the soldier-narrator's increasing candor as the crucial repeated phrase—"very much afraid to die"—tumbles out amid images of death and desolation:

> After that their manner changed a little toward me, although I was their friend against outsiders. I was a friend, but I was never really one of them after they had read the citations, because it had been different with them and they had done very different things to get their medals. I had been wounded, it was true; but we all knew that being wounded, after all, was really an accident. I was never ashamed of the ribbons, though, and sometimes, after the cocktail hour, I would imagine myself having done all the things they had done to get their medals; but walking home at night through the empty streets with the cold wind and all the shops closed, trying to keep near the street lights, I knew that I would never have done such things, and I was very much afraid to die, and often lay in bed at night by myself, afraid to die and wondering how I would be when I went back to the front again. (*Complete Short Stories* 208)

The thematic repetitions Hemingway had learned from Stein and the evocative images from Pound (italicized below) powerfully undergird the rising intensity of this passage: friend—friend—*citation*—different—different—things [they had done]—*medals*—wounded—wounded—*ribbons* —done things—they had done—walking *at night*—*empty streets*—*cold wind*—*all shops closed*—*near street lights*—things [I would never have done]—very much afraid to die—*in bed*—*at night*—*by myself*—afraid to die—*the front.*

In a remarkably short time, Hemingway polished and developed the thematic potential of techniques he had tried out in the short chapters. Consider the technique of presenting the sensation before explaining the conditions that create it:

> Nick sat against the wall of the church where they had dragged him to be clear of the machine gun fire in the street. Both legs stuck out awkwardly. He had been hit in the spine. (chapter 7)

Hemingway could easily have reversed sentences 2 and 3, making the legs sticking out awkwardly a clear consequence of Nick's having been hit in the spine. Instead, he gives us the physical fact ("stuck out awkwardly") before providing the explanatory cause. Experience is sensory—for characters and readers alike—before it is contextualized and understood.

The same technique appears often—and memorably—in the stories and novels. In "Indian Camp," for example, when Dr. Adams checks on the Indian father, "He pulled back the blankets from the Indian's head. His hand came away wet" (*In Our Time* 18). Not for another two sentences do we find out what this wetness signifies. In "Cross-Country Snow" the "sensations first" technique acquires thematic implications: "The rush and the sudden swoop as he dropped down a steep undulation plucked Nick's mind out and left him only the wonderful flying, dropping sensation in his body (*In Our Time* 107)." "Plucked Nick's mind out" ironically anticipates the story's conclusion, when paternal responsibilities now weigh on that mind and eliminate skiing's opportunities for lightening it in a rush of sensations. "The Battler" further develops the "sensations first" technique into an objective correlative for Nick's emotions. Having barely escaped a bad beating from ex-prizefighter Ad Francis, Nick heeds Bugs's advice to leave: "Nick climbed the embankment and started up the track. He found he had a ham sandwich in his hand and put it in his pocket." "He found" perfectly conveys Nick's dazed condition at this point, while the second action—"put it in his pocket"—reinforces this mental numbness with a mechanical action. Following his violent rescue by Bugs, Nick's questions about Ad gradually fade, while Bugs's answers expand to monologue. The physical fact of the sandwich in his hand thus establishes itself in his mind as a new reality but also conveys (along with Nick's growing silence) a mind that is still reacting to a powerful shock. In sum, a technique used to heighten the reader's physical perception in *in our time* evolves in stories written only a year or two later into a subtle method of suggesting a theme or conveying a character's psychological state.

The techniques discussed above were all legacies of the *in our time* experiments. Hemingway refined them in his stories and novels, extended their variety, deepened their complexity and subtlety, combined and recombined them in his prose to form a mature, intricate style of apparent simplicity. That style had not yet coalesced in *in our time*—the book explores too many directions to represent "the" Hemingway style. But the components of that style were clearly present. The characteristic rhythm of simple sentences intermingling with compounds and occasionally a complex sentence; the plain diction and precise rendering of physical details; the closely observed actions conveyed through calculated sentence rhythms; the narrative emphasis on sensation before context, on showing over telling; the unblinking stare at violent actions and previously unmentionable conditions, yet the calculated reluctance to describe emotions or state themes directly—all create a freshness and intensity of experience, both physical and psychological, that the earliest readers and critics of these chapters immediately felt. *in our time* provided the raw material for this style in a self-consciously avant-garde form that imposed rigorous discipline on these laboratory experiments. Hemingway's most distinctive achievement in moving from these chapters to the stories and novels that followed was not to retreat from the experiments of *in our time,* but to shape them into a style and technique that was simultaneously popular and modernist—his own style.

Appendix — Sentence Structure in *in our time*

Chapter	Sentences	Fragment	Simple	Simple‡	Compound	Comp.‡	Compound Predicate	Complex	Complex-Compound	Complex-Compound Predicate	Fusion F / FS	Run-on
1	11		5	2	2		1	1			0 2	
2	6		1		3				1	1		4
3	13	3	6	4								
4	8		5	1			1			1		
5	10	1	6		3							
6	11		8	1	1			1				
7	22	1	16	3	1		1					
8	10	2	3	1	1	1		1	1		0 1	
9	12		8		2			1	1		2 0	
10	40	1	9	8	5	7	2	5	1	2		
11	30	1	16	4	3	2	2	2				
12	9		3	1	2		3					
13	6		2		3		1				0 1	1
14	8	3			2		1	1	1			1
15	27	6	9		7	1	1	1	1	1	1 3	
16	19		10	2	1	1	4	1				
17	22		14	4				3	1			
18	16		12	2	1			1				
Totals	**280**	**18**	**133**	**33**	**37**	**12**	**17**	**18**	**7**	**5**	**3 7**	**6**
	100%	**6.4%**	**47.5%**	**11.8%**	**13.2%**	**4.2%**	**6.2%**	**6.4%**	**2.5%**	**1.8%**	**1.1/2.5%**	**2.1%**

Simple‡: Simple sentence with participles or clauses that do not qualify it as a complex sentence.

Compound‡: Compound sentence with participles or dependent clauses that do not qualify it as a complex sentence.

Fusion: Two sentences fused either with comma (F) or with speech tag ("he said": FS); categorized by nature of sentences.

Run-on: Three or more independent clauses run together; categorized by nature of independent clauses.

Sentence Structure in *in our time*

Classification Criteria

With the exceptions noted below, I followed the criteria in *A Comprehensive Grammar of the English Language,* by Randolph Quirk et al., for defining simple, complex, and compound sentences. The authors' definition of "complex" is conventional, that is, a main clause and a subordinate clause, but their definition of "subordinate" as "a constituent of the sentence as a whole" (987) excludes all clauses that fit within phrases:

> a simple sentence may have a clause functioning within a phrase. In that case the complexity is at the level of the phrase, not at the level of the sentence or clause. Thus ["You can borrow the car that belongs to my sister"] is a simple sentence [in which] the relative clause *that belongs to my sister* is a postmodifier within the complex noun phrase. (719 n. a)

Similarly, nonfinite clauses—participials and infinitives—do not constitute subordinate clauses at the sentence level. Most often, sentence-level subordinate clauses are introduced by a subordinating conjunction.

These criteria would categorize as "simple" many Hemingway sentences that *appear* complex. For examples:

> [The letters] were about the hospital, and how much she loved him and how it was impossible to get along without him and how terrible it was missing him at night.
> (chapter 10)

> In 1919 he was travelling on the railroads in Italy carrying a square of oilcloth from the headquarters of the party written in indelible

pencil and saying here was a comrade who had suffered very much under the whites and requesting comrades to aid him in any way. (chapter 11)

In the first example, the "how" clauses are all object clauses, completing the prepositional phrase beginning with "about." In the second example, the participial "carrying" (and hence *all* the clauses that follow) modifies "travelling." In neither example, would Quirk et al. define the additional clauses as directly "subordinate" to the sentence's main clause.

Exceptions

1. To avoid obscuring the categories and skewing their numerical totals, it seems essential to distinguish the potentially complicated yet *technically* simple sentences discussed above from simple sentences of one clause that are so prevalent in Hemingway's writing (for example, "We shot them.")
Accordingly, in Chapter Six and in this appendix, I have created a separate category and symbol—simple‡—for technically simple sentences with additional clauses, participles, and infinitives. Similarly, I distinguish compound sentences with additional clauses and so on as "compound‡."

2. In dialogue passages, I have excluded such speech tags as "I said" from analysis of the sentence (that is, the speech statement) except where the speaking verb seemed intrinsically part of the sentence action, for instance, "The lieutenant kept riding his horse out into the fields and saying to him. . . . " and "he lay very flat and sweated and prayed."

3. I have included several additional subcategories to reflect sentence patterns important to *in our time:*

- Compound Predicate:
  "He had so much equipment on and looked awfully surprised and fell down into the garden" (chapter 4)
- Complex-Compound Predicate:
  "He went inside when he saw me and came downstairs disgusted." (chapter 15)
- Fusion for sentences fused either with or without a comma (f):

"They're wops ain't they?" (chapter 9)
"He didn't listen to me, he was listening so hard for the music to start." (chapter 15)

or fused by a speech tag (f-s):

"You go down after him, said Maera, he hates me." (chapter 15)
"He was very short with a brown face and quite drunk and he said after all it has happened before like that." (chapter 13)

- Run-on sentences containing three or more independent clauses (typically, a multiple compound sentence):
  "The crowd came over the barrera and around the torero and two men grabbed him and held him and some one cut off his pigtail and was waving it and a kid grabbed it and ran away with it." (chapter 13)

4. Fusion and run-on sentences are also categorized by the structure of their individual sentences, that is, compound, compound-complex, and so on. The sentence above ("The crowd came over.") would be classified as "compound."

Notes

Introduction

1. To clarify briefly the two versions mentioned here:

1. *in our time,* a book published by Three Mountains Press in March 1924, comprises eighteen short chapters.
2. *In Our Time,* a book published by Boni & Liveright in late 1925, consists of these chapters (two converted to stories) interspersed with fourteen short stories.

An earlier version of the first six chapters, which appeared in the *Little Review* (Spring 1923) and was also entitled "In Our Time" need not be discussed here. Chapter Two sorts out the tangled publication history.

To avoid confusion between Hemingway's chapters and the chapters of this book, I shall refer to Hemingway's in lowercase followed by Arabic numbers, my own in uppercase with the numbers spelled out.

2. The holograph edition of *in our time,* published by Bruccoli Clark Books, was limited to 1,700 copies.

3. Even the much better known 1925 *In Our Time* has attracted only three scholarly books: Matthew Stewart's *Modernism and Tradition in Ernest Hemingway's In Our Time: A Guide for Students and Readers,* Wendolyn E. Tetlow's *Hemingway's In Our Time: Lyrical Dimensions,* and Michael Reynolds's *Critical Essays on Ernest Hemingway's In Our Time.* For a listing of the major articles on the *in our time* chapters, see n. 7 below.

4. Letter to Max Perkins, c. 10 Oct. 1924, *F. Scott Fitzgerald: A Life in Letters,* 82.

5. Letter to Edward O'Brien, 12 Sept. 1924, *Ernest Hemingway: Selected Letters,* ed. Carlos Baker, 123. Hereafter cited as *Selected Letters.*

6. Hemingway, of course, weighed in on this question, asserting vigorously (but not altogether convincingly) that "[w]hen they are read altogether [the chapters] all hook up. . . . It has form all right" (letter to Ezra Pound, c. 5 Aug. 1923, *Selected Letters,* 91–92). I consider the matter more fully in Chapter Two.

7. In addition to the chapters on *in our time* in the Stewart and Tetlow books cited in n. 3, the best stylistic examinations of the chapters appear in Richard Bridgman's *The Colloquial Style in America,* ch. 6, and Keith Carrabine's "Hemingway's *In Our Time:* An Appreciation," *Fitzgerald/Hemingway Annual 1979,* 301–26. Charles A. Fenton's *The Apprenticeship of Ernest Hemingway: The Early Years* astutely traces the influence of Hemingway's journalism on the chapters. Several excellent studies by Michael Reynolds examine *in our time*'s place in Hemingway's artistic development: "*In Our Time:* The Biography of a Book," in *Modern American Short Story Sequences,* ed. J. Gerald Kennedy; "Looking Backward," introduction to *Critical Essays*; and *Hemingway: The Paris Years.* Fenton's *Apprenticeship* is also very thorough in tracing the various stages of and influences on Hemingway's development.

E. R. Hagemann has contributed two invaluable works of literary scholarship: "A Collation, with Commentary of the Five Texts of the Chapters in Hemingway's *In Our Time,* 1923–1938" and "'Only Let the Story End as Soon as Possible': Time-and-History in Ernest Hemingway's *In Our Time.*"

Studies that assert an internal logic to the *in our time* chapters (all reprinted in *Critical Essays*) include: Clinton Burhans Jr., "The Complex Unity of *In Our Time*"; Jackson J. Benson, "Patterns of Connections and Their Development in Hemingway's *In Our Time*"; Linda W. Wagner's "Juxtaposition in Hemingway's *In Our Time*"; and David J. Leigh, S. J., "*In Our Time:* The Interchapters as Structural guides to a Psychological Pattern".

8. For examples:

> his first true style which he perfected in the *in our time* chapter. (Paul Smith, *A Reader's Guide to the Short Stories of Ernest Hemingway* xxvii)

> In these prose vignettes we can see the first example of what was to become Hemingway's characteristic prose style. (David Seed, "'The Picture of the Whole': *In Our Time*" 17)

> These qualities ["rigorous objectivity," "complete lack of 'thinking,'" and "unbelievably sharp and simple prose"] have never been more clearly marked than in a pamphlet called *in our time.* (Philip Young, *Ernest Hemingway: A Reconsideration* 180)

> [The chapters] show the mastery over craft in less than a year from the entry in the Paris 1922 notebook. (Charles G. Hoffman and A. C. Hoffman, "'The Truest Sentence': Words as Equivalents of Time and Place in *In Our Time*" 100–01)

> [The text of the chapters is] a monument in American prose. . . . With minimal vocabulary and maximal talent, Ernest Hemingway had invented what Edmund Wilson called, with exactitude, "a form of his own" (E. R. Hagemann, "Collation" 49)

> [The chapters are] the first real fruits of his genius. (Robert Brainard Pearsall, *The Life and Writing of Ernest Hemingway* 45)

> To describe [chapter 12] as apprentice work is again somewhat to miss the point, in that the very essence of Hemingway's early technique lies in such an intensity of concentration of the individual concrete details of a scene. (Peter Messent, *Ernest Hemingway* 20)

> [In contrast to the transitional *Three Stories & Ten Poems, in our time*] represents "his achieved hard, 'stripped' manner, the manner of an Imagist in prose" (Nicholas Joost, *Ernest Hemingway and the Little Magazines* 48).

For a contrasting view that emphasizes the experimental nature of *in our time,* see: Bridgman; Michael Reynolds, "Hemingway's *In Our Time:* The Biography of a Book"; and Carrabine. Carrabine's article is probably closest to the thesis of this study in stressing that the chapters "are all conscious experiments in making up voices and in testing narrative stances. . . . conscious experiments in voice and point of view" (309, 320) and that Hemingway "was at once forging an aesthetic and testing out the viability of themes that would dominate his literary career" (307).

9. Although Hemingway's publisher, Bill Bird, was responsible for much of this look—the lowercase titles and names; the small, centered texts surrounded by much white space; and the brilliant cover collage—chapter drafts show that Hemingway himself used the dashes, albeit inconsistently, to mark off speeches in some dialogues.

Notes to Chapter One

1. Although almost nothing from this period made it into print at the time, several stories and poems have survived. Five of these stories have been pub-

lished in Peter Griffin, *Along With Youth: Hemingway, the Early Years.* Surviving poems appear in *88 Poems.*

2. Cf. Stephen Crane's description of the Bowery's Maggie, who "blossomed in a mud puddle" (*Maggie: A Girl of the Streets* 141). In draft, "Up in Michigan" resembled "Pauline Snow" even more, as Paul Smith has shown ("Hemingway's Apprentice Fiction: 1919–1921" 137–48).

3. For his own part, Anderson agreed with Hemingway: "if others said I had shown Hemingway the way, I myself had never said so. I thought . . . that he had his own gift, which had nothing particularly to do with me" (*Memoirs,* qtd. in Fenton 89). Nonetheless, Fenton cites the recollections of several journalists who knew Hemingway in 1920–21 and who attest to his enthusiasm for Anderson.

In his discussion of Anderson's influence on the story, Paul Smith notes how the ambiguity surrounding the facts in "My Old Man"—just how crooked Joe's father is, how much Joe understands this—exceeds that of "I Want to Know Why" (*Reader's Guide* 13–14). I disagree, however, with his assertions that "Anderson's diction and syntax are more formal than Hemingway's" (note how Anderson's narrator digresses and interrupts himself midsentence) and that "[Anderson's] story is 'written,' rather than 'told' " (12).

4. Fenton's statement that "there was nothing imitative in [Hemingway's] impulse toward Paris" because "[t]he mass expatriation of young American artists had not yet begun" (98) is dubious in both claims. As Malcolm Cowley recounts in *Exile's Return* (79–81), 1921 was a peak year for the first wave of American expatriate writers going to Paris. For example, Pound arrived there in 1920, Cummings and Dos Passos in March 1921, and Cowley in late spring 1921. Anderson's enthusiasm over his own recent trip there in 1920 was Hemingway's immediate impetus.

5. Paul Smith notes that in the draft Hemingway likely completed in Chicago, the story's most Steinian paragraph (beginning "Liz liked Jim very much.") was already present (*Reader's Guide* 5). But his conclusion—and Fenton's (149)—that this proves that "it is unlikely that . . . Hemingway could have been influenced by Stein" is illogical since, as I argue above, Anderson surely recommended, perhaps even loaned, Stein's *Three Lives* to Hemingway. If Hemingway wrote the draft *after* he knew he would be meeting Stein (via Anderson's letter of introduction), he may also have boned up on her writing right away.

6. The image of the tyro humbly sitting at the feet of the tutor has been used by various biographers and biographical critics to describe Hemingway and Anderson, Hemingway and Stein, and Hemingway and Pound, attesting either to Hemingway's humility (and agility) or to the tenacity of a cliché.

7. Stein preceded nearly all writers in understanding the artist's rapidly

changing conception of time and space. As Stephen Kearns demonstrates, however, this conception also expresses a radically altered sense of time and space in everyday urban life in the century's first decade, largely through an influx of new inventions (*The Culture of Time and Space* passim).

8. Lisa Taylor, "Ernest Hemingway's Date Rape Story: Sexual Trauma in 'Up in Michigan,'" *The Hemingway Review* 13.2 (Spring 1994): 1–11.

9. Hadley R. Mowrer to Carlos Baker (Baker file, Princeton Univ. Library), qtd. in *The Paris Years,* 22.

10. "Imagisme," "A Few Don'ts by an Imagiste," *Poetry* (March 1913): 198–206; *Gaudier-Brzeska,* 88; letter to Harriet Monroe, January 1915, in *Selected letters of Ezra Pound* 49.

11. The Ernest Hemingway Collection of the John F. Kennedy Library, Boston MA. Hereafter cited as KL. Also reprinted in Reynolds, *The Paris Years,* 103.

12. The influence of Joyce—the author Hemingway later claimed to have most respected at the time (*Selected Letters* 696)—appears later, for example in the generic similarities between *In Our Time* and *Dubliners.* One may, however, hear an echo of Molly Bloom's repetitions of "Yes" from her closing soliloquy in the despairing Maera's repetitions ending chapter 15; the context and meaning, of course, are entirely different.

13. Carlos Baker states that the "Paris 1922" sentences were completed by the end of May (*Hemingway: A Life Story* 91); Michael Reynolds dates them as summer (*The Paris Years* 95).

14. Hemingway to Pound, 23 Jan. 1923, in *Selected Letters,* 77.

15. Reynolds, *The Paris Years,* 114. Reynolds does not give the source showing Hemingway's intent.

16. "All you have to do is write one true sentence. Write the truest sentence that you know. So finally I would write one true sentence, and then go on from there. It was easy then because there was always one true sentence that I knew or had seen or had heard someone say. If I started to write elaborately, or like someone introducing or presenting something, I found that I could cut that scrollwork or ornament out and throw it away and start with the first simple declarative sentence I had written." (*A Moveable Feast* 12)

17. In *Personae: The Shorter Poems of Ezra Pound,* ed. Lea Baechler and A. Walton Litz (New York: New Directions, 1990).

18. The fullest discussion of the nature and influence of Hemingway's journalism is in Charles Fenton's *The Apprenticeship of Ernest Hemingway.* See also: J. F. Kobler, *Ernest Hemingway: Journalist and Artist*; Robert O. Stephens, *Hemingway's Nonfiction: The Public Voice*; and Elizabeth Dewberry Vaughn, "'Truer Than Anything Else': *In Our Time* and Journalism" and "Hemingway's journalism and the realist dilemma."

19. Keith Carrabine disputes this view, arguing that Fenton "fails to recognize that the needs of the journalist and of the artist are not necessarily continuous but rather disjunctive, even at odds." ("*In Our Time:* An Appreciation" 302). Carrabine notes how few of the chapters derived directly from Hemingway's journalism.

20. "On the *Star* you were forced to learn to write a simple declarative sentence." George Plimpton, "An Interview with Ernest Hemingway," *The Paris Review* 18 (Spring 1958), rpt. in Baker, *Hemingway and His Critics,* 25.

21. *Kansas City Times,* Nov. 26 1940, qtd. in Fenton, 37.

22. Schuyler Ashley, "Another American Discovers the Acid in Language," 22.

23. Lincoln Steffens, *Autobiography,* 834. Jeffrey Meyers presents a slightly different account of Hemingway's enthusiasm for cablese:

> Steffens and [George] Seldes [another journalist] "gave him a quick course in cablese," Seldes recalled, "and within a week Hemingway mastered it. He came in one night and said: 'Stef, look at this cable: no fat, no adjectives, no adverbs—nothing but blood and bones and muscle. It's great. It's a new language.'" (Meyers, *Hemingway: A Biography* 94).

24. KL. "Stop" on line two is handwritten.

25. Hemingway illustrated the power and economy of these inversions in the angry wire he sent to his *Toronto Star* editor (quoted in Reynolds 92):

> SUGGEST YOU UPSTICK BOOKS ASSWARDS. HEMINGWAY

26. KL 633. The draft is typed, but the word count below it is handwritten in writing that does not look like Hemingway's.

Notes to Chapter Two

1. Reynolds notes that Pound "agreed to be the general editor" of the series by 1 August and "immediately began lining up authors" (*The Paris Years* 80). Pound to Williams, 1 August 1922, in *Selected Letters of Ezra Pound,* 183–84.

2. Pound Manuscripts, Lilly Library. A hand other than Hemingway's has written "1922] [late spring?]" on this undated letter. But Hemingway's reference to Pound's having "publicly" backed him (that is, in the published prospectus) would date the letter as October or later. Reynolds, on the other hand, allows for too much time in stating that "[b]y the first of March [1923], Hemingway told Pound that maybe Ezra had made a mistake under the pressure of friendship. Perhaps it would be better to take him off the list, for he had nothing worth printing" ("Looking Backward" 8). It seems more likely that Hem-

ingway would have alluded to the prospectus when it was still fresh in his mind—and when he hadn't yet produced any new work. By March 1923, he had finished several new pieces.

Another internal clue about the letter's dating: Hemingway alludes to Lincoln Steffens's admiration of his writing. In his *Autobiography,* Steffens identifies that writing as Hemingway's famous dispatch on the exodus of the Christians from eastern Thrace, "A Silent, Ghastly Procession," which Hemingway composed in mid-October 1922 (*Autobiography* 834–35).

3. E. R. Hagemann, accepting the questionable dating of this letter, speculates that the "samples" Hemingway has in mind might be the "Paris 1922" sentences ("Collation" 38). But if Hemingway wrote the letter after the prospectus was published in October, he could have immediately sent Pound these sentences or shown them to Pound earlier. They were, in any case, far too slight for the new book.

4. Baker's documentation is ambiguous. For facts pertaining to the composition of *in our time,* he cites a letter Hemingway wrote him (1 April 1951), but Baker's note does not specifically refer to the *Little Review*'s commission (*Hemingway: A Life Story* 580). I have not been able to locate Hemingway's letter to Baker, which may indeed contain the evidence of Heap's commission. The letter is in neither the Hemingway Collection of the John F. Kennedy Library nor the Carlos Baker Collection of Ernest Hemingway [materials] at Princeton University. In researching correspondence between Hemingway and Pound, Hemingway and Heap, and Pound and Heap (KL and the *Little Review* Records, Univ. of Wisconsin-Milwaukee), I have found neither Heap's commission nor references to it. Finally, Baker does not explain how Heap, living in New York at the time, would have even heard of Hemingway, much less want to publish his prose.

More recently, Hemingway's most comprehensive biographer, Michael Reynolds, also credits Jane Heap with the commission, adds that Heap's publication date was "April," and cites Baker's biography as his source (*The Paris Years* 114, 369 n. 49.) For a fuller discussion, see Milton A. Cohen, "Who Commissioned the *Little Review*'s 'In Our Time'?" *The Hemingway Review* 23.1 (Fall 2003): 106–10.

5. This letter is dated (presumably by curators of the *Little Review* collection) as "[Jan.–March 1923]." Precisely when Pound approached Hemingway with the magazine commission is uncertain, although February 1923, when Hemingway and his wife, Hadley, were visiting the Pounds in Rapallo, is a reasonable guess.

6. Pound, letter to William Carlos Williams, *Selected Letters of Ezra Pound* 183; prospectus for the *Inquest* series, *Little Review,* Spring 1923.

7. The precise contents of the stolen valise have been variously described,

the contents growing ever greater in Hemingway's successive recollections (Paul Smith, "1924: Hemingway's Luggage and the Miraculous Year" 41–42). Smith lists the items as part of an unfinished war novel, some short stories set at the Italian front, a sheaf of poems, and the "Paris 1922" sentences he had written a few months earlier. Two short stories finished in Paris escaped the theft: "Up in Michigan" (completed in early 1922) and "My Old Man" (summer 1922); the former was in a drawer Hadley had missed, the latter in circulation at the time. Hemingway soon recreated the lost "Paris 1922" sentences (KL 647).

8. Pound's actual response was more thoughtful and sympathetic than Hemingway had expected. He denied calling the theft a boon but said it would take ten years to know if the loss were truly a disaster. In the meantime, "nobody is *known* to have lost anything by *suppression* of early work." If the form of the lost pieces was good, Hemingway should be able to rewrite them from memory (letter to Hemingway, 27 January 1923, KL 69, qtd. in *The Paris Years* 95). Hemingway did just that with the "Paris 1922" sentences.

9. Though O'Brien did not succeed in placing the story, he did better: he included it in his anthology of *Best Short Stories of 1923* and even dedicated the volume to "Ernest Hemenway," giving the young writer (or his approximate namesake) much needed visibility.

10. The source of chapter 1 is unknown. Hemingway may have invented it from whole cloth, but it would be the only one of the six he invented (and one of only three or four in the entire book).

11. Qtd. in Paul Smith, "'Mons (Three)': An Unpublished *In Our Time* Chapter" 107–12.

12. Paul Smith speculates that if Hemingway intended the early vignettes to depict the war as "noble and clear," as he later asserted to Pound, then this one would be "inappropriate" ("'Mons (Three)'" 111). A related reason for deleting it may lie in the comparative expressiveness of the three vignettes. The calm, self-controlled voice of "Mons (Three)" falls between the polar extremes of chapters 4 and 5, muting the intensity of their contrast.

Regarding its date of composition, Smith notes that the three asterisks closing "Mons (Three)" group it with the six pieces in the *Little Review.* But it appears on the back of a draft for chapter 14, which was written in July 1923.

13. Reynolds presents this draft as the final revision of three (*The Paris Years* 127).

14. Precisely when Hemingway began to think of his prose experiments as the material for the "Inquest" book is not certain, but my guess is no later than March 1923 and possibly as early as November 1922, when he had declared to Pound regarding the "Inquest" commission that he now knew what he wanted

to achieve in prose and planned to show Pound some examples of the new prose in half a year's time (Pound Manuscripts, Lilly Library, c. November 1922).

Both Carlos Baker and Kenneth Lynn state that it was Bill Bird who encouraged Hemingway to devote the whole book to these pieces *after* Bird had read the six Hemingway composed for the *Little Review* (*A Life Story* 111–12; *Hemingway* 193). They err, however, when they state that Bird first read these pieces when "Jane Heap had printed [them] in *The Little Review*" (112). The "Exiles" issue did not come out until the fall, well after Hemingway had completed and sent all eighteen chapters to Bird. It is quite possible, of course, that Hemingway showed Bird the *Little Review* pieces in draft when the two were in Paris in March 1923.

15. "Four" sketches were really six (counting chapter 2). "Five" years were really three (*The Sun Also Rises* was published in 1926).

16. Both meanings of *l'envoi* fit: a conclusion or postscript to a literary work and a messenger or representative. In this case, the narrator is a messenger from the outside world; in one draft, he informs the king "how things looked along the Maritza and how changed the army was from last fall" (KL 94a). Critics have also noted the title's echo of "Envoi" in Pound's *Hugh Selwyn Mauberley* (the title of the closing poem in part one).

17. See Smith, *Reader's Guide,* 31–33, for the critical debate over the revolutionist's sensibility, which is also discussed in Chapter Six.

18. "The Complex Unity of *In Our Time,*" *Modern Fiction Studies* (1968), 313–28, rpt. in *Critical Essays,* 90.

19. "*In Our Time:* the Interchapters as Structural guides to a Psychological Pattern," 130–37.

20. The only apparent exception to this order of composition is chapter 18, which Hemingway wrote before chapter 17, as he mentions in his August 1923 letter to Pound (*Selected Letters* 91–92).

21. "Hemingway's *In Our Time:* The Biography of a Book," 35, 38–39, 47.

22. As Edmund Wilson observed, putting titles and names in lowercase was certainly not new by 1924; consider the title of the little magazine Hemingway helped edit, *transatlantic review.*

23. "The Emergence of Ernest Hemingway," rpt. in *Hemingway and His Critics,* ed. Carlos Baker, 59.

24. Mencken's review is not to be found where Jeffrey Meyers has cited it (*American Mercury,* August 1925, xxxviii) in *Hemingway: The Critical Heritage,* 60, n. 27. In fact, no Mencken review of any version of *in our time* is listed in the various editions of *The Mencken Bibliography.* Yet, the passage Meyers quotes and its title ("Quackery") sound like *echt* Mencken.

25. Warren Taylor, "Chiselled Prose Found in Fiction of Hemingway: Real-

istic Stories are Found 'In Our Time,'" *Nashville Tennessean* (10 Jan. 1926), rpt. in *Critical Essays*, 23–24. Other reviews noting the book's "experimental" style are those in the *New York City Sun* (17 Oct. 1925), *The New Republic* (Nov. 1925), and *Omaha World-Herald* (10 Jan. 1926), all rpt. *Critical Essays*, 15–26.

26. Miscellaneous reviews of *In Our Time*, rpt. in *Critical Essays*, 17, 20–21, 25–26.

27. Letter to Edmund Wilson, 25 Nov. 1923, in *Selected Letters*, 105; letter to Edward O'Brien, c. 20 Nov. 1923, in *Selected Letters*, 104.

28. In several letters written during the nine months he wrote these stories, Hemingway referred to the *number* of stories he had completed—as if marking off his progress toward the volume of material he would need for a book of stories. Michael Reynolds suggests that his converting chapters 10 and 11 into stories also helped "make the volume seem longer than it actually was" ("Biography of a Book" 41).

29. The exception is the Bruccoli holograph of *in our time* (1977). The textual alterations that the chapters underwent in their various editions will be discussed in Chapters Five and Six.

Notes to Chapter Three

1. Carlos Baker writes: "he was already tinkering with a series of short prose sketches. They were based in form and idea on the half-dozen 'I have seen' sentences . . . [of] *Paris, 1922*" (*Hemingway: A Life Story* 108). As noted in Chapter One, Michael Reynolds sees the "Cross Roads" sketches as antecedents ("Looking Backward" 7).

2. Letter to William Carlos Williams, 1 August 1922, in *Selected Letters of Ezra Pound*, 183, emphasis mine.

3. Letter to Edward O'Brien, 12 Sept. 1923, in *Selected Letters*, 123.

4. "Cameo stories"—Robert Pearsall, *The Life and Writings of Ernest Hemingway*, 45; "Impressions"—James Nagel, "Literary Impressionism and *In Our Time*," *Hemingway Review* 17 (Spring 1987): 17–26; "sketch[es]"—Nicholas Joost, *Ernest Hemingway and the Little Magazines*, 53; "experiment"—Michael Reynolds, "Biography of a Book," 38; "stylistic exercises"—Richard Bridgman, *The Colloquial Style in America*, 203; "tools of self-instruction"—Charles Fenton, *The Apprenticeship of Ernest Hemingway*, 180; "five-finger exercises" and Hemingway's "honor's thesis"—Earl Rovitt, *Ernest Hemingway*, 49.

5. Louis Cohn, *A Bibliography of the Works of Ernest Hemingway*, 21, qtd. in Fenton 180.

6. Hemingway's respect for concrete place-names finally expressed itself rhetorically in the much-quoted passage of *A Farewell to Arms:* "There were many words that you could not stand to hear and finally only the names of

places had dignity. Certain numbers were the same way and certain dates and these with the names of the places were all you could say and have them mean anything" (184).

7. "Greeks Execute Six of Old Regime," *Chicago Tribune Paris Edition,* 29 Nov. 1922, p. 1.

8. Even the evacuation from Adrianople (chapter 3) conveys violence in what the civilians flee from and in the childbirth the little girl witnesses.

9. Curiously, Hemingway in this same passage states that the "about to be" climax does not apply to executions (3). But chapters 6 and 17 argue to the contrary.

10. Though the queen's role is obviously different in *Alice in Wonderland,* both scenes share a surreal sense of menace in a garden setting: the card-painters will lose their heads if the queen discovers the white rose tree; Hemingway's queen and king will figuratively lose *their* heads if they wander outside the garden.

11. The point of view in chapter 7 (Nick's wounding) is third person but stays very close to Nick as protagonist. Hemingway first conceived of chapters 8 (the praying soldier under shellfire) and 10 (the recovering soldier and Luz) in first person and later changed them. Chapter 16 (Maera's death) was originally drafted with a first-person narrator. See Chapter Six for discussion of these changes.

12. Not all chapters with first-person narrators belong in this group, however. In chapters 11, 13, and 15, the first-person narrators are peripheral to the central characters (the revolutionist, the incompetent bullfighter, the irresponsible bullfighter and Maera), and I will consider these chapters further on as character studies.

13. *The Sun Also Rises* expresses this undercurrent eloquently: "It was like certain dinners I remember from the war: There was much wine, an ignored tension, and a feeling of things coming that you could not prevent happening" (151).

14. Only one experiential chapter, the third-person narrative of Nick's wounding (chapter 7), reads like a fragment of this bildungsroman, particularly when it is linked in *In Our Time* to the story immediately following it, "A Very Short Story" (formerly chapter 10), which extends the theme of wounding to hospital recovery and romance.

15. For example, after 1930 he would drop the British voices and experiences. But disorientation and drunkenness, tension, fear, and release, and sudden, unexpected lurchings into violence or calm mark many of his later stories, as do, of course, the archetypal experiences of being wounded and convalescing, all of which culminate in *A Farewell to Arms.*

16. "The Art of Fiction," 378.

17. At least, Hemingway considered it comic when "this animal instead of

doing something tragic, that is, dignified, gallops in a stiff old-maidish fashion around a ring trailing the opposite of clouds of glory." (*Death in the Afternoon* 6–7).

18. Hemingway quickly traded on his firsthand experience of World War I. See, for example, his letter to Edmund Wilson (25 Nov. 1923) accusing Willa Cather of plagiarizing her battle scenes in *One of Ours* from *Birth of a Nation:* "Poor woman she had to get her war experience somewhere" (*Selected Letters* 105).

Notes to Chapter Four

1. This list does not include the indirect speech of the officer in chapter 6, who is reported telling the soldiers to quit trying to make the sick cabinet minister stand up.

2. This ambiguity of the speaker's nationality can occur quite unexpectedly, as when one critic identifies the bullfighter-narrator in chapter 15 as "obviously an American friend of the matador, Maera" (Capellán 56).

3. According to the Paris edition of the *Chicago Tribune,* when King Constantine fled Greece after the failure of his war against the Turks, he knew that the cabinet ministers he left behind (who had brought him out of exile and supported him) would likely face a firing squad (see chapter 6). Allegedly, he even told one minister, "Sorry. There is no more room" on the plane whisking the king to safety ("Greeks Execute Six" 1).

4. Jeffrey Meyers, for example, writes of "On the Quai at Smyrna," the introduction Hemingway added in 1930, that it "is narrated by a British naval officer in the same tone of voice Hemingway adopted from Chink Dorman-Smith and used in the two Mons vignettes" (*Hemingway: A Biography* 101).

5. Robert Scholes, "Decoding Papa: 'A Very Short Story' as Work and Text," in *Semiotics and Interpretation,* 110–26.

6. In "The Bullfight Story and Critical Theory," Bruce Henriksen asserts that the chapter "is told in second person" (113). Alternatively, Richard Bridgman considers the chapter to be in first person (*The Colloquial Style in America* 203). Although neither critic supports his contention, both probably base their assertions on the two *yous* of the opening sentence. But *you* subsequently disappears and gives way to an anonymous narrator, ruling out second person. The first-person hypothesis is more plausible since the narrator appears to address the reader; but because the narrative voice does not characterize itself (except as knowledgeable), in contrast to the characterized voice in chapter 2, I consider it an anonymous narrator focusing on Villalta, hence a third-person point of view.

7. Michael Reynolds asserts that the point of view is omniscient primarily

because it leaves Maera's consciousness to focus briefly on the hurrying doctor (*The Paris Years* 140).

8. The first version of Maera's death supports the view that Maera infers these actions though he does not see them. The gored Maera tells the narrator (another bullfighter): "I kept waiting for Luis to do the quite and waiting for the quite to take him [the bull] away" (KL 564 ms.).

9. Whether or not the final sentence—"Then he was dead"—also reflects a shift out of Maera's fading consciousness, as Reynolds asserts (140), raises epistemological issues that cannot be resolved.

10. The narrator in chapter 4 refers to "Young Buckley," but this Briticism need not suggest much age difference between the speaker and Buckley. And Hemingway's source for this chapter, Eric Dorman-Smith, was a young officer.

11. Several modernist writers like Virginia Woolf, Katherine Mansfield and, of course, Joyce in *Dubliners,* successfully erased the boundary between third-person limited omniscient and first person, by sliding the narrative into and out of the voice of the protagonist although technically that protagonist does not narrate the story.

12. Richard Bridgman also identifies this chapter's point of view as first-person, but acknowledges the difficulty these ambiguous narrative voices pose: "The reader cannot really distinguish the journalistic chapters written in the third person from those written in the first. One is not often aware of a particular speaker in these sketches free of dialect and illiteracies, which means that the speaker can now be manipulated for special emphasis" (*The Colloquial Style in America* 203, 209).

The critical disagreement cited in n. 6 above affirms Bridgman's view (as do differing definitions of "journalistic"). His analysis of narrative voice and colloquial style in *in our time* is the best single study of the topic.

13. "'We went to work on the trench': Hemingway's Process of Appropriation in *In Our Time,* 'Chapter 7,'" in *Hemingway in Italy,* 61–67.

Notes to Chapter Five

1. Examples:

> It is a conspicuously American style, stressing the naturalness of language, syntax that fragments rather than unifies his predominantly simple sentences. (Waldhorn 32)

> In these prose vignettes we can see the first example of what was to become Hemingway's characteristic prose style. . . . the passages work

through a series of consecutive statements which generally avoid subordinate clauses and which give a superficial impression of naïveté. (Seed 17)

2. The criteria for these linguistically simple sentences, which may contain subordinate clauses but are not technically complex, are given in the appendix.

3. In the epilogue, I describe which *in our time* experiments Hemingway retained, altered, or dropped in shaping the early style of the stories and novels.

4. The aesthetic of indirect emotion comes from parallel theories in Pound and Eliot. The latter's "objective correlative" was a "formula" of "a set of objects, situations, [or] chain of events intended to evoke a particular emotion" ("Hamlet and His Problems" 100). Still earlier, Pound's "luminous detail"—"vigorously hostile to . . . the method of sentiment and generalization"—consists of "certain facts which give one a sudden insight into circumjacent conditions" and is presented "without comment" ("I Gather the Limbs of Osiris" 21–23). Louis Menand observes, "the same argument [for indirect emotion] appeared wherever Imagist practices needed justification" (*Discovering Modernism* 135).

5. E. R. Hagemann suggests plausibly that the correcting culprit for the first Scribner's edition (1930) was Max Perkins, Hemingway's editor ("Collation" 43, 45). *The Fifth Column and the First Forty-nine Stories* (editor unknown) restored a few of these fragments while "correcting" others, and the 1996 Scribner's Paperback Fiction edition of *In Our Time* has restored a few more.

6. Just who changed the fragments in the 1925 Boni & Liveright edition is not clear. Hemingway (in a letter accompanying the returned galley proofs) approved of the publisher's editing: "Whoever did the editing on the whole book was very intelligent and most of the changes of punctuation I agree with. Those I don't I have changed to their original form" (quoted in Hagemann, "Collation" 45, 51n). If Hemingway read the galleys closely enough to catch punctuation changes, he would certainly have spotted changes in his sentences. Thus, whether it was Hemingway or a Liveright editor who "corrected" the fragments, the changes were made with Hemingway's knowledge and approval. These conditions were far less likely to obtain for subsequent editions of *In Our Time,* such as the first Scribner's edition (1930), when Hemingway's concentration on his current writing made him impatient with proofing galleys for earlier books (Hagemann, "Collation" 43).

7. 31 March 1925, in *Selected Letters,* 155. Hemingway here compares his easily approachable style to E. E. Cummings's style in *The Enormous Room,* "the classic example of a really fine book that could not sell" because it "was written in a style that no one who had not read a good deal of modern writing could read."

8. Curiously, the *Little Review* version of chapter 2 places a semicolon after *sand,* yet the drafts originally had no punctuation there (KL 92, 94a). As Keith Carrabine observes, in converting the semicolon to a comma "Hemingway emphasized the ongoingness, the speed of the action." ("*In Our Time:* An Appreciation" 308).

9. Although chapter 10 is usually grouped in the war chapters because its male protagonist is a soldier recovering in a hospital, both its noncombat subject and, more importantly, its storytelling narrative mode (which relies heavily on complex sentences) separate it from the other war chapters. Therefore, I have excluded it from this count. Even including it, however, the total ratio of simple sentences for the war chapters is 44/101, significantly more than that of the bullfight chapters.

10. This was Wyndham Lewis's disparaging title for Hemingway in Lewis's 1934 essay. To demonstrate that Hemingway was "the enthusiastic amateur of rude, crude, naked force in men and women" and that his "art is an art of the surface," Lewis quotes all of chapter 4 of *in our time* (186–207).

11. Elizabeth Dewberry Vaughn observes that this "lack of historical context" underscores by its absence: it "draws attention to the function of verbal and imaginal context" ("'Truer Than Anything True': *In Our Time* and Journalism" 14).

12. For examples:

> Each of the vignettes . . . seems discrete and, even within its own confines, lacking a climax. (Waldhorn 46)
>
> There is no climax in any of these chapters; nor is there a sense of climax in their progression throughout the novel." (Clifford 21)

As I argue in "Highlighting Themes and Climaxes", Hemingway not only constructs subtle climaxes in many of these chapters, but highlights them with contrasting sentence structure.

13. Hemingway originally intended to give more play to this retrospective "That was when" closure. A draft of chapter 3 ends: "That was the beginning of the retreat" (KL 693). In a draft of chapter 8, following the terrified soldier's praying, the sentence appears: "That was during a ~~bombardment~~ shelling in the line near Fossalta." And chapter 1 originally began retrospectively with "I remember riding along in the dark," thus balancing the retrospective ending: "I was a kitchen corporal then and we were going to entrain for the champagne" (KL 92).

14. Part of this unity (or coincidence) was lost when chapter 6 becomes "Chapter V" in the 1925 *In Our Time* and thereafter.

15. Matthew C. Stewart, *Modernism and Tradition in Ernest Hemingway's* In Our Time: *A Guide for Students and Readers* 156–57; Wendolyn E. Tetlow, *Hemingway's* In Our Time: *Lyrical Dimensions,* chapter 2.

16. The crucial shift from "I" to "he" in this chapter and in chapter 8 is discussed in Chapters Four and Six.

17. Paul Smith goes so far as to argue that this beefing up of sentences was more typical of Hemingway's revision process than was compression and deletion ("1924: Hemingway's Luggage and the Miraculous Year" 44–45). My own research finds examples of both techniques in the chapters.

Notes to Chapter Six

1. "'Only Let the Story End as Soon as Possible': Time-and-History in Ernest Hemingway's *In Our Time*", rpt. in *Critical Essays,* 53.

2. In the draft, the sentence reads: "It was very funny going drunk along that road in the dark," emphasizing the comical meaning of "funny" (KL 92). Hemingway's revision creates a richer ambiguity.

3. Cf. Nick's depiction of himself as "stinking in every attack" in "A Way You'll Never Be" (*Complete Short Stories* 309).

4. As noted above, the draft makes their future combat less imminent than an all-night march *to* the battlefield would suggest. In any case, some critics, in my view, have overemphasized this ironic tension between the narrator's current, safe situation and his retrospective awareness of the battle to which he marches. Hagemann, for example, refers to the narrator as a "hapless *poilu* [who] relates a desperately comical incident as he heads for slaughter" ("Only Let the Story End" 53). Certainly Hemingway intended this tension by alluding to this battle site. But except for the last sentence, the present-time narrative prevails, giving us a mundane, slightly bizarre, yet eminently safe night march, not, as Hagemann concludes, the prelude to an "execution in battle" (53).

5. Critics have not resolved this ambiguity. Hagemann, for example, identifies the narrator of chapter 1 as a French *poilu* but does not try to account for his American usages ("Only Let the Story End" 53). Keith Carrabine, on the other hand, assumes the battery is American since the lieutenant is "proud of his French phrases" ("*In Our Time:* An Appreciation" 308). In a draft of this chapter (KL 92), the drunken lieutenant speaks more French than in the revised version.

6. The symbol ‡ marks sentences with additional clauses, participles, and infinitives that do not alter the sentence's category. See appendix for criteria determining these categories.

7. For the 1925 *In Our Time,* Hemingway placed this chapter as the first of the bullfight sequence (Chapter IX).

8. E. R. Hagemann claims that the episode described in this chapter "never took place," based on his review of *Los Toros: Tratado Técnico e Históroco* but then seems to contradict himself by noting that its author mentions the bullfighter Joselito "killing six bulls on six different occasions in 1915" ("Only Let the Story End" 57).

9. "Today is Friday," *Complete Short Stories,* 272. As noted above, Hemingway was fond of referring to a bullfighter as the "kid" and had various viewers (including his wife) use the term in his *Toronto Star* dispatches. In a different *Star* dispatch, the photographer Shorty Wornall refers to King George of Greece (see chapter 18) as "a fine kid" (15 Sept. 1923, *Dateline: Toronto* 295). "Kid" was also Agnes von Kurowsky's nickname for Hemingway, who sometimes referred to her as "Mrs. Kid" (see *Hemingway in Love and War,* chapter 3).

10. The permutations these two sentences have suffered in the various editions of the chapters make them virtually a case study in the problem of textual authenticity:

> *Little Review* 1923: " . . . he couldn't get the sword in. He couldn't hardly lift his arm."
> *in our time* 1924: " . . . he couldn't get the sword in. He couldn't hardly lift his arm."
> *In Our Time* 1925: " . . . he couldn't hardly get the sword in. He couldn't hardly lift his arm."
> *In Our Time* 1930: " . . . he could hardly get the sword in. He could hardly lift his arm."
> *First Forty-nine Stories* 1938: " . . . he couldn't get the sword in. He couldn't hardly lift his arm."
> *Short Stories of EH* 1954: " . . . he couldn't get the sword in. He couldn't hardly lift his arm."
> *In Our Time* 1956: " . . . he could hardly get the sword in. He could hardly lift his arm."
> *In Our Time* 1967: " . . . he could hardly get the sword in. He could hardly lift his arm."
> *Complete Short Stories* 1987: " . . . he couldn't get the sword in. He couldn't hardly lift his arm."
> *In Our Time* (Scribner Paperback Fiction) 1996: " . . . he couldn't get the sword in. He couldn't hardly lift his arm."

Presumably, an editor other than Hemingway (probably Max Perkins) gussied up the grammar—and eviscerated the sense—of these sentences in the first

Scribner's edition (1930), reprinted in 1956 and 1967. An unknown editor of the *First Forty-Nine* collection (1938) silently returned the sentences (and many other Perkins-inspired "corrections") to the Paris version, changes that the most recent editions have happily continued (Hagemann, "Collation" 39, 47).

11. The KL 92 draft reads: "the last bull *he killed* he was so tired" (emphasis mine), and this draft lacks "He couldn't hardly lift his arm." Another substantive difference in the *Little Review* version: the "kid" tries eight times, not five, to get the sword into his final bull. In keeping with his technique of repetition, Hemingway changed eight to five (which it had been in the KL 92 draft) to echo the five bulls the kid must kill.

12. The second bullfighter's unlucky fate undergoes an odd emendation in KL 94a and the *Little Review* version. Instead of the horn "came out" (as it does in KL 92 and in all other published versions), here we have "and the horn came and he lay in the sand"—in short, he's being gored again.

13. Hemingway's 1930 introduction to the larger *In Our Time,* entitled "On the Quai at Smyrna," also depicts an episode immediately following the Greco-Turkish War: the British naval evacuation of civilians from Smyrna.

14. Some critics have observed that Hemingway's shifting perspectives in this chapter have a dehumanizing quality. Keith Carrabine writes that "the changes of perspectives" provide "an overall shaping vision of timeless, anonymous suffering" ("*In Our Time:* An Appreciation" 310). And Kenji Nakajima goes a step further, arguing that eliminating the "humanity of the refugees" becomes Hemingway's "way of hardening his senses, to make them impervious to any human misery in any situation" ("To Discipline Eyes Against Misery: on Hemingway's 'Chapter II.' *In Our Time*" 13).

15. See Milton A. Cohen, "There was a woman having a kid"—From *Her* Point of View: An Unpublished Draft of *In Our Time,* Chapter II," *Hemingway Review* 22.1 (Fall 2002): 105–08.

16. Hagemann identifies the action in chapter 5 as occurring on 23 August 1914, in which Dorman-Smith's battalion prevented a German crossing of the Mons-Condé Canal at the Mariette Bridge, one of eighteen bridges over the canal that the British held. The historical source of the combat in the garden described in chapter 4, however, has not been identified ("Only Let the Story End" 53).

17. Jeffrey Meyers, for example, writes of "On the Quai" that it "is narrated by a British naval officer in the tone of voice Hemingway adopted from Chink Dorman-Smith and used in the two Mons vignettes" (*Hemingway: A Biography* 101). E. R. Hagemann is even more direct: "Dorman-Smith's battalion is responsible for the Mariette Bridge which *he* so jollily speaks of in Chapter IV [*in our time,* chapter 5]" ("Only Let the Story End" 53, emphasis mine).

18. Critics who are wont to slap a single label—typically "horrors of war"—on the depictions of combat in *in our time* might recall that only chapter eight portrays a terrifying situation (which fades like a bad dream the next morning). Nick is glad to be out of combat in chapter 7; the speakers in chapters 4 and 5 both encounter the easiest of combat situations, though their reactions are diametrically opposed; and the kitchen corporal in chapter one recounts bizarre events fifty kilometers from the front. As the diversity of these encounters undermines paradigm, resists stereotype, and opposes cliché, it becomes Hemingway's commentary on writing war fiction and on the experience of war (See Milton A. Cohen, "Soldiers' Voices in *In Our Time:* Hemingway's Ventriloquism?" *Hemingway Review* 20.1 [Fall 2000]: 28).

19. Historical facts about the incidents narrated in chapters 4 and 5 come from E. R. Hagemann, "Only Let the Story End," 53.

20. Paul Smith, in analyzing the relation of "Mons (Three)" to the other Mons chapters, draws a similar conclusion, noting the "understatement" of chapter 4 and the "overstatement" of chapter 5. Smith concludes: if "we assume a single speaker for all three chapters . . . [and that] the drama of the three chapters takes place within his character, . . . [then] its conflict and resolution are signified by opposed manners of speech and their implicit moral positions." Smith concludes that the voices in chapters 4 and 5 belong to different officers ("'Mons (Three)'" 109).

21. The unpublished "Mons (Three)" (KL 94A) appears to continue the action of chapter 5 but, again, in a different voice (see Chapter Two for a fuller discussion).

22. Ironically, this factuality is fictitious, since the real executions occurred at 11:30 A.M., not 6:30 A.M..

23. Words in brackets are my addition or represent a choice Hemingway left unresolved.

24. For example, Joseph Flora asserts that Nick is American because "he speaks mainly in English" (106). Flora does not explain why Nick speaks bilingually.

While the surname "Adams" first appears in the unpublished vignette "Did You Ever Kill Anyone?" (see Chapter Two), "Nick Adams" does not make his first appearance in Hemingway's fiction until early 1924 in "Three Shots," the original opening of "Indian Camp" (Reynolds, *The Paris Years* 165–66).

25. In Chicago after the war, Hemingway met a decorated Italian-American veteran, Nick Nerone, whose name he used in a pre-Paris story. (Reynolds, *The Paris Years* 126–27). Yet the fictional Nick's relief at no longer being a "patriot" scarcely matches Nerone's superpatriotism during the war.

26. Hemingway's subsequent novels and stories continue this "variations"

motif: Jake Barnes is wounded in the genitals; Frederic Henry in the knee and leg; and Nick, a lieutenant serving with the Italians in "Now I Lay Me," suffers from insomnia, a likely result of his war service. In "A Way You'll Never Be," Nick has suffered a head wound that has affected his mind. For an example of the critics' difficulty in maintaining a unified Nick Adams experience, see Joseph Flora's *Hemingway's Nick Adams,* in which Flora concludes that Nick must have been wounded "more than once" (115).

27. E. R. Hagemann provides no supporting evidence for his assertion that the Italian attack was really the counterattack of "early July 1918" in response to the Austrian offensive the preceding month. Presumably, he dates the chapter by biographically linking Nick's wounding to Hemingway's ("Only Let the Story End" 54).

28. In the first draft, Nick is "sitting" in a trench, "twisting a tourniquet around his ankle"—a good deal more in control of his situation than the Nick wounded in the spine (Kathryn Derounian 66–71).

29. Critics are sometimes reluctant to limit Nick's escape to combat and shows of patriotism. For Robert Slabey, Nick "deserts the army and resigns from society" (82). Kenji Nakajima, using the other chapters, Hemingway's letters home, and later writings as evidence, sees Nick's wounding as his red badge:

> Nick has passed an initiation ordeal successfully. Re-naming himself ("not patriots") is the privilege of a youth who has undergone symbolic death and rebirth. The wound is evidence of his adulthood. . . . He is joyous because he could suppress and rebuff his cowardly fear; he is prideful for he has attained manhood through a deadly trial." ("Shot, Alive, and Was Glad," *In Our Time*" 15–16)

Similarly, Nick's condition has received sharply contrasting descriptions. He is "joyous" (Nakajima), "in a state of shock" (Clifford 18), experiencing the "increased sensory perception that pain induces" (Carrabine, "*In Our Time:* An Appreciation" 312), and restricted by his wound to "his only comfortable position—looking forward" (Derounian 64).

30. "Alterations to Draft A," in Derounian, 66.

31. For example, the image evokes the benediction "May the countenance of the Lord shine upon you and give you peace"—the "peace in our time" that Nick can now look forward to from his wheelchair.

32. Joyce, Woolf, Katherine Mansfield, and, later, Katherine Anne Porter, among many others, used this "blending" point of view.

33. Derounian does not observe, however, an odd transference in the sentence, "Nick looked straight ahead brilliantly." Presumably he is squinting be-

cause "[t]he sun shone on his face." But "brilliantly" would logically describe the sun shining rather than Nick squinting.

34. The impact of this fragment is lost in the 1925 *In Our Time,* where it becomes the grammatically respectable "We're not patriots." Not only does the revised version fail to stand out, it also loses the breathlessness of the fragment, thus flattening Nick's characterization. Subsequent editions, beginning with *The Fifth Column and the First Forty-nine Stories* (1938), restore the Paris edition's fragment, which continues in the most recent editions of the chapters.

35. Hagemann, "Only Let the Story End," 54.

36. " 'We went to work on the trench': Hemingway's Process of Appropriation in *In Our Time,* "Chapter VII," 63.

37. A contemporaneous example illustrates this shock power: in 1920, the mother of Sibley Watson, publisher of the *Dial,* strenuously objected to E. E. Cummings's use of the word "Jesus" in his *Dial* poem "Buffalo Bill's."

38. Numerous studies of Allied soldiers in WWII show that of the many dangers they faced in combat, they most feared artillery shelling, during which they were helpless to affect their fate, even though artillery was not the deadliest weapon (John Ellis, *On the Front Lines* 68–71, 89–90). Ellis quotes a British infantry private, whose recollection is virtually identical to Hemingway's praying solider:

> We hit the earth with one thud where we had stood. I could feel the exact spot in the small of my defenceless back (I wish to God we had packs on, I thought, I wish to God we had packs on not because they're any *use* but it feels better) where the pointed nose of the shell would pierce skin and gristle and bone and explode the charge that would make me feel as if I had a splitting headache all over for a fiftieth of a second before I was spread minutely over the earth and hung up in trees. I held my breath and tried to press deeper into the earth and tensed every muscle as though by sheer will power I could abate the force of that disintegrating shock, cheat death, defy God (O God have mercy on me, please, please, *please* dear God, don't let me die!) (70)

39. An early draft (KL 94a) stresses even more the praying soldier's luck in the face of huge events he cannot affect; the sentence originally read: "The shelling moved further up the line and there was no attack."

40. In a provocative analysis of the tension between confessional "telling" and silence in this narrative, George Cheatham imputes gendered associations to these acts:

> Telling about Jesus, of course, would amount to admitting his vulnerability and dependency, his need for someone else. Through his silence, the soldier denies this vulnerability. . . . Thus the text encodes a series of dualities along the masculine-feminine axis: dependency, vulnerability, and talkativeness are encoded as "feminine" weaknesses and are projected onto the prostitute, while independence, control, and silence are encoded as "masculine" strengths and are appropriated for the soldier. ("Androgyny and *In Our Time*" 70)

Factoring in the text's narrative ambiguity as a suppressed confession and the absolutes of the final sentence (*never* and *anybody*), Cheatham concludes:

> Perhaps the [text's] most striking aspect . . . is the deep masculine anxiety which pervades it, signaled by the excess of these two absolutes. . . . The text, which is itself a telling, encodes telling as feminine weakness. . . . In this way "Chapter VII" strangely devalues itself while contradicting its own assertion of infinite control. (71)

Readers well-versed in Hemingway will recognize in Cheatham's thesis the author's lifelong bias against "talkiness," both in his fiction (for example, the soldier in chapter 10 "holding tight on to himself so he would not blab about anything during the silly, talky time [under the anesthetic]") and in self-descriptions of his inspiration: "If you talk about it, you lose it."

Yet Cheatham (and Scholes, too, whose *Textual Power* he quotes extensively) weakens his case somewhat by constructing overly neat antitheses that the text does not support. Thus, the praying soldier does not "project" the feminine weakness of being talkative onto the prostitute because the prostitute, a virtual cipher, is given no speech.

41. The complete news story appears in Michael Reynolds, "Two Hemingway Sources for *in our time,*" rpt. in *Critical Essays,* 33–34.

42. In the drafts for this chapter, Boyle is less sure of—and closer to identifying—the robbers' identity: "They're hunkies or wops ain't they?" (KL 94a). Hemingway's removal of "hunkies or" both strengthens the dialogue and sharpens Boyle's characterization.

Hagemann's assumption that the change of ethnicity to Hungarian anticipates the Hungarian protagonist of "The Revolutionist" (the story that immediately follows this chapter in the 1925 *In Our Time*) works well for *that* volume ("Only Let the Story End" 54). But the book for which Hemingway originally composed these chapters, *in our time,* lacks this juxtaposition because an entirely different chapter is interspersed between the two "Hungarian" episodes.

43. Hemingway's drafts at first followed the news story except for adding the colorful "off": "Boyle shot them both *off* the seat of the wagon." Then he penciled in the variation: "one off the seat of the wagon and one out of the wagon box" (KL 94a). The 1925 *In Our Time* enlarged Drevitts's slang ("bumped them") to "bumped them off"—perhaps more familiar to readers, but less radically slangy. The *First Forty-nine Stories* restored "bumped them." Thereafter, editions have seesawed, the most recent maintaining "bumped them." The 1925 *In Our Time* also corrected the earlier version's two spellings of "Drevitts."

44. Biographers disagree as to whether the affair was sexually consummated. Kurowsky, in a letter to Carlos Baker, flatly denied that it was, which would liken the fictional fantasizing here (for instance, "he thought of Ag in his bed") to that of chapter 7, where Nick is a combat soldier, fighting with the Italians.

45. The complete letter is reprinted in *Hemingway in Love and War,* 163–64.

46. The first draft (KL 633) is closer to Agnes's letter in this respect: "the letter came saying ours had been only a kid affair."

47. Besides *A Farewell to Arms* the theme appears in *The Sun Also Rises* (between Jake Barnes and Brett Ashley) and in the novel fragment *Along with Youth.*

48. Hemingway originally planned to dramatize the first paragraph's sexual episode, again stressing the bed:

> Ag sat
>
> She was cool and fresh in the hot night.
>
> on the bed. ~~I said I love you Ag. And pulled her over hard against me. And she said I know it and kissed me and got all the way up onto the bed~~ (KL 633)

49. The missing comma following "A short time after" allows the sentence to be misread as "A short time after he contracted gonorrhea." Ironically, Hemingway's revision in the 1925 *In Our Time* was even worse: "A short time after he contracted gonorrhea from a sales girl in a loop department store while riding in a taxicab through Lincoln Park." At first it appears that he contracted gonorrhea in the loop department store.

50. Scholes, "Decoding Papa," 110–26. See also Scott Donaldson's cogent comparison of the three versions of this chapter, "'A Very Short Story' as Therapy," 99–105.

51. Barbara Groseclose, "Hemingway's 'The Revolutionist': An Aid to Interpretation," 565–70.

52. Paul Smith, *Reader's Guide,* 32.

53. Hemingway registered his own views of Mussolini in a dispatch for the

Toronto Star (27 Jan. 1923), calling him "the biggest bluff in Europe." Observing the dictator at a press conference, the reporter described Mussolini as appearing lost in a book, which proved to be a French-English dictionary, held upside down. Hemingway adds: "There is something wrong, even histrionically, with a man who wears white spats with a black shirt" (*By-Line* 64).

54. *The True Believer: Thoughts on the Nature of Mass Movements,* reissue ed. (New York: HarperCollins 1989).

55. As Paul Smith points out (*Reader's Guide* 30), "In spite of Italy" should have been "In spite of Hungary"—where political events and the revolutionist's own bitter experience might well have disillusioned him. The chapter's typescripts (KL 94a) confirm this. Hemingway penciled into the second draft: "In spite of what had happened to him in Hungary, he believed altogether in the world revolution." He then shortened it to "In spite of Hungary." But somehow the phrase appeared as "In spite of Italy" in the proofs, and Hemingway missed the error. He corrected it for the 1925 *In Our Time.*

56. In his other descriptions—autobiographical or fictional—of this stage of the bullfight, Hemingway makes allowances for the spectator's likely revulsion. Michael Reynolds quotes him (letter to Greg Clark, c. June/July 1923) describing how he warned his wife about the goring of the horses and how she turned her attention to her embroidery at the crucial moment (*The Paris Years* 136). In *The Sun Also Rises,* Jake Barnes similarly warns Brett Ashley, who looks anyway. In *Death in the Afternoon,* Hemingway parodies this squeamishness by making his interlocutor, the little old lady, favor the goring of the horses above all else in the bullfight. Elsewhere in the book, however, he asserts that the goring is essential to the later stages of the bullfight.

57. McAlmon, *Being Geniuses Together,* 179, qtd. in Reynolds, *The Paris Years,* 130, n. 15. Quoting Hemingway's notes, Reynolds shows how he later used the material in the short story, "A Natural History of the Dead."

58. In *Death in the Afternoon,* Hemingway describes these comic possibilities:

> In the tragedy of the bullfight the horse is the comic character. . . . The comic that happens to these horses is not their death . . . but the strange and burlesque visceral accidents which occur. There is certainly nothing comic by our standards in seeing an animal emptied of its visceral content, but if this animal instead of doing something tragic, that is, dignified, gallops in a stiff old-maidish fashion around a ring trailing the opposite of clouds of glory it is as comic when what it is trailing is real as when the Fratellinis give a burlesque of it in which the viscera are represented by rolls of bandages, sausages and other things. If one is comic the other is; the humor comes from the same principle. (7)

59. Keith Carrabine notes that the shift from simple past tense to past modal ("could not make up its mind") in the last sentence suggests "that the horse's fate is part of an unfinished episode" ("*In Our Time:* An Appreciation" 315).

60. Ever the disciplined writer, Hemingway recognized that "bad" redounds "so much" and cut it from the 1925 *In Our Time.*

61. "The second bullfighter slipped and the bull caught him through the belly and he hung on to the horn with one hand and held the other tight against the place, and the bull rammed him wham against the wall and the horn came out, and he lay in the sand, and then got up like crazy drunk and tried to slug the men carrying him away and yelled for his sword but he fainted."

62. This draft begins with a salutation—"Dearest Old Izz"—as if Hemingway originally planned to describe Villalta to Pound in a letter.

63. Comparing Villalta's stance to a tree was essential in showing his absolute control over the body part most likely to yield to or signal fear: the legs. Thus Hemingway worked over these lines in the drafts:

> Villalta bends back like tree struck by sudden terrific wind, firmly rooted. (KL 414)
>
> . . . he swung back firmly like an oak when the wind hits it (KL 94a)
>
> . . . Then he cursed the bull, flopped the muleta at him and swung back the other way in the tree swing, the bull charging, and the muleta curving. (KL 94a)

64. See Chapter Four, n. 6.

65. In *The Sun Also Rises,* Hemingway also experiments with projecting this insider knowledge to another character, this time Brett Ashley, when it is clearly Jake's views that Brett absorbs: "I sat beside Brett and explained to Brett what it was all about. . . . She saw how Romero avoided every brusque movement. . . . She saw how close Romero always worked to the bull. . . . She saw why she liked Romero's cape-work, and why she did not like the others" (173–74).

66. Interestingly, the drafts had Villalta hating as well: "Then when he started to kill, all in the same rush hating" (KL 94a).

67. In all three drafts for this chapter (KL 94a), the sentence concludes: "and then it was *broken*" (emphasis mine), keeping the focus on the physical union.

68. Two changes from the drafts maintain this powerful parallelism. First, Hemingway cuts a colorful but unnecessary simile: "the bull roaring blood like a hydrant looking straight at Villalta and his legs going" (KL 94a). Second, he

changes the colloquial "going" to the vivid and precise "caving." For further analysis of structural effects in chapter 14, see Chapter Five.

69. A draft for this chapter strengthens these symbolic alternatives for Luis:

I grabbed his arm and he pulled loose
I'm dancing
and said Oh to hell with you and your bulls. xxxxxxxx . (KL 94a)

70. Curiously, the 1925 *In Our Time* retained this powerful fragment even though that edition had changed others. The anonymous editor of the 1938 *First Forty-nine Stories* made it a conventional sentence ("The street was full of them"). This, too, was strange, since that editor typically restored fragments of the 1924 *in our time.* Subsequent editions have followed both precedents.

71. See Chapter Four for a fuller discussion of this narrative perspective.

72. Another instance of Hemingway's precision is the singular "horn." The bull can gore so small a target only with one horn or the other.

73. Chapter Four discusses whether this digression from Maera's consciousness renders the point of view omniscient.

74. "The others stood around," a chilling detail of their useless and even voyeuristic presence, was omitted from the 1925 *In Our Time,* perhaps because it wasn't directly relevant to the narrative. Arguably, however, it is the ironic center of the chapter in its comment on Maera's death. Captioning a photograph of a similar death scene in *Death in the Afternoon,* Hemingway writes: "Granero dead in the infirmary. Only two in the crowd are thinking about Granero. The others are all intent on how they will look in the photograph."

75. Hemingway elongated this sequence in revision; originally, it lacked "Then it got larger and larger and larger and then smaller and smaller."

76. Hagemann, "Only Let the Story End," 55.

77. The absence of Cardinella's full name here suggests how familiar his name had become to the Chicago public, including Dr. Hemingway and his son.

78. Unpublished letter, courtesy of Nick Adams & Co. Rare Books, David R. Meeker, proprietor, P.O. Box 189266, Sacramento, CA 95818.

79. Compare also the cabinet ministers, who "stood very quietly against the wall," and the black prisoner in the poem who refuses to speak any last words.

80. As many explicators of the "Hemingway code" have noted, this losing or maintaining of self-control was to become—in fact, had already become—a significant theme in Hemingway's work. It appears in various guises throughout *in our time:* in the cabinet ministers' quiet courage just before their execution, in the desperate praying of the soldier under shellfire, in the recuperating sol-

dier's "holding tight on to himself so that he would not blab" under anesthesia, and in the matadors' contrasting responses to mortal danger.

81. Unaccountably, the Scribner Paperback Fiction Edition (first published in 1996) changes "skipped" to "stepped," thus losing the joke. I have not been able to trace their arbitrary change to any previous edition.

82. The draft's version is flatter: "When they pulled the cap over his head."

83. Subsequent editions have gone back and forth on which published version is "right." *The First Forty-nine Stories* follows the Paris *in our time* version, cutting the details of the rope around Sam's neck and the priest holding up the crucifix. The 1962 Scribner Library edition (following the first Scribner's edition of 1930) restores them, while the 1996 Scribner Paperback Fiction edition again cuts them.

84. The front-page headline for the *New York Times* of 30 Nov. 1922 reads: "Greek King Is Held Captive in Palace; His Plea to Leave Country Is Refused." A story the same day in the Paris edition of the *Chicago Tribune* states that "the king is now practically a prisoner."

85. "King Business in Europe," *Toronto Star Weekly,* 15 Sept. 1923, rpt. in *Dateline: Toronto,* 295–300.

86. The king's callousness here is Hemingway's invention. According to the *New York Times* (30 Nov. 1923: 1), the real King George "made every effort to prevent the executions of [the] ex-Ministers, even requesting the Ministers of Rumania and Jugoslavia to make efforts to save the condemned men. This led to a conflict between the ruler and the Gonatas Government."

87. The draft (KL 94a) clarifies that the king wishes to emigrate, not merely visit: "Like all Greeks he wanted most of all to get to America."

88. Wornall's story in Hemingway's dispatch mentions driving "into the palace grounds past a lot of those big tall babies in ballet skirts with their rifles held at the salute. I got out and [the King] came walking down the drive" (295). Hemingway's masterful understatement in the chapter evokes the menace of those lurking guns without ever mentioning them. Another slight change emphasizes the king's breezy facade: in the draft, he calls "Plastiras and those chaps" "hard men." In the chapter, Plastiris is "a good man."

Notes to Epilogue

1. *Hemingway and His Conspirators* 14. Leff overstates his thesis, however, in claiming that Hemingway sought only popular success: "Since *Three Stories* and *in our time* were small press books, printed in limited editions, they were not real books, at least not to the author" (13). Hemingway's pride in these books was genuine—recall his letter to Edmund Wilson declaring that "the *In Our*

Time stuff . . . is where I think I have gotten hold of it" (25 November 1923, *Selected Letters* 105). In the Paris of 1923, moreover, publication in small, avant-garde presses was all that was available to Hemingway, and he was happy to have it.

2. One could argue, however, that his interest never really left the short story and that he composed these prose experiments strictly for the commissions at hand. When he writes to Pound (c. November 1922) that he now knew what he was seeking in prose, he carefully qualifies the assertion to mean for the time being (Lilly Library).

3. Jolas's "Open Letter to Ernest Hemingway" (*Chicago Tribune Paris Edition,* 16 Nov. 1924, qtd. in *The Paris Years* 245) urged Hemingway to stick to short stories such as "My Old Man." Hemingway's reply appeared a week later in the same column, "Rambles Through Literary Paris," (*The Paris Years* 245, 381 n. 19).

4. Because Horace Liveright felt that this passage might cause the book to be suppressed, he deleted it and invited Hemingway to revise it. Hemingway docilely complied—another index of his eagerness to have the book published "by a good publisher." He restored the opening for the first Scribner's edition in 1930.

Works Cited

Primary Sources

Hemingway

Hemingway, Ernest. *88 Poems.* Ed. with introduction by Nicholas Gergiannis. New York: Harcourt/Bruccoli Clark, 1979.

———. "Bull-Fighting Is Not A Sport—It Is A Tragedy." *Toronto Star Weekly,* 27 Oct. 1923.

———. *By-Line: Ernest Hemingway: Selected Articles and Dispatches of Four Decades.* Ed. William White. New York: Simon & Schuster, 1967.

———. *The Complete Short Stories of Ernest Hemingway.* Finca Vigía ed. Scribner Paperback Fiction. New York: Simon & Schuster, 1998.

———. *Dateline: Toronto: The Complete Toronto Star Dispatches, 1920–1924.* Ed. William White. New York: Charles Scribner's Sons, 1985.

———. *Death in the Afternoon.* 1932. New York: Charles Scribner's Sons, 1960.

———. *A Farewell to Arms.* New York: Charles Scribner's Sons, 1957.

———. *The Fifth Column and the First Forty-nine Stories.* New York: Charles Scribner's Sons, 1938.

———. "Homage to Ezra." *This Quarter* 1 (Spring 1925): 221–25.

———. "In Our Time." *Little Review* (Spring 1923): 3–5.

———. *in our time.* Paris: Three Mountains Press, 1924. Holograph ed. Bloomfield Hills, MI: Bruccoli Clark Books, 1977.

———. *In Our Time.* New York: Boni & Liveright, 1925.

———. *In Our Time.* With an introduction by the author, "On the Quai at Smyrna." New York: Charles Scribner's Sons, 1930. Rpt. in 1956, 1967.

———. *In Our Time.* Scribner Paperback Fiction. New York: Simon & Schuster, 1996.

———. Interview. *Kansas City Times* 26 Nov. 1940, 1. Qtd. in Charles Fenton, *The Apprenticeship of Ernest Hemingway,* 37.

——. "King Business in Europe." *Toronto Star Weekly,* 15 Sept. 1923. Rpt. in *Dateline: Toronto.* 295–300.

——. "The Mercenaries." In *Along with Youth: Hemingway, The Early Years,* by Peter Griffin, 104–12.

——. *A Moveable Feast.* New York: Bantam Books, 1965.

——. [on Joseph Conrad's Death]. *transatlantic review* 2.3 (September 1924): 341–42.

——. "On Writing." *The Nick Adams Stories.* Preface by Philip Young. Scribner Paperback Fiction. New York: Simon & Schuster, 1999.

——. "Pauline Snow" ("Cross Roads—An Anthology"). In Peter Griffin. *Along with Youth: Hemingway, the Early Years.* 124–25.

——. "Refugees from Thrace." *Toronto Daily Star,* 14 Nov. 1922. Rpt. in *Dateline: Toronto.* 249–252.

——. "A Silent, Ghastly Procession." *Toronto Daily Star,* 20 Oct. 1922. Rpt. in *Dateline: Toronto.* 232.

——. *The Sun Also Rises.* New York: Charles Scribner's Sons, 1926.

——. *Three Stories & Ten Poems.* Paris: Contact Press, 1923. Holograph ed. Bloomfield Hills, MI: Bruccoli Clark Books, 1977.

——. *To Have and Have Not.* New York: Charles Scribner's Sons, 1937.

——. *The Torrents of Spring.* New York: Charles Scribner's Sons, 1926.

——. Unpublished drafts of *in our time.* Ernest Hemingway Collection. The John F. Kennedy Library, Boston MA.

——. Unpublished letters to and from Hemingway. Ernest Hemingway Collection. Kennedy Library.

——. Unpublished letters to Ezra Pound [1922–25]. Pound Manuscripts. The Lilly Library, Indiana University.

——. Unpublished letters to Jane Heap and Margaret Anderson. *Little Review* Records. University of Wisconsin-Milwaukee.

——. Unpublished writings, including "Did You Ever Kill Anyone?" "Heroes," "Paris 1922," and "Rapallo." Ernest Hemingway Collection. Kennedy Library.

——. "World's Series of Bull Fighting a Mad, Whirling Carnival." *Toronto Star Weekly,* 27 October 1923.

Primary Sources: *Others*

"Greek Ex-Premiers [sic] Shot for War Rout [. . .]" *New York Times,* 29 Nov. 1922: 1–2.

"Greek King is Held Captive in Palace; His Plea to Leave Country is Refused [. . .]" *New York Times,* 30 Nov. 1922: 1.

"Greeks Execute Six of Old Regime." *Chicago Tribune Paris Edition,* 29 Nov. 1922: 1.

"Greeks Take Steps to Arraign Prince [. . .]" *New York Times,* 1 Dec. 1922: 1.

O'Brien, Edward. *Best Short Stories of 1923.* Boston: Small, Maynard & Company, 1923.

Pound, Ezra. *Pound/The Little Review: The Letters of Ezra Pound to Margaret Anderson: The Little Review Correspondence.* Ed. Thomas L. Scott et al. New York: New Directions, 1988.

——. Unpublished letters to Margaret Anderson and Jane Heap. *Little Review* Records. University of Wisconsin-Milwaukee.

Steele, John. "British May Try to Rescue Greeks." *Chicago Tribune Paris Edition,* [1?] December 1922: 2

Influences

Anderson, Sherwood. "I Want to Know Why," "I'm a Fool." *Horses and Men.* London: J. Cape, 1924.

——. *Memoirs.* Qtd. in Charles Fenton, *Apprenticeship,* 89.

Crane, Stephen. *Maggie: A Girl of the Streets. The Great Short Works of Stephen Crane.* New York: Holt & Rinehart, 1968.

Eliot, T. S. "Hamlet and His Problems." *The Sacred Wood: Essays on Poetry and Criticism.* London: Methuen & Co., 1950.

——. "The Love Song of J. Alfred Prufrock," "Preludes," "Sweeney Among the Nightingales." *The Waste Land. Collected Poems and Plays, 1909–1950.* New York: Harcourt, 1962.

James, Henry. "The Art of Fiction." Rpt. in *The Norton Anthology of American Literature.* 5th ed. Vol. 2. New York: Norton, 1998: 370–84.

Pound, Ezra. *Gaudier-Brzeska.* New York: New Directions, 1970.

——. "I Gather the Limbs of Osiris." *New Age,* 7 Dec. 1911. Rpt. in *Ezra Pound: Selected Prose 1909–1965.* Ed. with an introduction by William Cookson. New York: New Directions, 1973. 21–23.

——. "Imagisme," "A Few Don'ts by an Imagiste." *Poetry* March 1913: 198–206.

——. "In a Station of the Metro," *Hugh Selwyn Mauberley,* "The Jewel Stairs' Grievance." Rpt. in *Personae: The Shorter Poems of Ezra Pound 1908–1925.* Ed. Lea Baechler and A. Walton Litz. Rev. ed. New York: New Directions, 1990.

——. *Selected Letters of Ezra Pound 1907–1941.* Ed. D. D. Paige. New York: New Directions, 1971.

Stein, Gertrude. *The Autobiography of Alice B. Toklas.* Rpt. in *Selected Writings.* 1–237.

———. "Composition as Explanation." Rpt. in *Selected Writings of Gertrude Stein*. Ed. Carl Van Vechten. New York: Vintage Books, 1972. 511–23.

———. *How Writing is Written*. Los Angeles: Black Sparrow Press, 1974. Vol. 2 of *Previously Uncollected Writings* of Gertrude Stein. Ed. Robert B. Hass.

———. "Melanctha." Rpt. in *Selected Writings*. 337–57.

———. *Narration: Four Lectures by Gertrude Stein*. Chicago: U of Chicago P, 1935.

———. *Picasso*. London: Charles Scribner's Sons, 1939.

———. *Tender Buttons*. Rpt. in *Selected Writings*. 459–509.

Secondary Sources

Books

Baker, Carlos. *Ernest Hemingway: A Life Story*. New York: Charles Scribner's Sons, 1969.

———, ed. *Ernest Hemingway: Selected Letters 1917–1961*. New York: Charles Scribner's Sons, 1981.

———. *Hemingway and His Critics: An International Anthology*. New York: Hill and Wang, 1961.

———. *Hemingway: The Writer as Artist*. Princeton, NJ: Princeton UP, 1990.

Beegel, Susan F., ed. *Hemingway's Neglected Short Fiction: New Perspectives*. Tuscaloosa: U of Alabama P, 1989.

Capellán, Angel. *Hemingway and the Hispanic World*. Ann Arbor, MI: UMI Research Press, 1985.

Cohn, Louis H. *A Bibliography of the Works of Ernest Hemingway*. New York: Random House, 1931.

Cowley, Malcolm. *Exile's Return: a literary odyssey of the 1920s*. New York: Viking Press, 1951.

Donaldson, Scott, ed. *The Cambridge Companion to Hemingway*. New York: Cambridge UP, 1996.

Ellis, John. *On the Front Lines: The Experience of War through the Eyes of the Allied Soldiers in World War II*. New York: John Wiley & Sons, Canada, Ltd., 1991.

Fenton, Charles A. *The Apprenticeship of Ernest Hemingway: The Early Years*. 1954. New York: NAL 1961.

Flora, Joseph. *Hemingway's Nick Adams*. Baton Rouge: Louisiana State UP, 1982.

Griffin, Peter. *Along With Youth: Hemingway, the Early Years*. New York: Oxford UP, 1985.

Hanneman, Audre. *Ernest Hemingway: A Comprehensive Bibliography*. Princeton, NJ: Princeton UP, 1967.

Hoffer, Eric. *The True Believer: Thoughts on the Nature of Mass Movements*. Reissue ed. New York: HarperCollins, 1989.

Joost, Nicholas. *Ernest Hemingway and the Little Magazines.* Barre, MA: Barre Publishers, 1968.

Kern, Stephen. *The Culture of Time and Space.* Cambridge, MA: Harvard University Press, 1983.

Kobler, J. F. *Ernest Hemingway: Journalist and Artist.* Ann Arbor MI: UMI Research Press, 1984.

Lewis, Robert W. *Hemingway in Italy and Other Essays.* New York: Praeger, 1990.

Lee, A. Robert, ed. *Ernest Hemingway: New Critical Essays.* London: Vision; Barnes & Noble, 1983.

Leff, Leonard J. *Hemingway and His Conspirators: Hollywood, Scribners, and the Making of American Celebrity Culture.* Lanham, MA: Rowman & Littlefield, 1997.

Lynn, Kenneth. *Hemingway.* New York: Simon & Schuster, 1987.

McAlmon, Robert. *Being Geniuses Together.* Rev. Kay Boyle. Garden City, NY: Doubleday, 1968.

Menand, Louis. *Discovering Modernism: T. S. Eliot and His Context.* New York: Oxford UP, 1986.

The Mencken Bibliography. Comp. Betty Adler. Baltimore: Johns Hopkins Press, 1961. Supplementary editions printed in 1962–7, 1972–81.

Messent Peter. *Ernest Hemingway.* New York: St. Martin's Press, 1992.

Meyers, Jeffrey. *Hemingway: A Biography.* New York: Harper & Row, 1985.

——, ed. *Hemingway: The Critical Heritage.* London: Routledge & Kegan Paul, 1983.

Noble, Donald R., ed. *Hemingway: A Revaluation.* Troy, NY: Whitston Publishing Co., 1983.

Quirk, Randolph, et al. *A Comprehensive Grammar of the English Language.* London: Longman, 1985.

Pearsall, Robert Brainard. *The Life and Writings of Ernest Hemingway.* Amsterdam: Rodopi NV, 1973.

Raeburn, John. *Fame Became of Him: Hemingway as Public Writer.* Bloomington, IN: Indiana UP, 1984.

Reynolds, Michael. *Critical Essays on Ernest Hemingway's In Our Time.* Boston: G. K. Hall and Co., 1983. Hereafter cited as *Critical Essays.*

——. *Hemingway: The Paris Years.* New York: Norton, 1989. Rpt. 1999.

——. *The Young Hemingway.* New York: Basil Blackwell, 1986.

Rovitt, Earl. *Ernest Hemingway.* New York: Twayne Publishers, 1963.

Sanford, Marcelline Hemingway. *At the Hemingways.* London: Putnam, 1963.

Smith, Paul. *A Reader's Guide to the Short Stories of Ernest Hemingway.* Boston: G. K. Hall, 1989.

Steffens, Lincoln. *The Autobiography of Lincoln Steffens.* Vol. 2. New York: Harcourt, 1931.

Stephens, Robert O. *Hemingway's Nonfiction: The Public Voice.* Chapel Hill: U of North Carolina P, 1968.

Stewart, Matthew C. *Modernism and Tradition in Ernest Hemingway's In Our Time: A Guide for Students and Readers.* Rochester, NY: Camden House, 2001.

Tetlow, Wendolyn E. *Hemingway's In Our Time: Lyrical Dimensions.* London: Associated University Presses, 1992.

Villard, Henry S. and James Nagel. *Hemingway in Love and War: The Lost Diary of Agnes von Kurowsky, Her Letters and Correspondence of Ernest Hemingway.* Boston: Northeastern UP, 1989.

Waldhorn, Arthur. *A Reader's Guide to Ernest Hemingway.* New York: Farrar, Straus, and Giroux, 1979.

Young, Philip. *Ernest Hemingway: A Reconsideration.* University Park, PA: Penn State UP, 1976.

Articles and Chapters

Baker, Carlos. "The Mountain and the Plain." *Ernest Hemingway: Critiques of Four Major Novels.* Ed. Carlos Baker. New York: Charles Scribner's Sons, 1962. 47–60.

Benson, Jackson J. "Patterns of Connections and Their Development in Hemingway's *In Our Time.*" *Rendezvous* (Winter 1970): 37–52. Rpt. in *Critical Essays.* 103–19.

Bridgman, Richard. "Ernest Hemingway." Chap. 6 in *The Colloquial Style in America* New York: Oxford UP, 1966. 195–230.

Burhans, Clinton, Jr. "The Complex Unity of *In Our Time.*" *Modern Fiction Studies* (1968): 313–28. Rpt. in *Critical Essays.* 88–102.

Carrabine, Keith. "Hemingway's *In Our Time:* An Appreciation." *Fitzgerald/Hemingway Annual 1979.* Ed. Matthew Bruccoli and Richard Layman. Detroit, MI: Gale, 1980. 301–26.

Cheatham, George. "Androgyny and *In Our Time,* Chapter VII." *Hemingway Review* 14.1 (Fall 1994): 67–71.

———. "'We went to work on the trench': Hemingway's Process of Appropriation in *In Our Time,* 'Chapter VII.'" *Postscript (Publication of the Philological Association of the Carolinas, Charleston, SC)* 12 (1995). Rpt. in *Hemingway in Italy.* 61–67.

Clifford, Stephen P. "Hemingway's Fragmentary Novel: Readers Writing the Hero in *In Our Time.*" *Hemingway Review* 13.2 (Spring 1994): 12–23.

Cohen, Milton A. "Soldiers' Voices in *In Our Time:* Hemingway's Ventriloquism?" *Hemingway Review* 20.1 (Fall 2000): 22–29.

———. "'There was a woman having a kid'—From *Her* Point of View: An Unpublished Draft of *In Our Time,* Chapter II," *Hemingway Review* 22.1 (Fall 2002): 105–08.

——. "Who Commissioned the *Little Review*'s 'In Our Time'?" *Hemingway Review* 23.1 (Fall 2003): 106–10.

Derounian, Kathryn. "An Examination of the Drafts of Hemingway's Chapters [sic] 'Nick sat against the wall of the church . . .'" *Papers of the Bibliographical Society of America.* 1982. Rpt. in *Critical Essays.* 66–71.

Donaldson, Scott. "'A Very Short Story' as Therapy." Beegel. 99–105.

Groseclose, Barbara. "Hemingway's 'The Revolutionist': An Aid to Interpretation." *Modern Fiction Studies* 17 (1971–72): 565–70.

Hagemann, E. R. "A Collation, with Commentary of the Five Texts of the Chapters in Hemingway's *In Our Time,* 1923–1938." *Papers of the Bibliographical Society of America.* 1979. 443–58. Rpt. in *Critical Essays.* 38–51.

——. "'Only Let the Story End as Soon as Possible': Time-and-History in Ernest Hemingway's *In Our Time.*" *Modern Fiction Studies* 26.2 (Summer 1980): 255–62. Rpt. in *Critical Essays.* 52–59.

Henrikson, Bruce. "The Bullfight Story and Critical Theory." Beegel. 107–21.

Hoffman, Charles G. and A. C. Hoffman. "'The Truest Sentence': Words as Equivalents of Time and Place in *In Our Time.*" Rpt. in *Hemingway: A Revaluation.* 100–01.

Leigh, David J. "*In Our Time:* The Interchapters as Structural guides to a Psychological Pattern." *Studies in Short Fiction* (1975): 1–8. Rpt. in *Critical Essays.* 130–38.

Levin, Harry. "Observations on the Style of Ernest Hemingway." *Contexts of Criticism.* Cambridge, MA: Harvard Univ. Press, 1957. Rpt. in *Hemingway: A Collection of Critical Essays.* Ed. Robert P. Weeks. Englewood Cliffs, NJ: Prentice-Hall, 1962.

Nagel, James. "Literary Impressionism and *In Our Time.*" *Hemingway Review* 17 (Spring 1987): 17–26.

Nakajima, Kenji. "Shot, Alive, and Was Glad—On Hemingway's 'Chapter VI,' *In Our Time.*" *Kyushu American Literature* 21 (1980): 13–17.

——. "To Discipline Eyes Against Misery: on Hemingway's 'Chapter II,' *In Our Time.*" *Kyushu American Literature* 26 (Oct. 1985): 11–19.

Plimpton, George. "An Interview with Ernest Hemingway." *Paris Review* 18 (Spring 1958): 61–89. Rpt. in Baker, *Hemingway and His Critics.*

Reynolds, Michael. "Hemingway's *In Our Time:* The Biography of a Book." *Modern American Short Story Sequences.* Ed. J. Gerald Kennedy. New York: Cambridge UP, 1995. 35–51.

——. "Looking Backward." Introduction. *Critical Essays.* 1–12.

———. "Two Hemingway Sources for *in our time.*" Rpt. in *Critical Essays.* 31–37.

Scholes, Robert. "Decoding Papa: 'A Very Short Story' as Work and Text." *Semiotics and Interpretation.* New Haven, CT: Yale UP, 1982. 110–26.

———. [on chapter 8]. *Textual Power: Literary Theory and the Teaching of English.* New Haven, CT: Yale UP, 1985: 26–38.

Seed, David. "'The Picture of the Whole': *In Our Time.*" Lee 13–35.

Slabey, Robert M. "The Structure of *In Our Time.*" *South Dakota Review* (August 1965): 38–52. Rpt. in *Critical Essays.* 76–87.

Smith, Paul. "1924: Hemingway's Luggage and the Miraculous Year." *The Cambridge Companion to Hemingway.* Donaldson. 36–54.

———. "Hemingway's Apprentice Fiction: 1919–1921." *New Critical Approaches to the Short Stories of Ernest Hemingway.* Ed. Jackson Benson. Durham, NC: Duke UP, 1990. 137–48.

———. "'Mons (Three)': An Unpublished *In Our Time* Chapter." Lewis 107–12.

Taylor, Lisa. "Ernest Hemingway's Date Rape Story: Sexual Trauma in 'Up in Michigan.'" *Hemingway Review* 13.2 (Spring 1994): 1–11.

Vaughn, Elizabeth Dewberry. "Hemingway's Journalism and the Realist Dilemma." *The Cambridge Companion to Hemingway.* Donaldson. 16–35.

———. "'Truer Than Anything True': *In Our Time* and Journalism." *Hemingway Review* 11.2 (Spring 1992): 11–18.

Wagner, Linda W. "Juxtaposition in Hemingway's *In Our Time.*" *Studies in Short Fiction* (1975): 243–52. Rpt. in *Critical Essays.* 120–29.

Wilson, Edmund. Introduction. *In Our Time.* By Ernest Hemingway. New York: Charles Scribner's Sons, 1930. ix–xv.

Reviews

"In Our Time." *World-Herald* [Omaha]. 10 Jan. 1926. Rpt. in *Critical Essays.* 24–25.

[Rev. of *In Our Time*]. *Cleveland Plain Dealer.* 6 Dec. 1925. Rpt. in *Critical Essays.* 20.

[Rev. of *in our time.*] *Kansas City Star.* 20 Dec. 1924: 6. Rpt. in *Critical Heritage.* 65–66.

Ashley, Schuyler. "Another American Discovers the Acid in Language." *Kansas City Star.* 12 Dec. 1925. Rpt. in *Critical Essays.* 22–23.

Fitzgerald, F. Scott. Letter to Max Perkins, c. 10 October 1924. Rpt. in *A Life in Letters: F. Scott Fitzgerald.* Ed. and annotated by Matthew Bruccoli. New York: Scribner's, 1994.

———. [Rev. of *In Our Time.*] *Bookman* 63 (May 1926): 264–65. Rpt. in *Critical Heritage.* 71–72.

Lawrence, D. H. [Rev. of *In Our Time.*] *Calendar of Modern Letters* 4 (April 1927): 72–73. Rpt. in *Critical Heritage.* 72–74.

Lewis, Wyndham. "The Dumb Ox: A Study of Ernest Hemingway." *Life and Letters* April 1934: 33–45. Rpt. in *Critical Heritage.* 186–207.

[Mencken, H. L.] [Brief review of *in our time.*] "Quackery." *American Mercury* 5 (August 1925): 38? Qtd. in *Critical Heritage.* 12–13.

[Miscellaneous reviews of *In Our Time.]* Rpt. in *Critical Essays.* 17, 20–21, 25–26.

M. R. [Ford Maddox Ford?]. [Rev. of *in our time.*] *transatlantic review* 1 (April 1924): 247–48.

Rascoe, Burton. [Reference to *Three Stories & Ten Poems*]. "A Bookman's Daybook." *New York Tribune,* 21 Oct. 1923. Qtd. in *Hemingway and His Critics.* 55.

Rosenfeld, Paul. "Tough Earth." *New Republic.* Nov. 1925: 22–23. Rpt. in *Critical Essays.* 18–20.

Seligman, Herbert J. [Rev. of *In Our* Time]. *New York Sun,* 17 Oct. 1925. Rpt. in *Critical Essays.* 15–16.

Stein, Gertrude. [Rev. of *Three Stories & Ten Poems.*] *Chicago Tribune Paris Edition,* 27 Nov. 1923: 4.

Taylor, Warren. "Chiselled Prose Found in Fiction of Hemingway: Realistic Stories are found 'In Our Time.' *Tennessean* [Nashville] 10 Jan. 1926. Rpt. in Critical *Essays.* 23–24.

Wilson, Edmund. "Mr. Hemingway's Dry-Points." *Dial* October 1924. 340–41. Rpt. in *The Shores of Light: A Literary Chronicle of the Twenties and Thirties.* By Edmund Wilson. New York: Farrar, Straus, and Young, 1952. 119–22.

———. "Emergence of Ernest Hemingway." In *Shores of Light.* 115–24.

Index

ambiguity in *in our time*
- in actions, 12, 14, 64, 95, 130, 144–45, 161–62, 177–78
- in agents, xiii, 22, 28, 64, 95, 111, 130–31, 153–54, 199
- in chapters, 22, 95
- in Hemingway's subsequent fiction, 206–7
- in sentences, 110, 135–36, 152–53, 160–61, 168, 170
- in setting, xi, 64, 129–30, 154, 177–78, 199, 201, 207
- in time, 129–30
- in voice, 22, 26, 27, 37, 91, 206
- of narrator, xii, 22, 26, 27, 82, 92–93, 131, 144–45, 157–58, 160–61, 199, 206–7, 232n6, 233n12, 236nn2, 5, 239n24, 242n40
- of nationality, 82, 131, 232n2, 236n5

Anderson, Margaret, 6. *See also* Heap, Jane; *Little Review*

Anderson, Sherwood, 4, 6, 10, 18
- Hemingway's denial of influence, 8–9, 18, 224n3
- influence on Hemingway's career, 9, 30, 224nn4–6
- influence on Hemingway's style, 7–9, 18, 28, 30, 31, 51
- "Strength of God, The," 8
- Winesburg, Ohio, 7, 72

Beach, Sylvia, 9, 10, 204, 205

Bird, Bill, 32, 33, 41, 42, 48–50, 223n10, 220n14

bullfights
- Hemingway's experience of, 8, 31, 38, 42, 77, 133–34, 176–77, 182, 189–90
- Hemingway's opinions on, 43–44, 75, 177, 244n58

bullfights in *in our time,* x, xi, 38, 40, 42–44, 46, 47–48, 49, 51, 60, 71, 108, 133–38, 176–93, 235n9
- crowd's behavior, 80, 82, 93, 115, 134–35, 179, 180, 182, 183
- diagram of Villalta's movements, 186
- importance to Hemingway's aesthetics, 43–44, 47, 75, 100, 177, 183
- observers of, 38, 69–70, 73, 81, 91, 93, 108, 134–36, 140, 183, 207–8 (*see also* voices in *in our time*)
- violence in, 177–78, 75, 233n17, 244nn56, 58

bullfighters in *in our time,* 76, 81, 82
- responsible vs. irresponsible, 48, 74–75, 76, 102, 186–88, 193
- skillful vs. incompetent, xi, 44, 45, 47, 48, 135, 179–81, 182–86
- "the kid," Maera, Villalta (*see individual chapters* 2, 14, 15, and 16)

Cézanne, Paul, 10

chapter 1 (the kitchen corporal), xi, 22, 36, 45, 71, 72, 81, 82, 88, 98–99, 108, 111, 112, 118, 129–33, 135, 140, 142, 146, 207, 228n10, 235n13, 235n5, 238n18
- drafts of, 132–33

chapter 2 ("the kid" kills five bulls), xi,

37–38, 46, 73, 83, 84, 89, 92, 95, 99, 106, 108, 112, 115, 117, 118, 121, 122, 133–38, 140, 177, 179, 180–81, 186, 207, 210, 235n8, 237–38nn7–12
drafts of, 136–38
chapter 3 (the civilian retreat), 3, 20, 27, 29, 30, 62–64, 65, 78, 82, 83, 99, 101–2, 112, 114, 115, 123, 129, 133, 138–43, 140, 144, 149, 150, 160–61, 177, 207, 231n9, 235n13, 238n15
drafts of, 27–28, 142–43
chapter 4 (combat in a garden at Mons), xii, 20, 52, 59, 71, 76, 98, 99–100, 103, 108, 112, 113, 115, 119, 123, 144–46, 147, 148, 207, 218, 233n10, 235n10, 238n16, 239n20
drafts of, 146
chapter 5 (the perfect barricade), 47, 71, 76, 83–84, 108, 112, 113, 115, 116, 123, 144, 146–148, 238nn16–17, 239nn20–21
chapter 6 (the cabinet ministers' execution), xi, xii, xiii, 20, 27, 42, 45, 51, 52, 53, 62, 64, 65, 66–67, 68, 70, 73, 75–81, 105, 115, 116, 129, 133, 138, 148–53, 155, 177, 200, 195, 232nn1, 3, 236n14, 246nn79–80
drafts of, 152–53
chapter 7 (Nick wounded), 50, 41–42, 43, 45, 71, 72, 76, 77, 81, 82, 85, 88–89, 101, 102, 103–4, 108, 111, 112, 115, 122, 124, 129, 153–57, 159, 165, 206, 213, 231nn12, 15, 239nn18, 24–25, 240nn27–34
drafts of, 154–55
chapter 8 (the praying soldier), xi, 26, 27, 59, 71, 72–73, 76, 77, 81, 84–85, 88, 89–90, 91, 95, 108, 112, 114, 116, 119, 121, 129, 155, 157–62, 165, 169, 171, 173, 174, 206, 208, 231n12, 235n13, 236n16, 241n39, 242n40
drafts of, 160–62
chapter 9 (Drevitts and Boyle), 27, 40, 42, 45, 62, 64, 73, 74, 81, 83, 101, 111, 112, 116, 117, 120–21, 162–64, 177, 199, 219, 243n43
drafts of, 164
chapter 10 (the recovering soldier and Ag), 68, 69, 81, 84–85, 107, 111, 112, 113–14, 116, 119, 121–23, 165–72, 173, 175, 208–9, 235n9, 242n40, 243nn44, 48
drafts of, 171–72
chapter 11 (the revolutionist), xi, 22, 27, 41, 42, 46, 56, 59, 73, 76, 81, 91, 111, 112, 114, 172–76, 208, 209, 229n17, 231nn13, 17, 242n42, 243n51, 244n55
chapter 12 (the gored horse), 27, 44, 62, 65, 68, 73, 79, 103, 104, 105, 110, 112, 115, 120, 121, 122, 176–79, 223n9, 244–45nn56, 58, 59
drafts of, 179
chapter 13 (the bad bullfighter), xi, 26, 27, 47, 73, 75, 79, 81, 89, 91, 106, 108, 111, 112, 115, 119, 120, 136, 179–82, 186, 201, 207, 210–11, 219, 231nn13, 17, 245nn60–61
drafts of, 180
chapter 14 (Villalta), xi, 15, 44, 47, 61, 73, 76, 77, 81, 84, 86, 100, 101, 108–10, 113, 115–16, 117, 119, 123, 134, 179, 189, 182–86, 187, 212, 221nn62–68, 228n12, 232n6, 245nn62–68, 246n68
drafts of, 186
chapter 15 (the drunken bullfighter), 47, 73–77, 81, 91, 92, 93, 101, 102, 106, 111, 115, 119, 179, 181, 186–89, 218, 219, 221nn69–70, 225n12, 231n17, 232n2, 232–33nn7–9
chapter 16 (Maera's death), 20, 44, 47, 71, 72, 76, 79, 80, 81, 87, 88, 93–94, 108, 111, 112, 115, 122, 182, 186, 187, 189–93, 208, 219, 225n11, 231n12, 232n2, 232–33nn7–9, 246nn71–75
drafts of, 192–93
chapter 17 (Sam Cardinella's execution), xi, 20–21, 22, 27–28, 45, 46, 48, 53, 62, 64, 68, 73, 76, 77, 78, 80, 81, 85, 107–8, 111, 116, 117, 124, 177, 193–99, 229n20
drafts of, 197–99
chapter 18 (the king in the garden), 27, 45, 46, 53, 68, 69, 70, 77, 83, 90, 92,

110, 112, 115, 123–24, 199–201, 229nn16, 20, 237n9, 247nn83–87
drafts, 201
chapters in *in our time,* ix
analyzed by critics in context of *In Our Time* stories, ix, x, 203
as experiments vs. synthesis of Hemingway's style, xii–xiii, xiv, 20, 44, 48, 50, 53, 56, 92, 96, 97, 99, 100, 124–25, 203, 206, 213, 214, 222n8, 223n9, 230n25, 233n1
as poetry, 117–18
comic elements in, 44, 45, 77, 78, 130, 131, 135, 146, 154, 178, 194–97, 199, 231n19, 236nn2, 4, 244n58
compressed, fragmentary form of, x, xi, 5, 29, 35, 37, 55, 56, 59–60, 124, 177
contemporaneity of, 61
cumulative impact in sequence, x–xiii, 56, 60, 61
description of, 37–38, 60–61
diversity in style, subject, 61, 72, 80–82, 110, 239n18 (*see also* voices in *in our time:* range and diversity in social class, nationality, and occupation)
experiments in, xi–xii (*see also* diction and phrasing in *in our time;* narrative modes; narrative techniques; point of view in *in our time;* sentence structures and rhythms; voices in *in our time*)
experiments transformed in later fiction, 206–14
form abandoned by Hemingway, 203
formal unity of, 41, 46–48, 61, 222nn7–8, 229nn18–19, 21
numbering of, 36, 40, 41, 56, 60, 61
subjects of, x, 37, 38, 60, 75 (*see also* bullfights; crime in *in our time;* politics in *in our time;* war in *in our time*)
synonyms for, 61, 230n4
titles for individual chapters, xx, 40–41, 61
chapters in *in our time,* revisions (*see also individual chapters*)
of diction (*see* diction and phrasing in *in our time:* revisions of)
of sentences (*see* sentence structures and rhythms: revisions of)
chapters in *In Our Time* (1925), ix, x, 54–56
differences from chapters in *in our time,* xi, 56, 101, 102, 125, 234nn5, 6, 237n10, 241n34, 247n81
jolting the stories, x–xi, 55–56
numbering of, 46, 56, 237n7
relationship to stories, Hemingway's view, x–xi, 55
chapters in *Little Review* ("In Our Time" 1923), 36–38, 131, 133, 136, 142, 144, 151, 205, 221n1, 228nn12, 14, 235n8, 237–38nn10–12 (*see also Little Review:* "Exiles issue" containing "In Our Time")
commissioning of (*see* Pound, Ezra: commissions "In Our Time" for *Little Review*)
individual titles of, 36
prospective titles for collection, 37
characterization in *in our time,* 37–38, 41–42, 95–96, 117, 121–22, 172, 241n34 (*see also* bullfighters in *in our time;* voices in *in our time:* range and diversity in social class, nationality, and occupation)
ambiguity of "Nick," 153–54, 239–40nn25–26
lacking development, 37
Chicago Tribune Paris Edition, 38, 65, 66, 67, 149, 150, 194, 231n8, 232n3, 247n83, 248n3
Complete Short Stories of Ernest Hemingway, ix, 237n10
Conrad, Joseph, 7
crime in *in our time,* x, 37, 40, 42, 44, 45, 46–47, 60, 64, 75, 76, 162–63, 193–95, 199 (*see also* chapter 9; chapter 17)
"Cross Roads" 5–6, 59, 230n1
Cummings, E. E., 19, 26, 34, 224n4, 234n7, 241n37

Death in the Afternoon, 43, 67, 75, 100, 177, 179, 232n19, 244nn56, 58, 246n74
Dial, 17, 19, 33, 51, 221n4, 241n37
diction and phrasing in *in our time,* 63, 80, 84, 89, 95, 97, 129, 140, 148, 186, 210, 214
compression of, 30, 122, 123–24, 139, 168, 169, 236n17
expansion of, 122, 197–99, 236n17, 246n75; level of, 92–93, 122–23, 134–36
precision of, xiii, 121–24, 137–38, 186, 245n68, 246n72
repetition of (*see* repetition in *in our time:* of diction and phrasing)
revisions of, 121–24
see also ambiguity in *in our time:* in sentences
Dorman-Smith, Eric Edward "Chink," 38, 129, 144, 147, 232n4, 233n10, 238nn16–17

Eliot, T. S., 4, 28, 30, 32
Hemingway's enmity toward, 21
influence on Hemingway's style and subjects, 21–23, 124, 150, 234n4
"Love Song of J. Alfred Prufrock, The," 23
"Preludes," 23
"Sweeney Among the Nightingales," 21–22
Waste Land, The, 16, 20–23, 77, 132
Ellis, Havelock, 7
Ernest Hemingway, 88 Poems, ix, 221–22n1
executions in *in our time,* 37, 38, 51, 52, 53, 62, 65, 68, 73, 75–76, 107–108, 133, 138, 149–51, 200, 201
botched, xi, 43, 45, 48, 65, 85, 105, 150–51, 195–96, 199
contrasting responses of the prisoners, xi, 45, 78, 85, 150, 194–99, 246–47nn79–80
described dispassionately, 38, 53, 64, 90–91
described in newspapers (*see in our time:* sources of, second hand)
(*see also* chapter 6; chapter 17; Greco-Turkish War; violence in *in our time*)

Fitzgerald, F. Scott, x, 8, 53–54, 89, 112
Flaubert, Gustav, 10, 72, 86, 131
Ford, Ford Madox, 19, 52, 205
Freud, Sigmund, 7

Galantière, Lewis, 9, 50
Greco-Turkish War, xi, 28–29, 47, 129, 148, 173
abdication of King Constantine, 148
execution of cabinet ministers, 129, 148–49
house arrest of King George II and his Queen, 199
retreat of civilians from Adrianople, 129, 138–39
Turkish brutality at Smyrna, 56
(*see also* executions in *in our time; individual chapters* 3, 6, and 18)

Heap, Jane, 34, 227n4, 229n14
Hemingway, Ernest
and Chicago Renaissance, 6–9
dedicatee of *Best Short Stories of 1923,* 54, 203–4, 228n9
determination to be popular, successful writer, xiv, 3, 4, 102, 203–4, 214, 247n1
first year in Paris, achievements, 3, 30–31
mastery of a subculture, 8, 31, 245n65
on importance of *in our time* to his stylistic development, x
pre-Paris fiction, 3–6, 224n1
suitcase debacle, 23, 34–35, 227–28n7
turns from chapter-vignettes to stories, 55–56, 203–4, 205, 206, 230n28, 248n2
wants major publisher, 55, 203–5, 248n4
Hemingway, Ernest, professional identities of, xiii, 3, 30–31

author of slick fiction, 3, 4–5, 30
in *our time* helps resolve, xiii–xiv, 34, 203, 205
journalist, 3, 4, 26–27, 30, 205
modernist, 30–31, 34–35, 102, 203–4, 206
opportunist, 204–5
parodist and satirist, xiii, 3, 9, 17–18, 27, 30, 31, 205, 208–9
poet, 3, 17–18, 30, 205–6; realist, 31, 40, 99, 72, 135
unresolved in 1922–23, xiv, 3, 31
Hemingway, Hadley Richardson, 10, 16, 32, 35, 42, 48, 55, 143, 225n9, 227n5, 228n7
Horne, Bill, 6
Howe, E. W. ("Anthology of Another Town"), 5

imagistic technique in *in our time*, 19, 28, 63–65, 67, 91, 111, 115, 141, 150–51, 167, 172, 195
in our time (1924), ix
autobiographical roots of, 41–42, 70, 88, 95, 160–62, 165–66, 171
composition of, 32–50, 226–27nn2–3, 228n14
critical views of, x, 50–54, 221nn22–26 (*see also* Wilson, Edmund)
Hemingway's uncertainty of conception, 23, 33–34
importance to Hemingway's work, ix–x, xii, 203, 210–14, 222–23n9
modernist appearance of, xii, 48–50, 59 (*see also* Bird, Bill)
printing of, 50
rejected pieces for, 38–40: "MONS (three)," 38–39, 144, 228n11–13; "Did You Ever Kill Anyone?" 39, 239n24; "Heroes" 40
sources of, second-hand, 38: from friends, 27, 38, 129, 144, 147, 199, 233n10, 247n87; from newspapers, 27, 42, 65–66, 67, 85, 138–39, 149–50, 162, 194
In Our Time (1925)
as Bildungsroman, xi
chapters in (*see* chapters in *In Our Time* [1925])
"L'Envoi," 45, 56, 90, 229n16
"On the Quai at Smyrna," 13, 17, 47, 238nn
stories, as more conventional genre than chapters, 203
thought to begin Hemingway's critical success, ix, 203

James, Henry, 73, 97, 106, 209
journalism
"cablese," 28–30
Hemingway's divergence from, 28, 39–40, 62–64, 65–68, 138–39, 149–50, 162, 193–94
influence on Hemingway's writing, 26–28, 49, 53, 62–65, 102, 138–39, 205, 222n8, 225–26nn17–18
Joyce, James, 7, 10, 19, 86, 93, 225n12, 240n32
"Dubliners," 233n11
Portrait of the Artist as a Young Man, A, 72;
Ulysses, 40, 60

Kansas City Star, 3, 26–27, 42, 53, 83, 162
"The Killers," 155, 208
Kurowsky, Agnes von, 165–66, 237n9, 243n44

Lawrence, D. H., 7, 19, 53
Little Review, 6, 19, 20, 23, 33, 205
"Exiles" issue containing "In Our Time," 34, 35, 36, 40, 50, 60, 205, 227nn4–6 (*see also* Anderson, Margaret; Heap, Jane; "In Our Time" in *Little Review;* Pound, Ezra: commissions "In Our Time" for *Little Review*)

Masters, Edgar Lee (*Spoon River Anthology*), 5
Mencken, H. L., 53, 229n24
"Mercenaries, The," 5
modernist painting, influence on Hemingway, 10, 60, 72

Monroe, Harriet (*Poetry* magazine), 6, 19, 33, 124
Moveable Feast, A 10, 15, 18, 19, 24, 36, 204, 206, 225n16
"Mr. and Mrs. Elliot," 209, 248n4
"My Old Man," 3, 8–9, 31, 33, 36, 54, 203, 224n3, 228n7, 248n3

narrative modes, xiii, 59–79
  action studies, 25, 39, 43–44, 53, 61–62, 67, 72, 73, 75–77 (*see also* violence in *in our time*)
  character studies, 74–75 (*see also* characterization in *in our time*)
  descriptive studies, 61–62, 72–79
  experiential, 61–62, 70–72
  mixtures, 61, 62, 196
  quasi-journalistic, xii, xiii, 27, 49, 61–68, 79, 111, 139, 140–41, 143, 149–51, 163–64, 195–96 (*see also* voices in *in our time:* range of emotion—objective and dispassionate)
    ambiguity in (*see* ambiguity in *in our time:* of narrator)
    violence depicted through, 27, 59, 62, 65–68, 95, 150–51, 164, 177–78, 193–96
  parody of fairy tale and nursery rhyme, xiii, 45, 68–70, 167–70, 172, 199–201, 208–9, 231n11
  satire, 46, 70, 107–8, 167–70, 171–72, 194, 195, 196, 198–99, 200
  scenic studies, 77–79
narrative techniques
  action, capture of (*see* narrative modes: action studies; sentence structures and rhythms: actions conveyed through)
  ambiguity (*see* ambiguity in *in our time*)
  beginning in medias res, 22, 25, 28, 36, 37, 64, 65, 102, 110–11, 139, 155, 177–78, 190, 199, 207 (*see also* sentence structures and rhythms: beginning sentences)
  cinematic, 94, 135, 190
  closings, deflated or missing, 37, 65, 78, 112, 131, 141, 145, 159, 177–78, 188, 196 (*see also* sentence structures and rhythms: ending sentences)
  emphasis on here and now, 65, 130, 139, 177, 179, 236n4
  forcing reader to look, 65, 67–68, 140, 142, 177–78, 195, 198, 211
  sensations before explanation, 103–4, 187, 212–13, 214
  showing over telling, 18, 65, 68, 86, 112, 118, 124, 167–68, 172, 209, 214, 235n9, 241n40, 241–42n40
  tension, building of, 65, 67, 68, 70, 90, 104, 111, 104, 130, 131, 177–78, 196, 200, 231n16, 236n4
  understatement and omission, xii, 18, 95, 99, 106, 139, 150, 152, 173, 187, 211, 239n20, 247n87
narrators in *in our time*
  ambiguous (*see* ambiguity in *in our time:* of narrator)
  detached (*see* voices in *in our time:* range of emotion—objective and dispassionate)
  knowlegeable vs. naive, xi, 7–8, 13, 31, 30, 43–44, 108, 134, 172, 207
  quick shifts of, xii, 157, 159, 180, 206
New York Times, 65–66, 149, 151, 247nn83, 85
Nick Adams stories, xi, 5, 72, 89, 139, 153, 154, 161, 208, 239n24, 240n26

O'Brien, Edward, x, 35–36, 51, 54–55, 203–4, 205, 228n9
"Oily Weather," 17

"Paris 1922," 22–26, 31, 33, 34, 59, 73, 132, 223n9, 225n13, 227n3, 228nn7–8
  scholars' estimate of, 23–24, 31
point of view in *in our time*
  first person, xiii, 25–26, 27, 70–71, 87–90: central, 87–88, 145, 147, 153; peripheral, 25–26, 71, 74, 89–90, 91, 157–58, 180–81, 187, 190, 192

first person changed to third person, 26, 41, 88, 158, 160–62, 171–72, 190, 192, 231n12
importance to narrative technique, 86, 95
inconsistency in, 157–58, 182–83, 190–91, 206, 208, 232n7, 238n14
multiple perspectives of, xii, 86, 206
objectification of, 160–61, 171–72
proximity to action, 61–62, 72, 73, 79, 108, 114, 134, 182–83, 190, 207–8
second person, 86, 182, 232n6
stream-of-consciousness, 87, 93–94, 190–91, 193
third person, 44, 71, 86–91, 169, 206, 233n12; objective, 89, 90–91; omniscient, 86–87, 88, 93; limited omniscient, 87, 88–89, 95, 155–56, 182–83, 231n12
politics in *in our time,* x, xi, 44, 60, 70, 75, 76, 138–39, 172–75, 200 (*see also* Greco-Turkish War)
futility of revolutionary idealism, 174–75
Pound, Ezra, 3, 4, 9, 10, 16–21, 30, 224n4
commissions *in our time* for "Inquest" series, 17, 20, 32–34, 35, 40, 54, 59–60, 226nn1–2, 227n3, 228–29n14
commissions "In Our Time" for *Little Review* 34, 35, 227nn4–6 (*see also Little Review:* "Exiles" issue containing "In Our Time")
consultant for *in our time,* 20, 21, 41, 45, 46, 49, 149, 190, 192, 193, 199, 229n16
"Hugh Selwyn Mauberley," 209
imagistic technique, 16–17, 60, 124, 150, 234n4
"In a Station of the Metro," 16–17
influence on Hemingway contrasted to Stein's, 20–21, 31
influence on Hemingway's career, 10, 19–20, 33, 205
influence on Hemingway's poetry, 17, 19, 33, 205
influence on Hemingway's prose style, 10, 15, 16–18, 21–22, 24–25, 34, 35, 54, 59–60, 63, 124, 150, 204, 212, 234n4
"Jewel Stairs Grievance, The" 24
relationship with Hemingway, 16, 18, 33, 35–36, 224n6, 228n8, 245n62

Rascoe, Burton, 50
repetition in *in our time,* 31, 86, 95, 125, 114–18, 212
and motion, 116, 185, 191
of diction and phrasing, 14, 15, 99, 116, 131, 132, 153, 163, 166–67, 168, 169, 191, 196, 209–10, 225n12
of imagery, 64, 115, 151, 167, 209–210
of numbers, 116–17, 151, 238n11
of sentences (incremental and overlapping), 13–15, 98–99, 184–85, 191
of sounds, 117, 151
"The Revolutionist" (in *In Our Time*), 41, 56, 242n42. *See also* chapter 11

sentence structures and rhythms, xi, xiii, xxx, 97–125, 209–12, 214
actions conveyed through, 100–1, 108–10, 115–16, 124–25, 163, 183–85
beginning sentences, xiii, 63, 64, 110–11, 125, 139–40, 141, 149–50, 156, 163, 177, 195 (*see also* ambiguity in *in our time:* in sentences; narrative techniques: beginning in medias res)
complex sentences, 98, 99, 100, 103–4, 105, 106–9, 113, 120, 124, 151, 164, 168, 184, 209, 210, 211, 214, 217, 218, 235n9
compound sentences, xiii, 5, 15, 98, 99–100, 104–6, 108–9, 113, 114, 118–19, 120, 124, 135, 151, 156, 168, 169, 178, 181, 183, 184, 188, 210–11, 212, 214, 215, 218, 219
contrasting sentence structure to highlight themes and climaxes, 113–14, 145, 156, 178, 181, 210, 212, 235n12

criteria for categories of sentence structure, 217–19
declarative sentences, 24, 26, 36, 97, 102, 145, 225n16, 226n19
diversity of, 97–100, 124
elisions in, xii, 49, 101–2, 124–25, 135, 188, 206, 246n70
ending sentences, 65, 111–12, 125 (*see also* narrative techniques: closings)
fragments, xi, xii, 28, 29–30, 49, 99, 100, 101–2, 108, 114, 124–25, 139, 140, 142, 147–48, 153, 156, 159, 160–61, 169, 184, 188, 206, 215, 234nn5–6, 241n34, 246n70
in relation to speaker's mood or consciousness, xii, 93–94, 104, 105–6, 108, 190, 191 length of, 113, 145, 181, 188
mistakenly thought simple, 97, 99
mixtures of, xi, 99–100, 108, 183–85, 188, 209, 212
participles, 12, 14–15, 20, 28, 31, 97–99, 100, 107, 108, 109–10, 124–25, 131, 141, 142, 168, 178, 184–85, 188, 198, 211–12, 215, 217, 218, 236n6
proportions of types in *in our time,* 97, 105, 106, 107, 108, 215
revisions of, 118–21 (*see also individual chapters:* drafts of)
run-ons, xi, xii, 92, 99, 106, 108, 133, 135, 140, 159, 169, 181, 184, 210–11, 215
simple sentences, 5, 28, 29, 36, 51, 63, 93–94, 97–98, 99–100, 101, 102–4, 105, 108, 112, 113, 114, 118–19, 120, 124, 140, 142, 145, 146, 147–48, 151, 153, 155–56, 159, 164, 169–70, 178, 181, 183, 185, 188, 196–97, 210, 214, 215, 217, 218, 225n16, 226n19, 233–34n1, 235n9
symmetry of, 106, 131–32, 139–40, 141, 178, 181
See also sentence structure analyses of individual chapters in Chapter Six and in Appendix

"Silent, Ghastly Procession, A," 29, 63
Smith, Y. K., 7, 9
"Soul of Spain, The," 17–18
Steffens, Lincoln, 28, 226n22
Stein, Gertrude, 3, 4, 9–10, 30, 17, 19, 34, 40, 49
"beginning again" in "Melanctha," 11–13, 31
cubist technique in *Tender Buttons,* 10, 11, 15–16, 31
influence on Hemingway's career, 9–10, 30, 31, 60, 203, 206
influence on Hemingway's style, 13–16, 18, 20–21, 28, 30, 35, 36, 51, 60, 72, 96, 115, 117, 131, 147, 175, 204–5, 211, 212, 224n5
influence on Hemingway's themes, 13–14, 42, 72, 133
modernist conception of narrative, 10–12, 60, 225n7
Strater, Henry ("Mike"), 36, 38, 42, 49, 133
Sun Also Rises, The, ix, 134, 174, 206–7, 208, 209–10, 223n9, 229n15, 231n14, 243n47, 244n56, 45n65

Three Stories & Ten Poems, ix, 9, 17, 33, 42, 50, 56, 60, 205, 247n1
Toronto Star, 3, 26–29, 32, 54, 62–63, 70, 134, 184–85, 199, 226n24, 237n9, 247n84
Torrents of Spring, The 18, 208
"To Will Davis," 194
transatlantic review, 19–20, 21, 52, 229n22
Turgeniev, Ivan, 7
Twain, Mark, 7, 80–81

unreality, sense of, in *in our time,* 45, 71, 99, 130–31, 144–46, 199–200, 207, 231n11, 236n4, 239n18
"Up in Michigan," 3, 4, 6, 7–8, 33, 143, 224n2, 225n8
Anderson's influence on, 7–8, 31
Pound's influence on, 18, 31
sexual explicitness of, 7–8, 13–14, 19, 31
Stein's influence on, 10, 13–14, 31

"Very Short Story, A" (in *In Our Time*), 41, 56, 117, 231n15. *See also* chapter 10
violence in *in our time,* xi, 48, 75–77, 231n16
anticipated, remembered, more than described, 38, 47, 68, 71–72, 75–76, 148, 150–51, 178, 195–99, 200, 231n9
fear of, 77, 130–31, 157–59, 180, 186–88, 195, 231n16
in bullfight (*see* bullfights in *in our time:* violence in)
in crime, 42 (*see* chapter 9; chapter 17)
in executions, 65, 67, 149 (*see also* chapter 6; chapter 17; executions in *in our time*)
in politics, 42, 149 (*see also individual chapters* 6, 11, and 18; politics in *in our time;* Greco-Turkish war)
in war, 43, 47 (*see also individual chapters* 1, 4, 5, 7, and 8; war in *in our time*)
pervasive, xi, 38, 45, 75, 79
rendered dispassionately (*see* narrative modes: quasi-journalistic—violence depicted through)
study of responses to, 68, 71, 75–77, 150, 194
tranquil settings of, xi, 45, 78
voices in *in our time,* xi, 80–96
ambiguity in (*see* ambiguity in *in our time:* in voice, of narrators)
British, confusion of number, 56, 71, 84, 144, 147, 232n4, 238n17, 239n20
importance to narrative technique, 80, 94–96
range and diversity in social class, nationality, and occupation, xiii, 22, 38, 79, 80–85, 95
range of emotion, 83–85, bemused, 130–33; callow, 165, 167, 168–69; fearful, 158–59, 187; hyperbolic, excited, 83–85, 134–36, 147, 175; laconic, 84; naive, 174–75 (*see also* narrators in *in our time:* knowledgeable vs. naive); objective and dispassionate, xii, 38, 42, 84, 85, 91, 140, 149, 155, 163–64, 177, 180; psychologically detached or dazed, 145–46; relieved, 154–55; skeptical and undercutting, 42, 90, 158–59, 173–75, 208
silent, 80, 85–86, 155, 195, 241–42n40

war in *in our time,* x, xi, 38, 39–40, 41, 44, 46, 47, 48, 70, 72, 88, 108, 124, 129–30, 144–48, 153–62, 165, 173 (*see also* Greco-Turkish War)
counter to stereotypes, 41, 72, 144–46, 154, 182, 239n18
emotive responses to (*see* voices in *in our time:* range of emotion)
Hemingway's reliance on secondhand accounts, 27, 144, 147
vs. Hemingway's experience of, 4, 37, 153–54
"Way You'll Never Be, A," 39, 147
Wilson, Edmund, x, xi, 9, 53, 54, 205
relationship with Hemingway, 50–52, 55, 204, 230n27, 232n20, 247n1
review of *in our time,* x, 49, 51–52, 54, 151, 221nn22–23, 223n9, 229n22